D1171519

Jürgen Joedicke A History of Modern Architecture

A History of Modern Architecture

by Jürgen Joedicke

Frederick A. Praeger, Publishers, New York

BOOKS THAT MATTER

Translated from the German by James C. Palmes

Published in the United States of America in 1959
by Frederick A. Praeger, Inc., Publishers
64, University Place, New York 3, N. Y.

Library of Congress catalog card number: 59-7459
Printed in Germany

Second Printing 1960

Contents

To my teacher, Professor Dr. Curt Siegel, in gratitude

Introduction

The nineteenth century, so rich in important works of music and painting, the great age of the novel and of lyric poetry, developed no characteristic art forms in spatial composition and planning. It was an epoch without a building style of its own. Self-confident reliance on the architectural forms of the past concealed an inner uncertainty. The past had become a store-house for hasty resurrections of every style, for the pseudo-Gothic and the neoromantic, for "renaissances of the renaissance" and resuscitations of Baroque and Rococo, to be plundered without restraint and often enough without any comprehension of the circumstances which had given rise to these particular forms. For religious structures Romanesque and Gothic models were preferred, for bank buildings Doric and Ionic columns were chosen to indicate stability and the dignity of wealth, and in the building of town halls middle-class vanity found expression in reminiscences of Late Gothic and Renaissance days, the golden age of towns. Even the ordinary middle-class home could not escape the carnival of styles and masqueraded in clothes borrowed from the Renaissance villas of the Florentine, Roman and Venetian nobility.

But even among followers of the cult of historical pageantry there were important architects like Semper and Viollet-le-Duc who stood head and shoulders above the sycophantic mannerists with their pattern books. There were architects who tried to speak a language of their own, even if they used the grammar and vocabulary of the past, but for the most part their efforts were condemned to failure. The intellectual revolutions and social upheavals which had taken place in the meantime could no longer find a response in concepts which were based entirely on traditional ideas of architecture.

The tasks which confronted nineteenth-century architecture, and which continued unsolved into our century, were unmatched in variety and magnitude. About 1800, with the onset of the industrial revolution, there occurred a rapid increase in population. Within 130 years the number of inhabitants in England rose from 9 to 45 million, in Germany from 24 to 66, and in the USA from 5 to 123. Simultaneously the proportionate distribution of town and country dwellers altered. In 1871 64 out of 100 Germans still lived in the country and 5 in cities, but by 1933 there were only 33 in the country to 30 in cities. London underwent an eigthfold expansion in 150 years, while Paris increased two-and-a-half times in half a century. The rise in population only affected towns.

1. Water works, Hanover, about 1900. Negation of function. Industrial building in historical trappings.

2. Walter Gropius and Adolf Meyer. Fagus Works, Alfeld an der Leine, 1911–16. New aesthetic conception; the work space is light and appropriate to its purpose.

In previous centuries architecture had been associated in its development with what were essentially unchanging building problems: the church, the castle, the town hall and the merchant's house. New tasks now began to appear, which hitherto had been without significance in architectural development: factories, workshops and administrative buildings; highways, stations and airports; hospitals and sports buildings; schools, libraries and exhibition halls. At the same time there arose an ever more pressing need to co-ordinate from the standpoint of overall control the immense multiplicity of requirements and regulations. The problem involved the technical, sociological and formal aspects of town planning, and finally national planning as well. Beyond the town boundaries regional planning sought a basis for individual planning by ordering the disposition of industrial and residential zones, highways and green spaces and of built-up and agricultural areas. Confronted with such an abundance of tasks eclecticism with its methods based upon historical precedents was certain to founder.

During the same period a complete change in production methods took place. Handicrafts were gradually superseded and supplanted by industry; technics began to appear as the determining factor. Manufacturing processes were increasingly mechanized. The staggering developments in natural sciences, which were leading to a different conception of our world, changed everyday activities in all respects. Seventy years ago in our grandparents' time, living and work rooms were still lit with gas; the motor car and the electric tram, the aeroplane, the radio and the telephone had not yet been invented. To-day, barely three generations later, we no longer measure the speed of the jet fighter in miles per hour, but by the speed of sound.

The pioneers of modern architecture could still know little of what the age of technics might bring. They instinctively sensed, however, the coming transformation in the social structure of the time and they recognized with absolute clarity that the new architectural problems could be solved only by contemporary means. Their protest against style mimicry and historical make-believe became audible for the first time when, in the last decade of the nineteenth century, Louis Sullivan in Chicago, Hendrik Petrus Berlage in Amsterdam, Henry van de Velde in Belgium and Otto Wagner in Vienna issued their simultaneous challenge, starting a movement which led to modern architecture.

If we look back at the history of modern architecture a number of decisive factors stand out. The search for a new language of form and the development of new concepts of space were stimulated by the introduction of building materials which took the place of conventional materials and were associated with new constructional methods. At the same time modern architecture was guided by a strong social sense, which influenced the thinking and conduct of leading architects and is seen in the changed attitude to important building problems. In the nineteenth century, housing, the real cardinal problem of a socially conscious architecture, had remained in the hands of building contractors and real estate speculators. The results were the wretched dwellings of our big cities, in which – cut off from natural surroundings, air and sunshine – a large part of the population had to live. The English Garden City movement tackled this problem. In 1898 Ebenezer Howard proclaimed his theory of settling factory and office workers in small garden towns, a prelude to the great housing schemes which grew up after the first world war.

The impetus given by new principles and materials of construction and the humanizing of the art of building are important forces in the history of modern

3. Backyards between Hussiten- and Acker Strasse, Berlin, behind a street elevation loaded with eclectic finery. Late nineteenth century.

architecture, but the change in approach to problems of form from that of the nineteenth century is fundamental. Form is not the only point of departure, the decisive factor to which all other considerations must be subordinated. It is no longer predetermined. As in all great architecture it takes shape from the problem itself. Only with such an attitude was it possible to master the multitude of tasks and give them a form corresponding to the outlook of the age.

The search for new forms of expression was increasingly determined by the creative opportunities afforded by adapting notions of form to the possibilities of new materials. For instance, artificial substances like steel and reinforced concrete, aluminium and glass, belong unmistakably to the sphere of the technical world in contrast to timber and stone. In the struggle between the creative work of the artist and the theories of the engineer, which distinguishes modern architecture, is reflected the problem of reconciling human aims to technical requirements, a problem characteristic of our entire age. Modern architecture has given proof that new values can be found by boldly grasping our technical resources and applying them with perception. Nowadays the creative artist and the technical theorist are no longer in opposition as they were in the nineteenth century, but form the piers upon which the arch of our present-day architecture is supported.

4. Walter Gropius. Housing, Berlin-Siemensstadt, 1929. Flats with big windows and balconies opening onto wide green spaces.

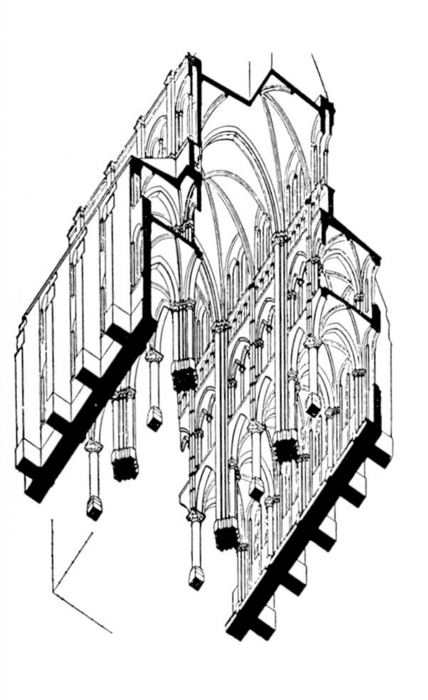

6. Noyon cathedral, begun about 1150. Section from below. Vaulted construction of the Gothic cathedral with stresses carried by arches and flying buttresses, in contrast to the post-and-beam method of Greek temples. In Gothic buildings the system of buttresses and columns bears the load; walls are glass.

There appears to be a secret connection between the notions of form characteristic of each period and the means at its disposal. The age of every historical style, in pursuit of its own particular brand of expression, found the material which suited its wishes. Until our day, however, the choice of materials available for building was confined to natural substances: freestone of various kinds from hard granite to sandstone, soft and easy to work, the material from which the Gothic master-masons carved the delicate arabesques of the cathedrals of the middle ages: timber, which in its material characteristics is similar to the substances which we employ for building to-day – and clay used in the form of dried and baked bricks. The baking of clay already indicates an attempt to alter the inherent qualities of a building material. But only in our time did the really significant change occur. With iron and reinforced concrete[1] new constructional materials were introduced into architecture which, in their technical properties as materials, in their high degree of strength and in their structural possibilities, differed fundamentally from conventional natural materials. They can be described as artificial, since a highly developed industry is needed for their production. In them the architecture of our day has found the means of realising its ambitions.

The first appearance of iron as a building material occurred at a time of general decline in creative inspiration. So it was only natural that a tremendous impetus towards a future architectural style was seen in this new building material. "An appropriate architecture will arise immediately when use is made of the means which the new industrial techniques offer. The application of iron permits and demands many new forms, as can be seen in railway stations, suspension bridges, and the arches of conservatories."[2] (Théophile Gautier, 1850.)

At first these hopes were not to be fulfilled. The use of a new kind of building material only contains a potentially new structural language if theories of form and constructional possibilities are complementary and interrelated. In the first half of the nineteenth century and even in the later decades this was not yet the case. Moreover iron only became a highly valuable building material, economically and structurally, as we know it to-day, in the second half of the last century,

←
5. Acropolis, Athens. Parthenon, 447–437 B. C. The Greek temple – starting point and model for centuries of Western building tradition.

[1] All notes are grouped together on pages 238–240.

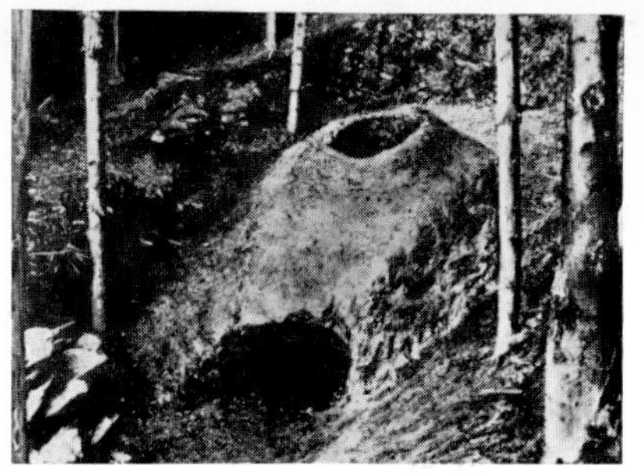

7a. Smelting furnace of the ancient Egyptians, who probably acquired their knowledge of "the wonder of heaven" from meteorites.

7b. Crude early furnace. Built on a hill-side. Wind supplied draught. After eighth century replaced by small shaft furnace with bellows, which made higher temperatures possible and yielded more iron.

after the introduction of the Bessemer (1855) and Thomas (1879) processes. After the middle of the century, too, people were still quite content to dress iron in the decorative forms of past styles. But even then there were architects and engineers who visualized new possibilities and anticipated many of the later solutions in their buildings and projects.

Steel in nineteenth-century buildings

Iron as a multi-purpose material has been known for nearly five thousand years, as discoveries in Mesopotamia and Egypt prove [7a][3]. But production methods were so primitive that it could only be manufactured in very small quantities. It was also extremely valuable and was never considered for use in large-scale activities like building. After iron had been smelted for the first time in blast-furnaces in the fourteenth century, it could be produced in larger quantities, but any significant rise in iron production in the following centuries came to nothing, because the charcoal needed for smelting was not available in anything like sufficient amounts[4]. The mighty forests of Central Europe and England began to recede, and men tried, by reducing iron production and by forbidding the clearing of timber from specified areas, to prevent this stripping of the forests.
Attempts to use pit-coal instead of wood failed at first. But Abraham Darby, after earlier attempts by Dud Dudley (1621), succeeded in 1713 in partially substituting coal for charcoal. His son carried this process further, using – as is still customary to-day – coke in place of natural coal. In contrast to wood, coal was widely available, and iron could, therefore, be produced in greater quantities. Thus was laid one of the essential foundations of the Industrial Revolution in England. Manpower could be replaced by the machine.
The coke-processed pig-iron, however, was inordinately brittle, unmalleable and of little practical use. For this reason it had to be subjected to further treatment in

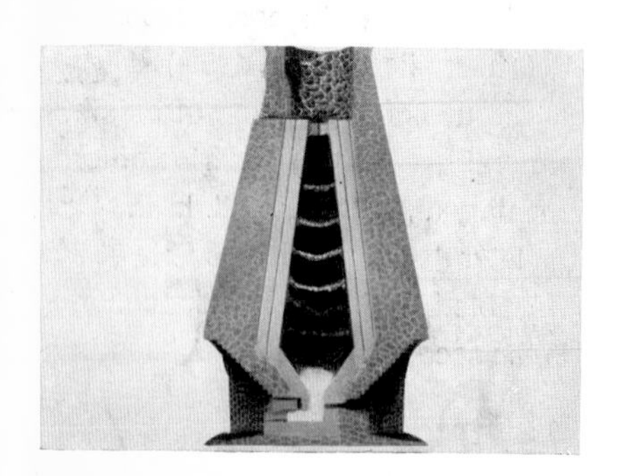

8. Section through coke blast-furnace, end eighteenth century. Fuel is now coke instead of charcoal. Temperature of iron raised to smelting point. Pig-iron obtained in molten form, instead of pasty lumps (blast furnace smelting since fourteenth century). To produce wrought (malleable) iron, a refining process was necessary, for which charcoal was still needed.

9. Section through puddling-furnace. Invented in England, end eighteenth century; refinement now possible with coke. Fuel and ore no longer in immediate contact. A hot draught of air is carried through the reverberatory furnace, in which the liquid pig-iron was "puddled" (stirred) to prevent formation of slag. Later replaced by the Bessemer Converter (1855).

0. First cast-iron bridge at Coalbrookdale (England), 1779. The semicircular arch recalls masonry bridges, but is also suited to the characteristics of the new material, cast-iron being only resistant to compression.

11. Thomas Paine. Sunderland Bridge (England), 1793–96. Small cast-iron components are connected with wrought-iron bars; wider span, flatter arch.

12. Robert Stephenson. Bridge over the Menai Straits (Wales), 1846. In place of arches, pure beam construction of steel web plate girders. The massive piers show none of the stylistic decoration characteristic of the later nineteenth century.

which charcoal was needed. It was Henry Cort's great achievement to have introduced the "Puddling" process, in which coal was also used. This puddle-iron provided the material for the tremendous development of the English machine industry [9].

But in building work also the possibilities offered[5] by the new material were soon recognized. In 1779 the first cast-iron bridge was erected over the Severn at Coalbrookdale [10]. It had a span of a hundred feet and its construction comprised five semi-circular cast-iron arches. The rings in the spandrels of the middle arch, which serve as decoration, strengthen the frame, the plain form of construction revealing at the same time an aesthetic quality.

In 1796 Sunderland bridge was built to the designs of Thomas Paine, with a single span measuring 236 feet, an extraordinary width for those days [11]. The roadway rests upon six segmental ribs which are held together by wrought-iron tie bars and bolts. In the meantime the first cast-iron on the Continent had been erected in 1794 over the Striegauer Wasser at Laasau in Silesia. The boldness with which constructional problems were solved at this period is shown by the project of 1801 for a bridge over the Thames. The engineer Thomas Telford evolved a structure with a span of 600 feet, which was not built, although a commission confirmed its feasibility [14].

These bridge projects were principally based upon the use of cast-iron, a material with a tensile strength which is low in relation to its strength in compression. Next to cast-iron, wrought-iron or, to use the present-day term, steel was also available in increasing quantity. The characteristic of this material is its high

13. Thomas Telford. Conway Castle Bridge (Wales), 1822–26. One of the first suspension bridges, made possible by the tensile strength of steel.

tensile strength, and the constructional consequences of this attribute were quickly appreciated. In 1796 the first wrought-iron suspension bridge was built over Jacob's Creek in America. Modern suspension bridges, the supreme achievements of our latter-day engineering techniques, are based on very similar calculations.

In 1846 Robert Stephenson built the bridge over the Menai Straits as a simple girder bridge of steel tubes which, with a span of 460 feet, is to-day still among the widest-spanned constructions of this kind. The principle of the girder (or beam) is a typical form for steel and reinforced concrete, which would be unthinkable for stone, since it demands a material which allows both compression and tension. The beam, however, was later to achieve its most important place as a structural element in the steel frame building.

In the construction of other buildings, too, the possibilities of the new material began to be recognized. In Salford, Lancashire, a cotton mill was built in 1801, in which the internal load-bearing frame was formed of cast-iron stanchions and beams developed by the engineers Matthew Boulton and James Watt. The

14. Thomas Telford. Project for a bridge over the Thames, London, 1801. Daring, but an entirely feasible, design. The span of 600 feet requires massive abutments and consequently high road way ramps.

15. Matthew Boulton and James Watt. Cotton mill, Salford (England), 1801. Contemporary representation of brick carcass. The iron supporting frame is inserted in the strong load-bearing external walls. T-beams, between which the floor is fixed, rest on slender columns.

16. Thomas Telford. St. Katherine's Docks, London, 1824–28. Cube-like compactness is characteristic of early industrial building. The construction consists of an inner iron frame, the beams supporting the floors resting upon external load-bearing walls.

7. K. L. Althans. Casting shop, Sayn (Rheinland), 1824–30. The ornamental arrangement of the gable end reflects the disposition of the structural members.

external walls consist of load-bearing masonry into which the delicate iron skeleton is inserted as though into a shell. In the following decades a large number of factory buildings were built in accordance with this principle. In this early building the girders already resemble the double-T form, characteristic of steel beams to-day [15].

Whilst in this building the iron frame is only used inside the wall as a substitute for load-bearing masonry, in the casting shop built in 1824–30 by K. L. Althans at Sayn (Rheinland), the construction is revealed externally as a formal element of the structure [17].

The building is planned with three aisles, the middle one higher than the other two. At the gable end the cast-iron columns, copied from models of past days, and the arched skeleton frame of the roof, are clearly visible. The ornamental arrangement of the window surfaces is related to the pattern of the structural elements and is obtained by disclosing the curved outlines traced by the iron frame. In the Sayn works tendencies are anticipated which were to be developed by the protagonists of Art Nouveau in an entirely different context.

8. Jules Saulnier. Chocolate factory, Noisiel-sur-Marne, 1871–72. One of the first real skeleton frame buildings. The diagonals of the lattice framework which serve as wall reinforcement are also used ornamentally. Cladding of coloured wood tiles.

19. Joseph Paxton. Crystal Palace, London, 1851. View over the roof towards the entrance hall. A design of extraordinary clarity and simplicity composed of standardized units.

→

21. Palm House, Kew Gardens, 1844. French and English conservatories of the first decades of the nineteenth century already constructed as transparent buildings of glass and iron, foreshadowing the exhibition halls of the second half of the century.

20. Crystal Palace, London. Set back in three steps, the walls of the building were entirely constructed of glass and iron. The Crystal Palace initiated a series of important buildings for international exhibitions, in which new structural processes were given their first practical trial.

In 1851 Joseph Paxton's Crystal Palace was built, that unique structure which had no counterpart in the nineteenth century except for the Machinery Hall of the Paris Exhibition of 1889. For the first time a building was erected which, in principle, consisted solely of iron and glass. The dimensions are impressive. The exhibition hall covered an area of 18 acres and was constructed in barely four months. These figures must be compared with the times which were normal at that period, in order to appreciate the importance of the new system. In a traditional stone building of similar size the process of erection would have lasted years, even decades. The impression made by the Crystal Palace on contemporary opinion was overwhelming. Instead of the usual massive masonry, the space was enclosed by only a slender network of iron and glass, through which there shone the natural light of the sky with the ever-changing pageant of the clouds [19, 20]. The daring of the conception, however, lacked one of the characteristics of later steel buildings: the unsupported spanning of large areas. The arch of the middle aisle bridged a mere 70 feet. The side aisles rested upon a great number of closely placed columns. All components were standardized. For instance, the window units of the side elevations were all the same size, so that they could be replaced easily if damaged. The Crystal Palace was not an isolated development. It had precedents in English and French hothouses. Architects like the Frenchmen, Flachat and Horeaux, devised schemes which show a fundamentally similar approach. At the same period Henri Labrouste (1801–1875) was working in Paris. He had turned away from the rigid formalism of the teaching of the École des Beaux-Arts and founded a school of his own. In 1843–50 he built the Bibliothèque Sainte-Geneviève in Paris [22], in the thick external walls of which there is a steel structure of arch-shaped lattice girders carried on cast-iron stanchions. The reading room of the Bibliothèque Nationale (built 1858–68) is conceived on similar principles [23]. It is lit by roof-lights in the vaulted ceiling. While in the reading room historical decoration was more strongly emphasised, Labrouste achieved a solution in the stackroom in which the construction contributes decisively to the spatial effect. The entrance to the reading room is startling. A glass wall, about thirty feet high, its only features being a few steel guides, separates the reading room from the bookstacks. The stack is a combination of column, beam and grid which is so modern in its suitability to purpose that it might have been built to-day.

22. Henri Labrouste. Sainte-Geneviève reading room and library, Paris, 1843–50. Light inner steel skeleton and heavy load-bearing walls.

How far ahead of his contemporaries Labrouste was in his analysis of the problem is proved by a letter, in which he tells his brother about his teaching methods. "I tell them (the students) repeatedly that the arts have the power to make everything beautiful, but I stress most emphatically that architectural form must correspond to the purpose for which it is intended."[6] We are reminded of the later axiom of the Chicago architect, Louis Sullivan, that "form ever follows function". In 1855, 1867 and 1878 various international exhibitions took place in Paris [27]. Architecturally speaking, they provided nothing new, but they offered opportunities for using steel in typical structural forms. The exhibition hall of 1855 already revealed a span of 155 feet, and gradually men learned how to exploit the tensile strength of steel and to design individual building components in the most economical way. This progress was made possible through a deepening knowledge of construction and refinements in methods of calculation. Karl Culmann(1821–81) succeeded, by graphic systems of calculation, in determining exactly the moments of resistance in transverse members of a frame. In 1889 Gustave Eiffel erected the gigantic Eiffel Tower, in which he utilized his experience in bridge-

23. Henri Labrouste. Main reading room of the Bibliothèque Nationale, Paris, 1858–68. The steel construction rests upon stanchions placed in front of the walls. Their extremely slender proportions do not break the unity of the room. Modern spatial conceptions are thus anticipated. Good natural lighting through sky lights in the domes. In the background a 30 foot high glass partition with the entrance to the bookstack behind.

building[7]. The Eiffel Tower became a monument to modern architectural engineering, and even to-day remains the symbol of the city of Paris [25].
The culmination of all these endeavours was represented by the daring project of the Machinery Hall of the World Exhibition of 1889 in Paris (Engineer Contamin, Architect Ferdinand Dutert), which spanned a width of 375 feet [28, 282][8]. Whilst we recognize an increase in wall strength at the bottom as typical of a masonry structure, in a steel building it is possible for the supporting frame to be smaller, and not broader, at the base. Contamin built the Machinery Hall of three-pinned arches, which means that the thrust was exerted equally on the hinges at the crown and the two abutments. Stanchions and beams were no longer separate units. The structure rises in one movement from base to crown. This building is of great importance because it offers a consistent practical demonstration of a new structural theory and also because of the revolutionary aesthetic ideas which are fundamental to it.

24. Gustave Eiffel and L. A. Boileau. Bon Marché department store, Paris, 1876. Sense of movement in space created by raised bridges; unifying effect of huge glass roof.

25. Gustave Eiffel. Eiffel Tower, Paris, 1889. Pier Engineers' architecture, with no practical purpose, builds itself a monument.

26. I. K. Brunel and M. Digby Wyatt. Paddington Station, London, 1854. New structural techniques applied to new tasks in building. Vast scale of the spatial conceptions of the train sheds of railway-stations of the fifties and sixties contrast with the historical stylistic treatment of the reception areas.

→

28. Ferdinand Dutert and Contamin. Machinery Hall of Paris International Exhibition, 1889. Transparency, lightness, impression of floating. Pioneer example of three-hinged arches. Frame secured at base and apex. Dimensions reduced towards the ground – exact opposite of previous aesthetic conceptions.

27. Frédéric Le Play. International Exhibition, Paris, 1867. Exhibition building of seven concentric galleries; elliptical ground plan.

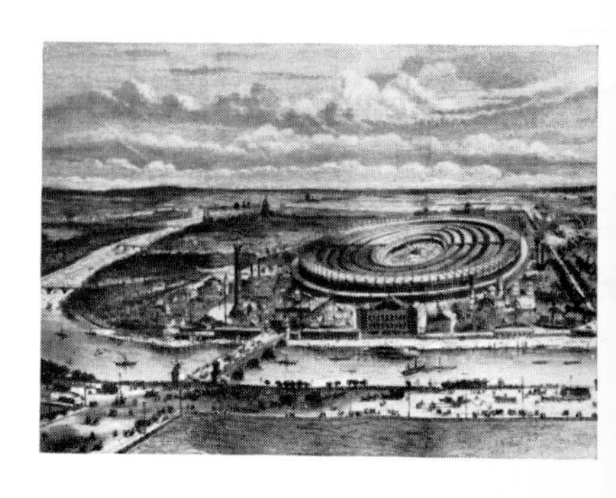

29a. James Bogardus. Cast-iron factory, New York 1848. Prefabricated cast-iron components replace masonry. Excellent natural lighting. Precursor of skeleton frame construction.

The Chicago School

The theory of using a steel skeleton in the construction of multi-storey buildings originated in Chicago. The first steps in this direction had already been taken in English factories at the beginning of the nineteenth century, the load-bearing structure consisting of cast-iron piers and beams with external walls of masonry. In the middle of the century the American James Bogardus went still further, composing even the outside walls of cast-iron units and obtaining, in comparison with masonry walls, a high degree of transparency [29a]. The really significant contribution of the Chicago school lay in the logical development of the steel skeleton as a load-bearing structure and in evolving a characteristic architectural form for this new type of construction. Essential to this purpose was the exclusive use of steel as a building material which, in contrast to the cast-iron chiefly used by Bogardus, possesses both compressive and tensile resistance. Stanchions and

29b. H. H. Richardson. Marshall Field store, Chicago, 1885–87. Traditional masonry construction; but, in its rejection of Victorian Gothic and pseudo-Renaissance ornament, usual in contemporary commercial buildings, and in its clear straightforward idiom, strongly influenced by the School of Chicago.

beams can be connected in such a way that the skeleton forms a rigid load-bearing structure from foundation to roof. The first "skeleton" (or steel frame) construction was used by William Le Baron Jenney for the Home Insurance Building in Chicago (1883–85) [32], but the elevations were still handled in a heavy, monumental, fashion. On the other hand in the Reliance Building in Chicago by Burnham and Root, of which four storeys were built in 1890 – it was later increased in height –, the lightness of the structural idiom evolved logically from the steel construction. The elevational treatment of the Home Insurance Building, copied from historical models, is abandoned for a form which is now simplified and is beginning to be an architectonic expression of the structure [31].

The new conception of form with its tendency towards elements which are clearly defined and developed from their function was also applied to traditional masonry buildings. In 1891 Burnham and Root erected the Monadnock Building, a sixteen-storey block with external walls of load-bearing masonry [30]. The fenestration, projecting bays and curved edges and cornices, which are as elegantly

30. D. H. Burnham and J. W. Root. Monadnock Building, Chicago, 1891. Masonry construction with load-bearing external walls. No structural innovations, but elegant lines and striking effect of unadorned mass. Uncluttered appearance as in skeleton frame buildings.

Boston Store
LOANS
HILLMAN'S
RESTAURANT

shaped as they are structurally logical, give a rhythmic movement to its bold silhouette. No pilasters, and no projections or mouldings disturb the coherence of these cleanly modelled surfaces. Traditional masonry construction is adapted here to a new conception of form and rises to splendid heights.

Louis Sullivan (1856–1924), however, had given the most searching consideration to the construction and functional problems of skyscrapers, and his theoretical principles are as important as his buildings. "All things in nature", said Sullivan, "have a shape, that is to say, a form, an outward semblance, that tells us what they are, that distinguishes them from ourselves and from each other."[9] Comparison with nature leads him to the conclusion that it must also be the object of architectural creation to give to every building its fitting and unmistakable form. "Whether it be the sweeping eagle in his flight or the open apple-blossom, the toiling work-horse, the blithe swan, the branching oak, the winding stream at its base, the drifting clouds, over all the coursing sun, form ever follows function and this is the law." And he underlines these ideas in his final assertion: "Where function does not change form does not change".

32. William Le Baron Jenney. Home Insurance Building, Chicago, 1883–85. Logical development of the steel skeleton, which is hidden behind the historical treatment of the exterior.

←

31. D. H. Burnham and J. W. Root. Reliance Building, Chicago, 1890; further floors added 1894. Classic instance of the early American skeleton frame. Glass tower with wide "Chicago windows"; narrow horizontal terra-cotta bands; lively effect of bays.

33. Louis Sullivan. Guaranty Trust Building, Buffalo, 1895. Sullivan's theories in practice. The sky-scraper is built in three parts: ground and first floors for shops, the remainder for offices, with a final floor for services. Vertical character stressed by recessing the horizontal panels below the windows.

In order to be able to develop the typical form of a high office building, Sullivan examines its functional character as a basis for defining the architect's problem: "Wanted – 1st, a storey below-ground, containing boilers, engines of various sorts, etc. – in short, the plant for power, heating, lighting, etc. 2nd, a ground floor, so called, devoted to stores, banks, or other establishments requiring large area, ample spacing, ample light, and great freedom of access. 3rd, a second storey readily accessible by stairways – this space usually in large subdivisions, with corresponding liberality in structural spacing and expanse of glass and breadth of external openings. 4th, above this an indefinite number of storeys of offices piled tier upon tier, one tier just like another tier, one office just like all the other offices – an office being similar to a cell in a honey-comb, merely a compartment, nothing more. 5th, and last, at the top of this pile is placed a space or storey that, as related to the life and usefulness of the structure, is purely physio-

34. Louis Sullivan. Carson, Pirie, Scott Department Store, Chicago, 1899; additions 1903-04. Detail. Strictly organized network of horizontal and vertical lines as an expression of the skeleton frame. The relief pattern of the surface is obtained by setting back the long windows and by the sharply defined ornament of the surrounds.

35. Carson, Pirie, Scott Department Store. General view.

logical in its nature – namely, the attic. In this the circulatory system completes itself and makes its grand turn, ascending and descending. The space is filled with tanks, pipes, valves, sheaves and mechanical etcetera that supplement and complement the force-originating plant hidden below-ground in the cellar."

From these considerations it follows, for Sullivan, that the building should have three parts. The ground and first floors form a single unit, for they fulfil similar functions. Above them rise the offices, which are all treated in the same way externally, and the building is completed by a floor for services, usually provided with only a few openings. Sullivan's question about the expressive value of such a building and his answer did not seem so self-evident in his day as they may appear to us: "What is the chief characteristic of the tall office building? And at once we answer, it is lofty... It must be every inch a proud and soaring thing, rising in sheer exultation that from bottom to top it is a unit without a single dissenting line." And in order to indicate this feeling of height, he stressed the vertical organization of the building. These theories of Sullivan found expression in the Wainwright Building in St. Louis (1890–91) and the Guaranty Trust Building in Buffalo (1895) [33].

By accentuating the vertical elements which projected beyond the horizontal members, he emphasised the upward thrust of the structure. In the Schlesinger-Meyer Department store (now Carson, Pirie, Scott) erected between 1899 and 1904, Sullivan concentrated on the provision of unobstructed sales space [34, 35], in this commission he developed an external articulation which displays the structural skeleton with great precision, creating a strongly defined network of horizontal and vertical lines which correspond to the pattern of the steel frame. In this way, in contrast to earlier office buildings, the long windows and wide sills underline the horizontal arrangement of the building.

Sullivan's ideas had a revolutionary effect in his day. Even the notion that a building should be planned from the inside outwards, and that the similarity of office spaces must, therefore, be reflected in a corresponding structural treatment, was at that time new. The prevailing eclecticism decided the elevational treatment in accordance with an overall scheme without bothering about the functional needs of the building. And this eclectic attitude was to smother the tendencies in Chicago which had led to the first logically conceived high buildings of our time.

The World Fair took place in Chicago in 1893. Out of lath, plaster and timber frames a make-believe world of historical forms was conjured up. The so-called abstract beauty of form triumphed over functional form in Sullivan's sense. McKim, one of the leading American architects of this movement, maintained that the construction of a building should not be apparent in the completed work, the contention being that in order to create "pure forms", one must be free of any connection with the structure. Instead forms, typical of masonry construction, were used unconsciously[10]. A massive effect was applied to the corners, where in masonry construction it is essential for rigidity, the corners being stressed with projecting freestone blocks and the windows kept narrow. These buildings, however, are pure steel frame structures. The forms used are in complete opposition to the changed sociological requirements. Their incompatibility with the new materials was too great for another renaissance of historical forms to have resulted; while the creative link between construction and form was so openly severed that no encouragement towards a new architecture could emerge from this blending of empty forms with novel structural materials.

36. Ernest R. Flagg. Equitable Building, New York, 1915. Eclecticism prevails in the U. S. A. The School of Chicago seems to have had no influence. Lack of proportion, arbitrary mixture of styles (Renaissance and Baroque features piled one on top of the other).

In 1887 Frank Lloyd Wright[11], then eighteen years old, came to Chicago and in 1888 entered the architectural office of Sullivan and Adler. Only a few years earlier in 1885 William Le Baron Jenny had completed the Home Insurance Building as the first steel frame structure and in so doing paved the way for the tremendous developments in the form of the skyscraper in Chicago. In this stimulating atmosphere, among architects who were striving as their first objective to create an architecture which grew out of structure, the young Wright absorbed impressions which were to have a decisive influence on his later development.

In 1894 Wright left the office of Sullivan and Adler to practise independently. There followed in quick succession a series of domestic buildings which soon revealed the individuality of his idiom as an artist. The identification of the building with its natural setting, and development of the house from the inside outwards without regard for traditional canons of form, are the marks of his architectural language, symbolised in the concept of "organic building".

This principle had already appeared in Sullivan, who exemplified with it the interdependence of form and function and used this idea especially to distinguish his own architecture from the eclecticism of the time. The notion of organic building is ambiguous and does not lend itself to precise definition. It has, however, nothing to do with imitating organic forms. Its meaning theoretically implies that the architect should be creative like nature, that is to say that "the inner nature of the problem always carried the solution in itself"[12]. But in practice and above all this concept meant for Frank Lloyd Wright harmony with the natura attributes of the site, the use of primary materials like wood and stone, and consideration for human needs and feelings.

All these tendencies found exemplary expression in the Jacobs House, Middleton, Wis., built in 1948 [37–39]. Organic building is clearly manifested here. As a contrast to this fundamental approach it is worth looking at the almost exactly contemporary Farnsworth House of Mies van der Rohe (1950) which, detached from the ground, open on every side, and with its consistent use of inorganic materials like steel and glass, ushers in a more rationally conceived stereometric architecture [40].

37. Frank Lloyd Wright. Herbert Jacobs House, Middleton, Wis., 1948. View from north east. The house as "a safe stronghold". Complete integration with the site. Semi-circular building crowning a gently sloping hill. A mound raised on the north side acts as a wind-break. Use of natural materials from local sources: sandstone and fir.

8/39. Herbert Jacobs House. View from south-ast and of interior of large living-room. The Sun-semicircle-house" (Wright) opens out owards the south. The projecting roof allows nly the winter sun to penetrate. The 50-foot-ong living-room is divided naturally into different ving areas without losing its unity. Bedrooms, in he gallery storey above.

About 1910 there appeared in Germany and Holland publications on Wright which excited the greatest interest. It was apparent that here was an architect working on his own on another continent who had long known how to solve the problems which engaged the minds of Europe's leading architects. By putting his ideas into practice Frank Lloyd Wright demonstrated that he was able to build upon the theories of the most progressive architectural school of the period, whilst reaching back to the living tradition of the simple Anglo-Saxon country house.

In 1902 there appeared the Willitts House in Highland Park, Chicago [41, 42]. The ground plan is freely developed in the form of a cross disposed about a central fireplace as the principal feature. The wings of the building reach out like arms over the surrounding tree-studded site which has lawns running right up to the walls of the house. The projecting roof emphasises the horizontal effect and the blending of the house with its setting. Wright's living rooms are often linked with the outside world by large openings, whilst preserving their feeling of intimacy. This tendency is very noticeable in the principal room of the Coonley House 1908) in Riverside [43], where the ceiling follows the gentle slope of the roof and

40. Mies van der Rohe. Farnsworth House, Plano, Ill., 1950. The house as a glass cube; separated from the ground and open on all sides. The right angle as a design principle; use of inorganic materials – steel and glass.

41. F. Lloyd Wright. Willitts House, Highlan
Park, Chicago, Ill., 1902. "Prairie House". Spa
cious layout; the wings of the building reach ou
into the park; horizontal bands of windows unde
heavy eaves; mixture of one and two storeys
"open and closed" wall surfaces.

gives the room the desired feeling of being enclosed. The living room becomes a safe place, a den. Wide, projecting eaves diminish the intensity of the light. Instead of many separate rooms Wright often provided one principal living room which is divided into sections and is sometimes two storeys high with a gallery. The great importance of these early buildings lies in the daring conception of this new way of moulding space, in the escape from the cold splendour of un-needed rooms, in the unconcern with which natural building materials are left visible on the inside – nowadays a conspicuous expedient of modern architecture – and in the logical way in which an appropriate architectural expression is sought for the internal structure.

These domestic buildings made Wright immediately famous in Europe, where he stood as the outstanding modern architect of the house. It was, therefore, all the more astonishing to European observers at this time that in America Wright was completely isolated. Indeed as Bruno Taut has said in his book "Die Neue Baukunst" (1929), which is based on his own experiences, even "to mention his name was shocking".[13] The revival of eclecticism in America meant not only the end

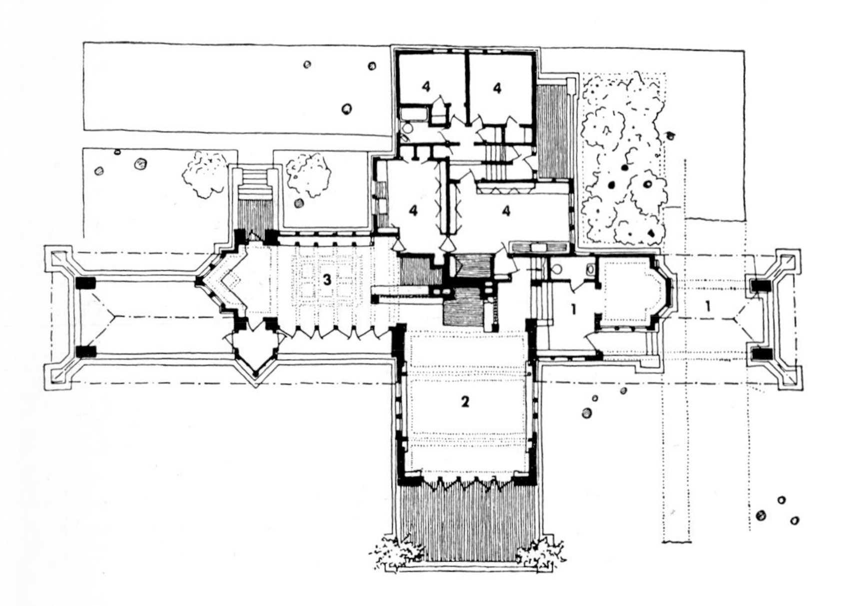

42. Willitts House. Ground floor plan. "Windmill-sail" layout. The various building parts form a cross about the chimney, the central feature of the house. 1. Entrance. 2. Living-room. 3. Dining-room. 4. Kitchen and utility rooms.

43. F. Lloyd Wright. Avery Coonley House, Riverside, Ill., 1908. Living-room. Windows on three sides provide close contact with nature. Intimate feeling ensured by low ceiling, which follows pitch of the roof.

of the School of Chicago, but also the stemming of all other modern currents. Only with the rising influence of the new European architecture did Americans begin again to take interest in Wright's work. He is now recognized as one of the great pioneers of modern architecture.

A danger to which the organic conception of architecture is exposed can lie in a sentimental enthusiasm for nature which ignores the technical possibilities of our time. Wright moved further and further away from any such standpoint. He endeavoured to apply the resources of technology rationally: "Technics must not enslave us, we must make them our servant"[14]. It is true that Wright used reinforced concrete and steel in later buildings, but he hardly employed these materials as constituent elements of a new architectural form. Above everything else he stuck to his conception of natural materials, and characteristically paid little or no attention to the invention of the steel frame which had been decisively important for the architecture of the Chicago school. Even the office building for the Larkin works in Buffalo (1904), sublime in its cubist simplicity, was constructed of load-bearing masonry, and when in 1906 Wright used reinforced concrete for

44. F. Lloyd Wright. Martin House, Buffalo, N. Y. 1904. Horizontal emphasis; shady projecting roofs; early example of the horizontal ribbon window, an important feature of form in the twenties.

the Unitarian Church in Oak Park, Chicago, the form of the building shows no indication of this. The architectural elements are heavy and monumental and display none of the elegance proper to forms evolved from reinforced concrete.
After World War I Wright went on with his series of domestic projects. In the twenties came houses in California constructed with precast concrete units which acquire a singular texture with their stamped patterns [48]. Between 1930 and 1940 followed the "Usonian" houses, small dwellings in which, despite deliberately low construction costs, Wright evolved remarkably ingenious planning solutions [45, 46].
The administration building of S. C. Johnson & Son Inc. (Racine, Wis., 1936–39) was built as a self-contained group with no visual connection with the world outside [49–52]. Natural light enters through the ceiling and through bands of glass tubing laid high up into the walls. This effect of seclusion is increased by the shut-in form of the buildings. The construction of the main office hall consists of conical piers tapering towards steel bases and merging above into circular discs, ties to the pier heads ensuring rigidity. The room is lit by roof lights between the cylindrical discs: a remarkable structural device, unique of its kind. The spatial impression obtained is, as Giedion rightly says, "magic"[15]. Is there any point, however, in generating emotional values of this kind in an office block? Perhaps this building more than any other illustrates the division which lies between Wright and the main stream of modern architecture. Wright did not pass through the phase of matter-of-fact utility construction and purpose fulfilment which was

45. F. Lloyd Wright. Catherine Winkler and Alma Goetsch House, Okemos, Mich., 1939. "Usonian House" prototype. Ingenious plan with low building costs. The principal living-room accommodates a variety of activities. The kitchen forms part of it. Brick construction and wood panelling. Part of the garden is enclosed with wooden walls.

→

47. F. Lloyd Wright. Fallingwater, Bear Run, Pa., 1936. Vertical core of ashlar, around which the house is disposed in terraces. In its emphasis on horizontal, vertical, projecting and recessed surfaces, the house shows tendencies similar to those in European architecture (De Stijl, Le Corbusier). Reinforced concrete used by Wright for the first time.

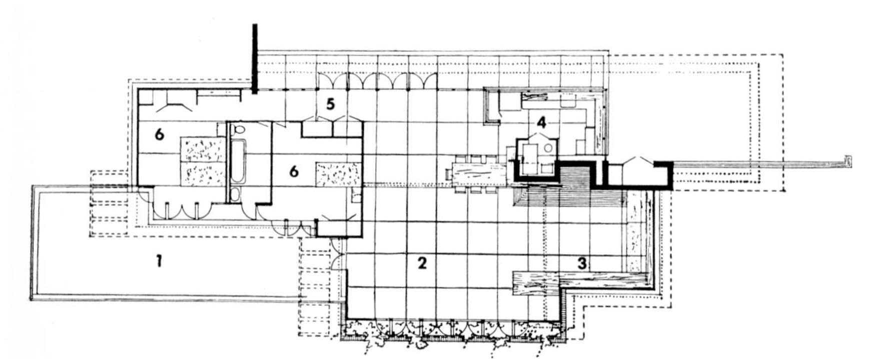

46. Catherine Winkler and Alma Goetsch House Floor plan. 1. Enclosed yard. 2. Living-room. 3. Inglenook. 4. Kitchen. 5. Passage to bedrooms 6. Bedrooms.

→

48. F. Lloyd Wright. Mrs. George Madison Millard's house, Pasadena, Calif., 1923. Concrete block walls. The stamped relief patterns aim at an ornamental effect through the play of light and shade.

an essential stage for architecture in Europe. He has remained a great individualist continually causing surprise by the power of his imagination. Wright's grammar of form is too strongly tinged with his individuality to lead to the formation of a school of any considerable size. But the influence of his ideas which strove to break away from accepted forms – and also from geometrical exactitude – and turned towards nature, towards flexibility and adaptability to widely differing conditions of environment, is to-day as vital as ever. For the constantly quoted opposition between organic and rational architecture to-day no longer seems to exist to its former extent. Rational architecture, the primary object of which is to achieve simpler forms evolved out of the purpose of the building, advanced very soon beyond this stage, bringing greater coherence to the newly developed structural elements and an enriched formal scale.

49/50. F. Lloyd Wright. S. C. Johnson and Son Inc., Racine, Wis., 1936–39. Interior of administration building. The office space, in accordance with American tradition, is a single unit. An introverted spatial conception, isolated from the outside world. Cone-shaped columns widen at the top into umbrella-like slabs to form the roof. Ceiling panels and bands of glass tubing provide even lighting without dazzle.

51. S. C. Johnson and Son Inc. Main entrance. The completely enclosed interior is reflected in the compact, starkly plastic, effect of the building masses. Contrasts of straight edges and curves, and of red brick and white cement bands.

52. S. C. Johnson and Son Inc. Laboratory tower.

The trend away from Eclecticism

At the beginning of the nineties movements appeared in Belgium, France, Holland, Austria and Germany which, despite their differences, have features in common. Shared by all was a complete rejection of past styles, and also a search for new forms of ornament which would be an expression of their own time. In their emphasis upon ornament these movements still clung to the nineteenth century, but they built up their own vocabulary of form upon flower movement and tensely curved lines. In the course of time, however, there arose an ever stronger aspiration which led beyond the search for a contemporary language of ornament, a consciousness of the fundamental basis of architectural design towards which Otto Wagner, Adolf Loos, Hendrik Petrus Berlage and Henry van de Velde were groping.

In 1896 there appeared in Munich the magazine "Jugend" which gave its name to the new movement in Germany. The word "Jugendstil" implies not only something new, a breaking-out of eager youth, but conveys a sense of the topical urgency of such endeavours, whilst suggesting a picture of successive generations. Equally clearly set out was the programme of this young movement in its customary West-European conception as "Art Nouveau" = new art; by which was intended a search for an art free from all historical ties[16].

Two things should be distinguished in the currents of opinion of the time. There is first the unquestionable feeling that nineteenth-century eclecticism must be done away with. It is an attack by individuals upon a whole era. But besides this emotional hostility is a clear recognition that "every new style originates gradually from the previous style; new methods of construction, new materials, new human problems demand a change... from existing forms"[17]. These words were spoken by Otto Wagner in 1895 at the time when Louis Sullivan was insisting that "form ever follows function".

The emphasis on ornament springs from an attitude which is still a long way from modern architectural thinking. But the same attitude, no longer taking a dead tradition for granted, led also to new solutions in architecture. As the ornament of Jugendstil follows a rhythm of line of its own, so each individual building is no longer subordinated to the limitations imposed by a symmetrical "show front"

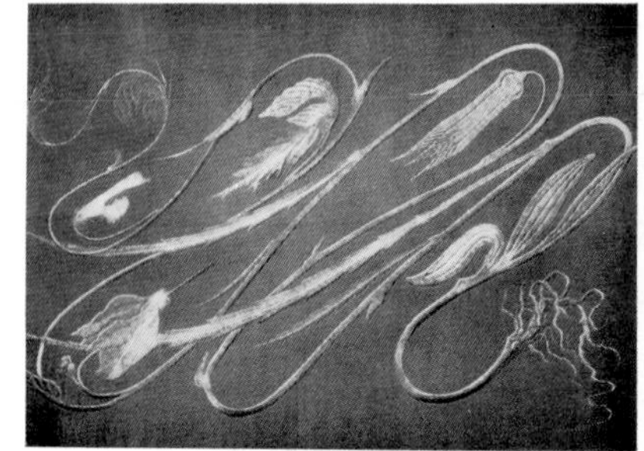

53. Henry van de Velde. Door handles, Folkwang Museum, Hagen i. W., 1901. Ornament developed from structural characteristics.

54. Hermann Obrist. Whip-lash pattern, embroidery, 1893.

55. Middle-class living-room about 1890. Overdressed imitation of historical styles.

56. Henry van de Velde. Study, 1899. Pure "Jugendstil".

57. Living-room after 1900. Debased "Jugendstil".

elevation, but is governed by the particular needs and space requirements of the building programme. Houses now begin to appear in which a basically changed conception is revealed in the free asymmetrical plan and in the flexible arrangement of space on different levels.

For purposes of comparison the significance and tendencies of Jugendstil in Germany and also its swift vulgarization must be recognized. The sitting room of 1890 was stuffed with furniture, the form of which was copied from the styles of the past. Heavy curtains darkened the windows. Contrast this with a study by van de Velde! It contains a few pieces of furniture of clean-cut design and good craftsmanship, appropriate to the requirements of the room. The wall comes into its own right; bright colours give a sense of light. The furniture still provides a decorative note with its vertical lines, but the difference between this and the normal middle-class sitting-room is glaringly obvious. The forms of Jugendstil in the hands of imitators were copied as a purely money-making fashion and grew into a tasteless type of luxurious decoration [55–57].

Art Nouveau and Jugendstil had their forerunners in England, where John Ruskin (1819–1900) and William Morris (1834–1896) had been active in the second half of the nineteenth century. Both strove to counteract the confusion of forms prevailing at that time by the purifying effect of simple handicrafts and the beauty of natural materials. Morris established workshops in which handmade furniture, handwoven materials, wallpaper and household utensils were produced. As early as 1859 the architect Philip Webb built the Red House, Bexley Heath, for Morris [58, 59, 264], which in its spatial composition and fresh and unconventional layout stood in the greatest imaginable contrast to the overdressed stucco villas customary at this period. Viewed historically it is also one of the first attempts to bring a new and constructive approach to domestic building. C.F.A. Voysey and R. Norman Shaw, two of the best known English architects, continued along the path first taken by Morris and Webb [60].

The architectural significance of these experiments in England lies above all in a new conception of the house, which is now regarded as an organism of which the external expression grows out of its internal requirements. Two-storeyed halls often formed the principal spatial feature, around which the other rooms were loosely grouped. These buildings indicate a break-away from the convention of the symmetrical plan and of outward display; the frequently expressed claim of a later period that function should be regarded as the supreme originator of form, found its first expression in domestic building here. At the same time these architects designed not only the house itself, but its fittings, furniture and household equipment as well. The emergence of the modern architect as the creator of the entire environment of man was for the first time an understood fact.

Besides Webb, Shaw and Voysey, the Scotsman Charles Rennie Mackintosh

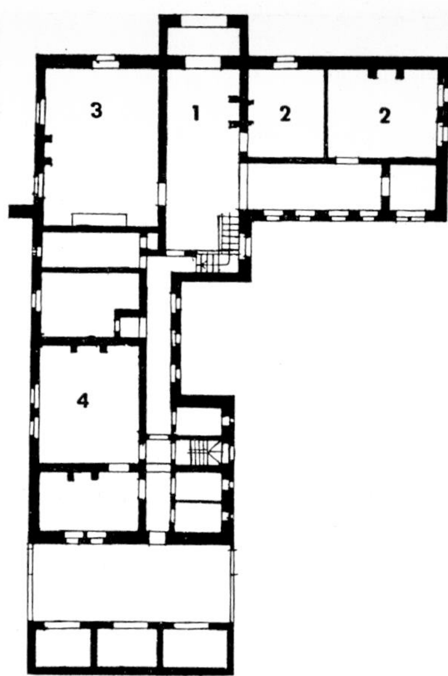

58. Philip Webb. Red House, Bexley Heath, Kent 1859. A new conception of the house. Freedom from the tyranny of symmetry; planning from the inside outwards; rich variety characterizes the building mass. Details still Gothic in feeling. Colour and texture. Plain brick surfaces inside and out.

59. Red House. Floor plan. 1. Entrance hall 2. Sitting rooms. 3. Dining room. 4. Kitchen.

(1868–1928) was especially well known in Europe. With his work in the field of the applied arts he had a particularly strong influence on Otto Wagner's circle and the Vienna "Sezession". His most important achievement as an architect was his building for the Glasgow School of Art (1898–99), to which a library wing was added in 1907–09 [61].

The scheme still shows a symmetrical floor plan, but the form of the façade points in new directions. The effect depends upon an abrupt contrasting of plain wall and glazed surfaces, but still on a solid monumentality of form as well.

The artistic struggles of Europe were lastingly influenced by England. There was a fundamental difference, however, between the aspirations of Morris and the continental movements which started later. Morris and Ruskin saw in the machine the enemy of all culture.

Honest craftsmanship was their protest against mass production by machines, which threatened to lead to the decay of all form. Morris saw clearly the danger of the factory product undermining civilized values, but he did not see that with

→

61. Charles Rennie Mackintosh. Glasgow Art School, Library wing, 1907–09. The bays and vertical windows add a lively plastic quality to the massive block.

60. C. F. A. Voysey. Living-room of "The Orchard", Chorley Wood, 1900. Various levels to the same floor. Convenient allocation of space. Simple clear forms without style-mimicry.

the machine a tool had been given to mankind which – rightly used – offered splendid opportunities for the future.
The work of the Belgian Henry van de Velde (1863–1957) now comes into the picture at the beginning of the 1900s. Van de Velde was a painter, but he was very soon confronted with a problem of conscience; whether, in face of the challenging demands of his time, he was justified in living by painting alone. Moreover, his attention had been drawn to Morris and Ruskin and their circle. From them he derived a positive inspiration, whilst recognizing also that without technics a new culture was impossible: "The completely useful object, which is created according to the principles of rational and logical construction, fulfils the first condition of beauty, achieves the very essence of beauty"[18]. Functional excellence is assumed from the aesthetic effect.
In his early furniture designs the influence of this sort of statement of belief is hardly detectable. Their general form consists largely of ornamental lines which, in contrast to the delicate curves of purely floral decoration, are far more strongly determined by structural principles and mutually reinforce, support and grasp each other [53, 56]. Their effect, however, depends upon the objects on which they appear and they are still often applied to architecture. But in this early period it was not so essential for far-reaching theoretical principles to be realized in practice. The important thing was that such fundamental claims were put forward at all.

62. Henry van de Velde. Dining-room, Weimar 1902–03. Considered in relation to his early furniture designs, functional and practical virtues now replace ornament.

63. Henry van de Velde. Weimar Art School, 1906. Large glass surfaces set in steel frames of standard sections. The windows in the mansard roof light the studios.

54. Henry van de Velde. Werkbund theatre, Cologne, 1914. The various parts of the building are moulded into a unified cubic effect.

Van de Velde's real sphere of influence was to be in Germany, where he first became known through his participation in the Dresden Art Exhibition of 1897. Karl Osthaus invited him to Hagen to complete the Folkwang Museum, until he was able to put his ideas as an artist and teacher to work as Director of the School of Applied Art at Weimar. He reorganized the school buildings and established workshops in which the students acquired practical experience. The products of the workshops were sold, so that an unbroken connection with the professional world was provided. Walter Gropius, who took over the school in 1919 and founded the Bauhaus there, was to find much on which he could build.

In his architectural work, as in the Weimar Art School (1906) and the Werkbund Theatre in Cologne (1914), van de Velde succeeded in translating the problems posed by the functional needs of the building into vigorous expression. The glass surfaces of the Weimar Art School, placed between heavy pillars, and the roof lights set in the steep mansard roof, have the same expressive power as, in another context, van de Velde's furniture. In the Cologne Werkbund theatre he devised a structural form, which moulded all the individual building parts into

55. Victor Horta. Maison du Peuple, Brussels, 1897. Exposed, delicately articulated, supporting frame; light appearance; structural integrity.

66. Victor Horta. House in the Rue de Turin, Brussels, 1893. Flexibility in use of space emphasised by differences in floor level. Iron now also used in domestic building, although still decoratively interpreted.

a single whole and reduced the ornament to a few lines and surfaces which enhance rather than diminish the cubelike compactness. The structural conception, already apparent in his early furniture designs, now enabled the whole richly varied building mass to take shape.

In Belgium van de Velde was not alone in his endeavours. In the nineteenth century a circle of adventurous artists, known as "Les XX", had already appeared in Brussels, who were strongly influenced by William Morris and his followers. In 1893 Victor Horta (1861–1947), who belonged to this group, built the house in the Rue de Turin [66] in Brussels at a period when there were still few signs of the new movement on the Continent. Many things found expression here for the first time. In this building and in the Maison du Peuple (1897) iron was systematically used [65], which up till now was only to be found similarly applied in factories and exhibition buildings. Iron as a building material, which permitted a more open floor plan, now made its undisguised appearance in domestic building. While in the Rue de Turin the cast-iron stanchions were still, decoratively speaking, derived from plants, their sprouting tendrils merging into the painted ceiling, the

67. August Endell. Elvira photographic studio Munich, 1897–98. The exuberant movement conveyed by the ornament on the façade acted like a rallying call to "Jugendstil".

3. Richard Riemerschmid. Theatre, Munich, 901. Original interpretation of traditional theatre. Moulded space. Ceiling and wall become one. oat-shaped form of ceiling, with light fittings reating an ornamental pattern of light points. eeling of intimacy.

horizontal, vertical and diagonal members of the structural frame of the Hall in the "Maison du Peuple" is connected to a delicately articulated network, which in its transparency and lightness goes beyond ornamental effect and becomes an expression of the principles of construction.

One of the chief centres of Jugendstil was Munich, where in 1897–98 August Endell built the Elvira Studio for a photographer [67]. On one wall surface is placed a huge decorative feature of delightfully exuberant lines. Its effect must have been like a rallying call in Munich at that time. The ingenuity of their ornamentation of applied art and furniture was the important contribution made by the Munich group, to which Behrens, Eckmann, Obrist, Pankok, Paul and Riemerschmid belonged. To start with – with the possible exception of the work of Riemerschmid [68] – no significant architectural ideas sprang from this circle. For this it needed the stimulus of another country, Austria. The place where architectural problems were worked out in Germany was not Munich, but Darmstadt. Moreover, the particular member of the Munich group whose change-over to architecture was crucially important for industrial building, found his true place away from the Bavarian capital.

69. Joseph Olbrich. Hochzeitsturm, Darmstad 1907. Chief feature of the group of buildings the Mathildenhöhe and of the view of Darmstad The bands of windows, extended round th corners, give a rhythm to the brick surfac Colour effects of materials; red brick, light ashl and green oxydized copper.

In 1901 a comprehensive exhibition of contemporary art was opened on the Mathildenhöhe at Darmstadt [69–71]. Instead of the usual museum type of display, the participating artists were to have the opportunity of building and furnishing houses according to their own ideas. The patron was Archduke Ernst Ludwig of Hessen, who had set the aim of this exhibition as the revival of the arts under the leadership of architecture. The artist's colony on the Mathildenhöhe may be considered as an experiment in collaboration between art and architecture. It stated a problem which is highly significant for the social importance of architecture in our time. With its artists' houses, exhibition building and park the Darmstadt Mathildenhöhe sought to provide a city with a vital centre of culture. Joseph Olbrich's Hochzeitsturm, visible a long way off, was its architectonic expression and to-day it still dominates the view of Darmstadt.

The Deutscher Werkbund[19] was founded on a much broader basis in 1907, with architects, artists, manufacturers and sociologists acting in unison. Its object was to bridge the gulf between creative artists and practical industrialists. In contrast to the reformative attempts of Morris, the Werkbund did not reject machines

70. Peter Behrens. His own house, Darmstad 1901. Only building in the artists' colony nc erected by Olbrich. Strong lines emphasised b pilasters. Feeling for materials, and instinctiv sense of the texture of brick and tile, whic stimulated Mies van der Rohe, the young assistar of Behrens.

1. Joseph Olbrich. Ernst-Ludwig-House, Darmstadt, 1901. Studio building and common rooms. The vertical lines of the monumental figures and the exuberant ornamental relief of the moorish arch of the entrance contrast with the deliberately plain, horizontal, arrangement of the elevation.

and their products, but strove to bring the artist and manufacturer together, for only in this way was it possible to combat shoddy industrial standards effectively. With its demands for fitness for purpose and genuine materials, the Werkbund exercised the greatest influence on later developments. After 1918 it became the meeting point of modern architectural currents. The Weissenhof housing scheme built in 1927 in Stuttgart on the occasion of a Werkbund exhibition brought together all the architects who had acquired a name in the "new building" and enabled them to give a representative display of its possibilities [72, 149a, 149b]. The Weissenhof scheme symbolises the long road between Darmstadt and Stuttgart, between 1901 and 1927. Supported by wide publicity the "new building" had opened the way to town-planning and housing schemes, stated the relationship between house and landscape and set itself the problems of prefabrication and domestic building. A princely patron had invited a few enthusiastic artists to an experiment in Darmstadt, but Stuttgart represented a movement which very soon affected all social levels and many nations.

The Darmstadt experiment would hardly have been possible without Austria.

72. Weissenhof housing scheme, Stuttgart, 1927. Instead of the artists' colony, the general community; in place of homes for the few, homes for the many. Housing for everyman, the logical application of the steel frame and of reinforced concrete, and prefabrication are the new tasks.

Joseph Olbrich who, with the exception of the house by Behrens (for himself), designed and built the whole artists' colony, came from the Vienna of Otto Wagner. A well-known architect, until then strongly influenced in his buildings by the Renaissance and the Baroque, Wagner had been appointed in 1894 to the staff of the Vienna Academy. But it was at precisely this time that he was in the act of radically changing his views. In the book "Moderne Architektur", which appeared in 1895, he gave an interpretation of architectural design, recognizing that a modern form was only possible by using the materials and methods of construction of one's own time.

In the first of his buildings erected after 1894, a delight in ornament preponderates, as it did with his like-minded contemporaries. Out of the linear characteristics of iron, forms were developed which still display a stylistic pedantry, as in the stations of the Vienna underground [73]. But beneath the superimposed ornament the construction and simple form of the building is apparent. The Post Office Savings Bank in Vienna, built in 1905, shows what Wagner could do [74]. The banking hall is noteworthy for its clarity of line. All ornament is abolished.

73. Otto Wagner. Station for the Vienna metro politan railway, 1896–97. The Baroque tradition o Vienna lingers in Wagner's work: central dom with oval windows, volutes and cartouches – bu under the decoration the simple, stereometric form is already discernible.

74. Otto Wagner. Vienna Post Office Savings Bank, 1905. Compare Wagner's earlier buildings; all ornament now eliminated, rigidly disciplined form. Glass and steel as the determining materials.

Every part – the rectangular stanchions tapering towards the base, or the longitudinal and transverse members supporting the glazed surfaces – are reduced to their simplest form. Glass and steel are put to the service of a modern structural theory.

Besides Wagner (1841–1918), Adolf Loos (1870–1933), whose views on architectural theory were deeply prophetic, was active in Vienna. Whilst Wagner never rejected ornament entirely, Loos turned against it from the beginning, launching a vigorous attack upon Jugendstil decoration in the work of Olbrich and Hoffmann[20]. His buildings assume a puritanical, but elegant, austerity from their lack of ornament. The simple stereometric block, which in Wagner's buildings was already discernible, emerges undisguised. In his design for the Steiner House in Vienna (1910), Loos renounces all ornamentation and display. The windows are inserted straight into the bare wall surfaces [75]. The stronger his rejection of all ornament, the greater significance he attached to proportions, especially in the relationship of the glazed openings to the plain wall. By achieving fundamentally simple cubic forms, Loos – who had spent much time in England and the United

75. Adolf Loos. Steiner House, Vienna, 1910. Seen from garden. The cube theme. Windows without glazing bars, set in the bare wall surface. The aesthetic effect is obtained by the interplay of transparent and opaque surfaces.

States – completely overcame eclecticism of form and the attitude which went with it, and accomplished one of the greatest pioneering achievements of our architecture.

In Holland H. P. Berlage (1856–1934) laid down the need for simplicity and clarity and for materials of genuine quality, for which Wagner and later Loos had pleaded among the Viennese. "We architects must try to get back to truth, that is to say to grasp the essentials of architecture. This is, and always remains, the art of building, which means the joining together of various elements into a whole in order to enclose a space"[21]. Berlage once more subordinated the individual elements, which had acquired a predominating significance in nineteenth-century architecture, as parts of a disciplined structural whole. Buildings with him also begin to assume a cubic form, the wall becoming a surface in which the separate architectural elements are integrated.

In the interior of the Amsterdam Stock Exchange (1898–1903), Berlage's most important building, the piers of the arcaded area, the freestone abutments, the masonry of the wall areas and the parapets of the galleries are set in one plane [76, 77]. The wall surface springs to life, not because of its plastic qualities, but thanks to Berlage's supreme sensibility in handling materials, his meticulous masonry technique and the dramatic contrast between brick and ashlar. New materials are used by Berlage for covering the room, but two worlds of form – the masonry of the walls and the steel and glass construction of the roof – still abruptly confront each other. At the same time, with its galleries, round windows and denticulated frieze, the building brings back memories of Romanesque architecture.

Through the efforts of these pioneers the endless rotation of stylistic imitations was broken. Although much, like the emphasis on ornament and the heaviness of form, stemmed from a nineteenth-century attitude of mind, the decisive change in outlook was already basically accomplished. The significance of the new structural materials had been experienced and recognized; only from a foundation of absolute straightforward practicality could a new architectural language arise". We have had enough of originality. What we need is the self-evident"[22] (Karl Scheffler).

The new architecture had to grow out of its own age. Hermann Muthesius, one

→

76. H. P. Berlage. Stock Exchange, Amsterdam 1898–1903. Romanesque echoes. The wall surfaces, almost bare of plastic features, come close to the conception of the cubic space. Masonry and glass-steel-construction come abruptly face to face.

→

77. Stock Exchange, Amsterdam. Exterior. The lower floors of the tower blend with the elevational treatment of the building as a whole.

of the founders of the Werkbund, expressed in the clearest way in 1902 the facts of the situation at that time: "The result of the machine can only be unadorned practical form"[23]. Unadorned practical form, however, could be introduced most effectively at that time in the field of factory building which was ignored by "official" architecture. "We found only in industrial building the line of least resistance, a field surrendered to us all the more readily since it appeared unimportant to official architecture"[24] (Hans Poelzig). Thus it was that in the first decade of the new century a series of industrial buildings took shape, which became a model for subsequent generations. Horta, Berlage, the Viennese and the artists of Darmstadt had in their various ways liberated architecture from the convention of the showy façade and historical ornament and indeed from the recapitulation of past styles in general. They had come close to achieving buildings of a simple geometrical basic form and evolved the first syllables of a language derived from new structural materials and methods. The Spaniard Antoni Gaudí (1852–1926) opened the way to other possibilities contained in the art of the 80s and 90s, with his inexhaustible fantasies and the wealth of his

often extraordinary inventions. He translated the flowing line of Jugendstil into the three-dimensional form of a consistently directed plastic art and achieved a supremely expressive architecture. As with the predilection for plant forms displayed in particular by Art Nouveau in France, Gaudí too – after a series of buildings in the moorish-oriental style – turned towards organic natural forms, and devoted himself intensively to their study, often working with plaster casts. Directly borrowed organic forms do not appear on Gaudí's later buildings. His interests were increasingly attracted towards the internal structure, rather than the outward aspect, of nature.

The material in which Gaudí designed his buildings was usually stone. But he broke away from the conventional, centuries-old, structural methods, in order to be able to develop new forms. By preliminary studies, in which he used scale models of wire and paper loaded with metal weights, he sought to clarify his spatial conceptions and to calculate the load stresses involved in his complicated vaulted shapes. For the most part his work is still an exposition of Gothic forms and construction methods, which are particularly conspicuous in the un-

78. Antoni Gaudí. Chapel of the Colonia Güe Barcelona, 1898–1914. Gaudí realizes his aim continuing the work of the great architects of th middle ages. He replaces the Gothic vau system of vertical columns and arches by obliqu supports aligned to the direction of the shea forces of the vault.

. Antoni Gaudí. Casa Milá, Barcelona, 1905 1910. The building as a single expression of rm. Plastic modelling of entire building mass; owing "Jugendstil" lines; fantastic and eccentric inventions of form.

completed church of the Sagrada Familia, a work of fantastic imaginative power. In his efforts "to take up the work of the great master builders of the middle ages where they had left it"[25], Gaudí belongs to the nineteenth century. For our time the significance of his œuvre lies above all in the comprehensive plastic modelling of the entire building as one whole, which in its structural unity – but only in this characteristic – can be compared with the buildings of Otto Wagner and Adolf Loos. Furthermore the rich inspiration derived from organic forms seems like an early anticipation of the vigorous shapes which began to appear in the thirties in architecture and town planning. A piece of plastic originality like the balustrade of the Parque Güell which follows the contour of a hill and comprises, in addition to ceramic tiles and coloured glass, undressed locally quarried natural stone, is as closely linked in its linear pattern with the structure of the landscape as Aalto's students' residential hall in Cambridge, Mass. [198], or the elongated curves of Reidy's block of flats in Rio de Janeiro [81].

). Antoni Gaudí. Casa Milá, Barcelona, 1905 1910. Roof.

. Affonso Eduardo Reidy. Pedregulho flats, Rio e Janeiro, 1950–52. Whole building linked rganically to the undulating contours of the site.

The beginnings of reinforced concrete in building

To the nineteenth century steel was the only new form of building material. Reinforced concrete had indeed been known in theory since the second half of the last century, but the decisive structural basis for its general use in building was established only in the last decade of the nineteenth century by the Frenchman, François Hennebique. The elevation of reinforced concrete to the level of a structural material of high value occurred at the same time as a widespread endeavour to develop simple, straightforward, architectural forms. This co-incidence of formal aims and new structural possibilities found far more propitious conditions than had been vouchsafed to steel building in the previous century. For one should not overlook in any appreciation of the Machinery Hall in Paris of 1889, or of other important steel structures of the nineteenth century, that they remain more or less isolated achievements measured by the number of buildings erected. Not until the end of the century did a change take place, when a new generation grew up who – pupils of Wagner, van de Velde, Perret and Behrens – were to stride forward in the 1920s to the new architecture. This was the generation of those born about 1885: Gropius (1883), Mies van der Rohe (1886) and Le Corbusier (1887).

Reinforced concrete consists of steel – or more precisely, of thin round steel rods, varying in thickness as a general rule between $^{5}/_{16}$″ and $1^{1}/_{4}$″ (8 and 32 mm) – and concrete. The latter is usually made up of a mixture of sand, shingle, cement and water, and is, therefore, simply an artificially produced mineral. Reinforced concrete combines the compressive and tensile strength of steel. The concrete provides fire protection also by enclosing the thin steel reinforcement rods, protecting them at the same time from rust [84].

Joseph Monier (1823–1906), a Frenchman, was one of the first to use this new material[26]. He made every kind of object out of it, like transportable tanks, pipes and railway sleepers. His first patent, by which his building system was protected, dates from 1867. But he failed to grasp the structural function of steel in reinforced concrete.

More important in this respect were the experiments of the Frenchmen Lambot and Coignet, and the American Thaddeus Hyatt. Lambot exhibited a boat built of reinforced concrete at the Paris World Exhibition of 1855. Coignet described the great significance of this building material in a paper[27] in 1861, while Hyatt

82. Anatole de Baudot. St. Jean de Montmart Paris, 1894. First sacred building in reinforc concrete. The spatial form still exemplifies t vaulted construction of the middle ages, b signs of originality appear in the decoration.

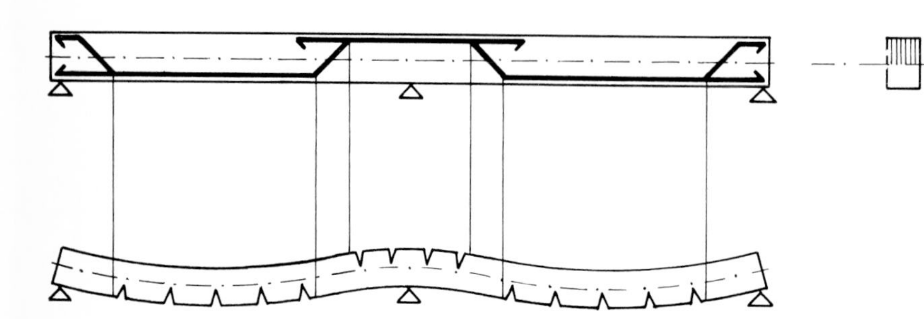

83. Principle of reinforced concrete. Tensi stresses occur in the loading of reinforced co crete beams. The reinforcement bars must l in the beam at the side where the tensile stresse operate.

84. Reinforced concrete construction. Hennebique system, 1892. Typical structure of columns, main beams, secondary beams and slabs.

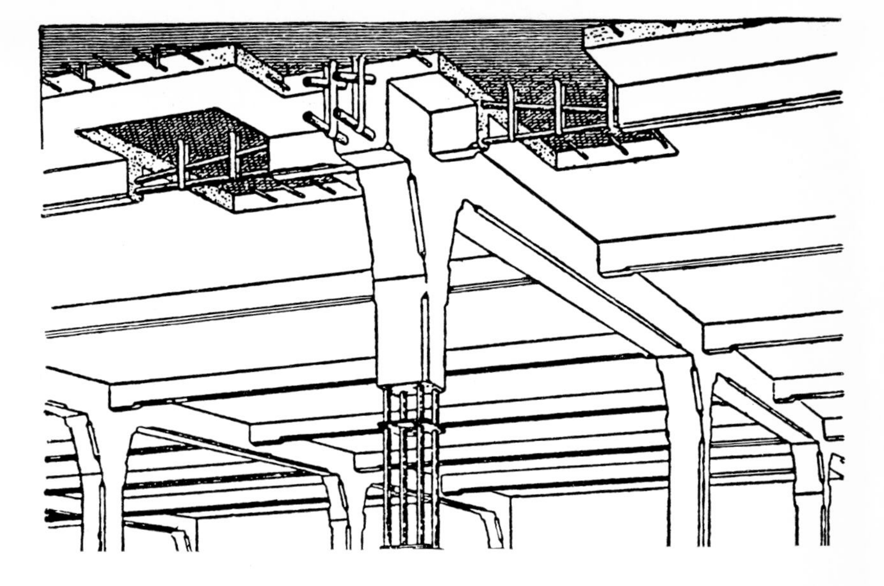

was the first to recognize the structural function fulfilled by steel in reinforced concrete. His experiments, about which he reported in 1877, go back to the 1850s[28]. In his American patent No. 206112 of 16 July 1878 he gives an exact description of the structural conditions: "Iron or steel may be combined with concrete or with bricks as tie-metal, capable of furnishing all the tensile strength needed to balance the compressive resistance of the other materials when the beam or structure is subjected to bending stress" [83].

The credit, however, for having introduced reinforced concrete as an exclusively structural material for buildings (above ground) belongs to François Hennebique (1842–1921). He was the first to construct a building from foundation to roof as a reinforced concrete frame, and also developed the beam and slab, a typical construction form of reinforced concrete, in which the slab in addition to its function as a ceiling (or floor) contributes to an appreciable extent to the load-bearing effectiveness of the beam[29] [84]. Reinforced concrete can be poured into any desired shape, and so offered great possibilities in the creation of form. Of course there was a danger here that a material so easy to mould would be used to imitate forms which were out of date and structurally inappropriate. Hennebique, outstanding as a designer, used it only as a designer should.

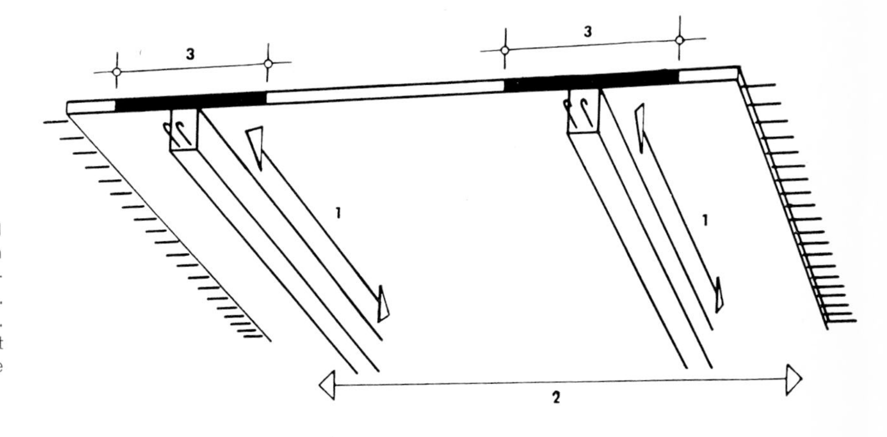

85. Principle of the beam and slab. Slab and beam form a homogeneous whole. In addition to its function as ceiling (floor), the slab contributes to the supporting function of the beam. 1. Direction of span of beam (longitudinal). 2. Direction of span of floor (transverse). 3. Part of slab, which adds compressive strength to the bearing capacity of the beam.

Auguste Perret (1874–1954) was the first who succeeded in developing a characteristic form for reinforced concrete. The straightforward practical quality of his early buildings has lost none of its effect to-day. In 1903 he built the house in the Rue Franklin in Paris [86, 88]. By reducing the supporting vertical elements to a few columns Perret made it possible to arrange the plan of each floor as he wished by means of partitions. The first step towards an open floor-plan had thus been taken, a floor-plan unobstructed by load-bearing walls. Le Corbusier later instanced the open plan as one of the essential bases of his aesthetic philosophy. The façade of the house in the Rue Franklin is faced with thin slabs; the skeleton of the load-bearing frame is discernible, however. The elegance of the architectural conception and the slenderness of the structural elements still surprise us to-day.

With Perret's design for the garage in the Rue de Ponthieu in Paris (1905) unconcealed frame construction as an architectural form makes its appearance – structure and form at the same time [87]. In the areas between the visible structural members huge sheets of glass are inserted, the effect emphasising the

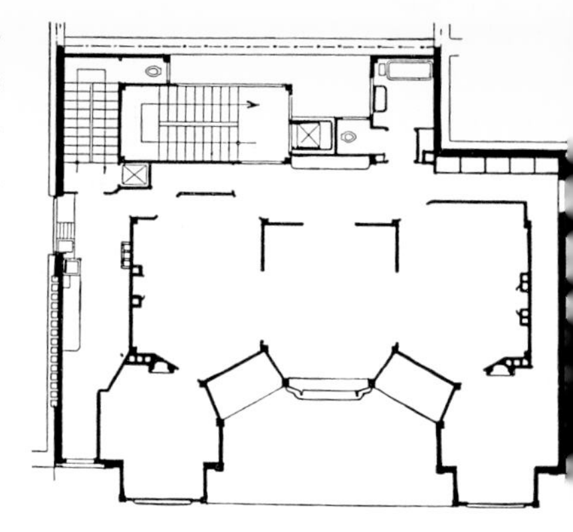

86. Auguste Perret. House in the Rue Franklin, Paris, 1903. Floor plan. The few stanchions upon which the construction depends, permit a high degree of freedom in the organization of space by means of partitions. The flexible plan becomes an essential factor in modern architecture.

87. Auguste Perret. Garage in the Rue de Ponthieu, Paris, 1905. The reinforced concrete frame determines the exterior. The non-bearing wall is made of glass.

3. AEG Turbine factory, Berlin. Section. Light ree-hinged arch construction. Unity of the terior in contrast to the conspicuous separaon of wall and roof in the exterior.

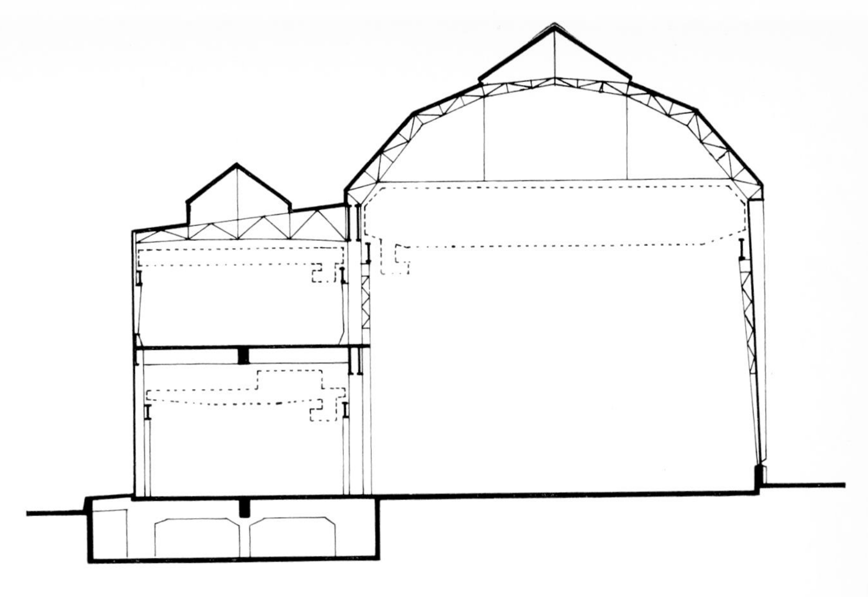

revealing the construction leads Behrens to show the hinge point on the façade. In this way points of intersection between structural members are given architectural prominence.

The principle used here of creating form out of structure is not consistently followed out, however. By canting the glass surfaces inwards a conspicuously projecting cornice is formed, which divides the building into two halves – a heavy roof looming over a building which is set back. This form is justifiable in traditional building, in which the cornice forms a structurally correct division between roof and house. The three-hinged arch used by Behrens, however, swings in one movement from base to crown, recognizing no division between roof and building any more than the interior which consists of a single spatial conception. The monumental effect is heightened by the massive corners where the long façade and gable-ends meet, suggesting an essential reinforcement of the structure. In reality the corners have nothing to do with the construction of the building, but are purely formal elements placed in front of the real load-bearing steel construction. Behrens dramatises form; the building loses its straightforward, practical, character and becomes a monument.

In later buildings an increased tendency to monumentalise functional form is still more apparent. The Berlin AEG factories of 1910 [102] display a markedly symmetrical arrangement, in which an imposing effect is obtained by the stark three-dimensional aspect of the staircase towers. The entrances to the workshops, which are located between the multi-storey sections of the building, are conspicuous for their bold, simplified, classical forms; but at the same time they are combined with expressions of straightforward functionalism, as in the glass-and-column articulation of the side façades.

9. Masonry construction. Diagram. Functional nd structural division between the body of the ouse and its roof, emphasised by the cornice.

00. Three-hinged arch. Diagram. New structural nd spatial form. No division between the body f the house and its roof.

01. AEG Turbine factory, Berlin. Diagram. Despite the use of the three-hinged arch, the conception of form is inspired by masonry construction. The cornice separates the body of the building rom its roof, although there is no structural ustification for this.

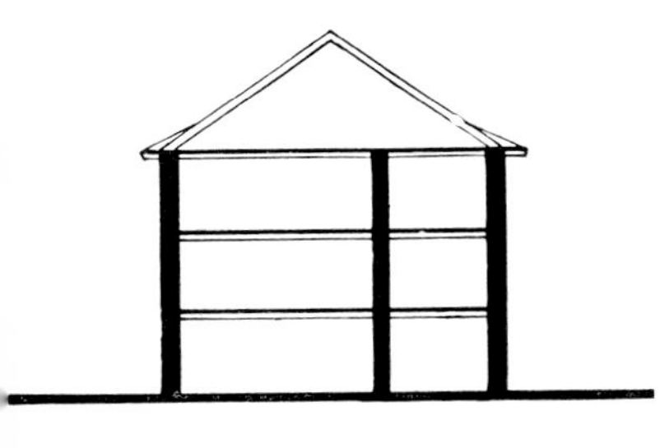

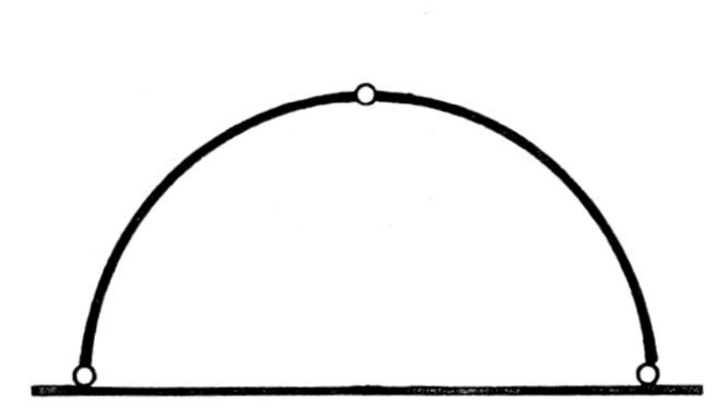

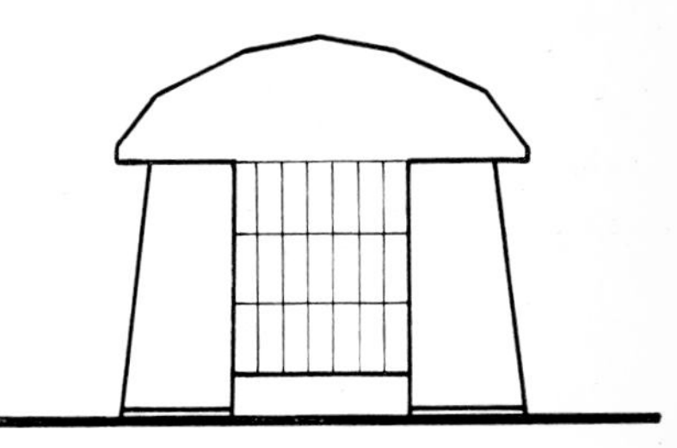

The tendency indicated here towards a classical conception of form is similarly noticeable in the German Embassy in St. Petersburg (1912). Later buildings, especially those of the period after the first world war, like the administrative block of the dye works at Höchst (1920–24) [103], show a decidedly monumental approach, which is expressed in heavy, archaic forms and goes hand in hand with neo-classical tendencies in other designs.
Hans Poelzig (1869–1936), who in his early buildings (contemporary with Behrens) represented a straightforward practical architecture, developed on similar lines. In 1911 his water tower was erected in Posen, which was at first used as an exhibition building before being finally applied to its primary purpose [104]. In its later function as a water tower it exemplifies compactness and symmetry in its external shape. The steel load-bearing frame has no cladding of any sort, either on the inside or the exterior. The windows are inserted as horizontal and vertical elements in the conspicuous pattern of the steel frame. The masonry is treated as in-filling between the load-bearing members. The dynamic form emerges from an objective interpretation of the structural plan. The building is in the line of

102. Peter Behrens. AEG High Tension factory Berlin, 1910. Classical inspiration of the main entrance flanked by massive towers. The factory becomes a monument.

103. Peter Behrens. Administration building of Dye Works, Höchst, 1920–24. Heavy building masses, marked individuality of the romantic forms.

104. Hans Poelzig. Water tower, Posen, 1911. The building rises in a pattern of "steps", which enliven its compact, self-contained, form.

105. Hans Poelzig. Administration building of IG-Farben, Frankfurt-am-Main, 1928–31. Monumental solution of an office building for several thousand employees. Unlike that of the Posen water tower, the steel construction is hidden.

06. Hans Poelzig. Grosses Schauspielhaus, Ber-
n, 1919. Dome over the arena stage (stipulated
y the theatrical impresario, Max Reinhardt).
Poelzig transformed the old Circus Schumann
nto a fantastic grotto of light.

07. Bernhard Hoetger. Paula-Modersohn-Bek-
er House, Bremen, 1927-28 (rebuilt). Eccentricity
t any price.

08. Otto Bartning. "Star" Church, 1922. Model.
Chancel and altar form the central feature of this
rotestant church. The separation of the wall
nd the vault of the roof is eliminated by con-
erging parabolic columns in reinforced con-
rete.

Perret's garage in the Rue de Ponthieu, Paris. Just as Perret in his later work adopted a classical convention, so Behrens and Poelzig tended towards a monumental or exuberant architecture. This last characteristic comes out very clearly in Poelzig's transformation of the Grosses Schauspielhaus in Berlin [106].
The administrative building for I. G. Farben in Frankfurt am Main (1928–31), the most important of Poelzig's late works, follows on the other hand the monumental tendency [105]. Six evenly spaced blocks radiate from the main body of the building which is in the form of an ellipse. The construction is steel frame and the building is faced with thin travertine panels, but the impression of heaviness and monumentality given by this form of cladding recalls massive stone buildings, although structurally it consists of no more than a skin.
The significant contribution, which architects like Perret, Behrens and Poelzig made to modern architecture, came from their work before 1914. In the second decade the picture became confused owing to a development which ran parallel with the emergence of Expressionism in literature and which affected a number of architects in Germany and North Europe. The tradition of modern building,

109. Fritz Hoeger. Chile House, Hamburg, 192
Pictorial architecture. The east corner of t
building assumes the form of a ship's pro
Gentle undulations and sharp edges used
deliberate contrast.

110. Michel de Klerk. Housing, Amsterdam, 192
De Klerk belonged to a group of architect
known as "Wendingen" – turning point –, wh
had sympathies with German "Expressionism"
and especially with Mendelsohn.

which had evolved gradually – even if it was still a tradition of individuals –, seemed in jeopardy, the renunciation of decoration and ornament appeared to be forgotten, the preference for the cube and the plain surface and the honest attitude towards function and construction checked.

Expressionist architecture was an attempt to extend the stark eloquence of the contemporary art of the plain surface to three-dimensional architectural form. The boldly defined silhouette and a restless plastic interpretation of mass were means which gave the building its expressive effect. Above all striking use was made of light, both natural and artificial. It was no accident that this search for an architectural style lasted longer in the field of cinema building than for other building types. Often the building adopted features which might suggest associations with particular objects. Hans Poelzig patterned the dome of the auditorium of the Berlin Schauspielhaus with rows of denticulations which, when the lights changed, produced a fantastic impression through the multifarious interplay of shadows, recalling stalactites in a dripping cave [106]; Fritz Hoeger's Chilehaus (1923) points to a sharp street corner like the prow of a ship [109]. Build

ing has become sculpture. In the architectural fantasies of the Futurists, like Sant' Elia (1888–1917), the idea of movement was added as an additional source of form. Streams of traffic pulsate through buildings in strikingly depicted giant lifts, and along roadways and over turntables, changing the architectural conception from moment to moment and placing the art of spatial composition in the dimension of time [111, 399].

Expressionism in architecture remained an interlude. It was important only in theatre and church building, in which Otto Bartning designed a church as a rotunda in the shape of a star (1922), a moving exercise in irrationalism [108]. Of the architects who had an appreciable influence in determining the path of modern architecture, Erich Mendelsohn was the most lastingly affected by Expressionism [112, 330]. But even Gropius paid his tribute to it in his Memorial to the Fallen at Weimar (1920), in which concrete assumes a striking sharp-angled sculptural quality in forming an obliquely pointed symbol of remembrance.

11. Antonio Sant'Elia. Design for a "Futurist" own, 1913–14. The Futurists discovered the expressive value of movement in architecture. mphasis on traffic ways: streets at various evels, bridges, lifts.

12. Erich Mendelsohn. Einstein Tower, Potsdam, 920–21. Dome observatory and astrophysical aboratory. Sculptural architecture inspired by he formal possibilities of reinforced concrete.

BENSCHEIDT

Walter Gropius

Walter Gropius, born on 18 May 1883, belongs like Le Corbusier and Mies van der Rohe to the generation who absorbed the knowledge of the pioneers, and created the architecture of our time[31]. Working in the office of Behrens, Gropius became familiar with the elements of modern architecture, but he reacted against the superimposed monumentality which, in his later years, led Behrens ever further away from the principles of modern architectural form.

In 1911 Gropius began the building of the Fagus Works in Alfeld/Leine [113, 114], where he had had the rare good fortune to find a client whose views coincided with his own. A preliminary scheme on traditional lines had already been put forward, but Karl Benscheidt, who owned the Fagus factory, wanted to put up a building which reflected modern thinking. It so happened that he knew Gropius, whose proposals pleased him so much that he gave him the job. In his plan Gropius preserved the essence of the original scheme, but his individual approach and treatment of the elevations were completely new.

In contrast to the Turbine shop by Behrens (three-hinged steel arches) and Sullivan's department store, for the Carson, Pirie Scott Co. (steel frame), Gropius did not use a new structural system. The office block of the Fagus Works is built (much in accordance with centuries-old structural methods) of masonry with columns in front and a load-bearing wall at the back[32]. Only for the floors are steel beams used. The novelty lies in the conception of form, the free-standing nature of the external wall between the columns demonstrating aesthetically that it is composed of a thin sheath hung from a steel framework. The glazing bars serve no structural purpose, but merely hold the glass and panels in place. Gropius has succeeded here in creating a new and enduring form for industrial building and at the same time anticipated a discovery which, as the curtain wall, has become one of the most important formal elements in the multi-storey block. The Fagus Works exemplifies that the fundamental impetus of modern architecture did not only come from novel structural systems, but just as often, and to a decisive extent, from particular conceptions of form.

Moreover the absence of support at the corners of the office building springs less from structural considerations than from an instinctively correct interpretation of

13/114. Walter Gropius and Adolf Meyer. Fagus Works, Alfeld/Leine, 1911–16. The stanchions are located inside, the walls consisting argely of a transparent glass skin. Behrens oncentrated massive masonry at the corers [97]. Gropius avoids even slender corner upports. A daring architect and an undertanding client created a light and elegant uilding.

a complicated architectural problem. The typical form of a traditional masonry building shows a concentration of masses at the corners. Unconsciously this idea of form was still in Behrens's mind, when he designed his turbine shop. Gropius, however, seems to have felt that the form of a modern building must be clearly distinguished from the massiveness of masonry structures. Logically, he "dematerialized" – Giedion's word – the corners by his use of glass and dispensed with the rigid corner support.

The building of the Fagus Works established the reputation of Walter Gropius. He was invited to erect a factory with offices at the Werkbund Exhibition at Cologne in 1914 [115, 116]. A single-storeyed glass enclosure fits like a clasp round the office building; embracing three sides and merging at the front into projecting semi-circular staircase towers. The feature of the glass-walled staircase tower, which appears here for the first time, was developed by Gropius with great imagination. The staircase is suspended from an internal core, so that there is no load on the outside wall. The delicate pattern of glazing bars with their horizontal emphasis contrasts with the vertical lines of the pilasters on the façade.

115. Walter Gropius and Adolf Meyer. Wer bund Exhibition, Cologne, 1914. General vie of model layout for an average firm (wi offices); back view of open garages and fa tory building. Contrast between glass stai case towers and completely plain brick façad

116. Werkbund Exhibition, Cologne. View fro entrance court towards the administratio building. Offices completely glazed. The fla roof was used as garden and restaurant.

7. Walter Gropius. Bauhaus, Dessau, 1925 1926. Workshops and students' building. ich variety in grouping achieved by high ocks, passages, bridges and courts. No iowy elevations. Only by altering his position in the onlooker appreciate the ever-chang- g architectural patterns.

The world war interrupted further activities. In 1919 Gropius was called to Weimar in succession to van de Velde and founded the Bauhaus there, the "High School for Creative Art". The aim of his teaching at the Bauhaus was to bring about a modern architecture, which like human nature, embraced every aspect of life[33]. The methods of instruction were devised to remove the barriers separating architecture, applied art and technology, "to bridge the gulf ... between art and industrial production" (Giedion). Gropius succeeded in attracting many of the leading modern artists to the Bauhaus. Among them were Feininger, Kandinsky, Klee and Schlemmer. Itten, and later Moholy-Nagy, supervised the basic course in which artistic sensibility was awakened and encouraged by studying structural principles and the nature of materials. Particular value was placed on practical training. Gropius believed in the theory of a workshop education, which van de Velde had already applied, and organized workshops in which students were taught. In 1925 the Bauhaus moved to Dessau, as it had been subjected to increasingly violent attacks in Thüringen. It became a centre of many-sided intellectual endeavours, and Gropius's far from simple task was to co-ordinate

8. Bauhaus, Dessau. Workshops. The wall as become a glass curtain.

119. Walter Gropius. Housing scheme, Berlin-Siemensstadt, 1929. Terrace blocks with wide green spaces between.

120. Maxwell Fry and Walter Gropius. Impington College, Cambridgeshire, England, 1936. Loose grouping of school buildings. From left to right: rooms for adult education, assembly hall, (behind) classroom wing.

these varied activities. He tried to "draw everything in and leave nothing out", because he felt that the welfare of architecture depended upon the co-operation of a team actively working together for a common purpose. The significance and nature of the Bauhaus have been summarized by Mies van der Rohe: "The Bauhaus", he said, "was not an institution with a clear programme – it was an idea, and Gropius formulated this idea with great precision . . ."[34]. This idea was a union of art and technics as the basis of a modern creative art.

The transfer of the Bauhaus to Dessau offered Gropius an opportunity to realise his architectural theories in the new buildings for the school and in the accommodation for the teaching staff [117, 118, 222][35]. The programme included, besides the Bauhaus proper with its workshops, lecture rooms and students' living quarters, a trades school for the town of Dessau. Gropius succeeded in giving architectural unity to this extensive project. The means which he used to achieve this were a consistent vocabulary of form and a clear differentiation between the building masses according to their function.

In 1928 Gropius resigned his position as Director of the Bauhaus and went to

121. Impington College. Early example of the single-storey school building. The individual classrooms have natural lighting from both sides and open directly into the countryside.

22. Walter Gropius and Joost Schmidt. Exhibi-
on of "Non-ferrous Metals", Berlin, 1934. Spiral
f various metals in a large metal drum.

Berlin as an independent architect. His efforts at this time were principally devoted to town-planning questions [178]. The urban population in Germany rose rapidly at the end of the twenties; housing was an urgent matter. In 1927 the Werkbund Exhibition, which was largely concerned with this problem, took place on the Weissenhof in Stuttgart. Ernst May carried out modern housing schemes in Frankfurt on a large scale. But the centre of activity was Berlin, where Hugo Häring, Erich Mendelsohn, Ludwig Mies van der Rohe, Bruno and Max Taut, and Hans Scharoun were working. In 1929 Gropius won the competition for an experimental housing scheme at Berlin-Haselhorst, in which he developed further the conception of multi-storey flats as elongated, high-rising slabs, determining both the form and ground plan from the possibilities offered by the steel frame. In the same year was built the Berlin-Siemensstadt housing scheme, four-storey terrace blocks with wide green spaces between [4, 119].

In 1934 Gropius left Germany for England, where he worked with Maxwell Fry. This collaboration produced Impington College in Cambridgeshire (1936), a secondary school which also contains space for adult education [120, 121]. Here the single-storey pavilion type school is perfectly exemplified. The classrooms open directly onto the countryside. Access is provided at the back by means of an open corridor, and cross-ventilation and natural lighting from two sides are already features of a building, which has become a model for schools since 1945.

In 1937 Gropius was invited to teach in the department of architecture at Harvard University, Cambridge, Mass. This was hardly expected. American architecture and architectural schools still laboured for the most part under the after effects of eclecticism, which had ousted the School of Chicago. The invitation of modern architects from Europe, however – Mies van der Rohe was appointed professor at the Illinois Institute of Technology, Chicago, at the same period – had such a fruitful influence on American architecture in general that from now on one can speak of a wide diffusion of modern building [124, 126, 179, 180, 442, 443].

Gropius's work as a teacher of architecture was of the greatest importance. He recognized that, in an age of increasing specialization, it was essential to avoid becoming lost in technical details, but to keep open the doors between the different fields of expert knowledge. His policy was to get rid of the boss-and-employee mentality and build a team of equal partners. In 1945 he founded with several young architects "The Architects' Collaborative" (TAC), and there followed a series of important buildings and projects, such as the Harvard Graduate Center in Cambridge, Mass., completed in 1949–50, which includes students' accommodation and common rooms [124]. The scheme for the Harvard Graduate Center splits up a big spatial programme into a succession of low buildings. As in the Bauhaus at Dessau the individual buildings are differentiated according to their various functions, but the much larger complex permits a richer "interplay of solids and voids" (Giedion). The spatial composition is tremendously enlivened by the attractive surface treatment of the building materials, and by the shadow patterns cast by the open ground-floor rooms and sharply jutting balconies. Gropius had an opportunity here to combine with architecture the works of modern artists, like Joan Miró and Hans Arp, and to give practical reality to a principle of his Bauhaus Programme of 1919: "the ultimate goal of all artistic endeavour is the building".

The work of Gropius possesses universal significance – significant both in its effect and in the broad foundations upon which his philosophy is based. From his architecture, which formed only one side of his life-work, there came new aesthetic and structural solutions in factory building, and in housing and school construction which involve accurate scientific research, solutions of the most varied architectural problems. Gropius has turned frequently to the problem of the modern theatre and in 1927 developed the theory of the Total Theatre [123], in which the various possibilities evolved in the history of the theatre were combined – the conventional deep stage, the apron stage and the central arena stage. The change from one form of stage to another is effected by a turntable. An equally important subject for Gropius is the Exhibition. The Cologne Werkbund Exhibition of 1914, the Paris Exhibition of 1930 and the "Non-Ferrous Metals" Exhibition of 1934 in Berlin, were all opportunities to combine a less rigid interpretation of form, permissible in exhibition architecture, with the education of the public in a sense of community [122]. Just as he systematically set out principles for a new attitude towards environment, so Gropius made an intensive study of the technical problems which would aid in putting his principles into practice. Gropius has made important contributions to the rationalization of house building by industrial methods of standardization. He devoted himself again and

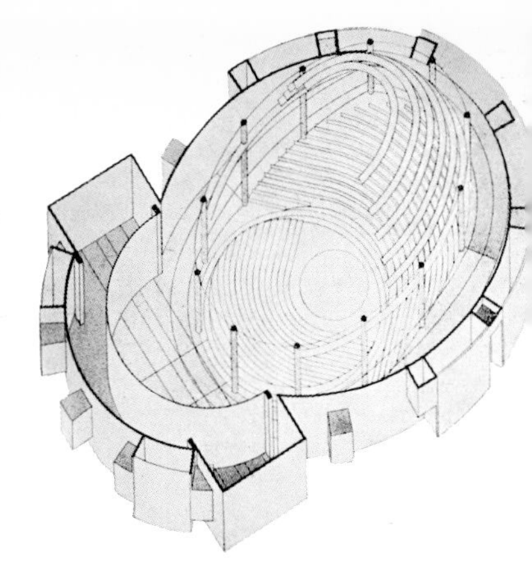

123. Walter Gropius. Total Theatre, 1927. Projec
By turning the larger of the lower platforms (wi
part of the stalls) through 180° a central aren
stage can be created.

124. The Architects' Collaborative (Walter Gro
pius and a group of young architects). Harvar
Graduate Center, Cambridge, Mass., 1949–50
Open forecourts and "an interplay of solids an
voids". The scheme includes seven dormitorie
and common rooms (Harkness Commons).

125. Walter Gropius and Wils Ebert. Flats. "Inte
bau" Exhibition, Berlin, 1957. Curved bloc
accessible by four lifts and staircases at th
back. Delicate colours: white wall surfaces, whit
enamelled steel balcony panels, loggias coate
blue (inside).

again to the problem of prefabricated building components and, as early as 1909, had reached the conclusion that such a system was only practical if it was applied to the smallest parts of a building. Only in this way is it possible to obtain a wide variety of ready-made house types from a limited number of components. The use of interchangeable, mass-produced parts leads to a form of house which can be adapted with great flexibility to differing family needs. In his evenly balanced interest in social, technical and artistic questions Gropius is noteworthy among the great modern architects for the way in which his personality is subordinated to his work. Conceptions of form which do not grow out of an intensive analysis of the practical aspects of building he describes as the "I-cult" and he contends "that the architect to-day must direct his efforts to a search for the typical and for what is of general value, and not for the sensational." Any dogmatic assertion about style means for Gropius the danger "of classifying art and architecture and of arresting processes before they have assumed definite shapes"[36]. His work as an architect and an educator will not produce results which can be taken over by others. What it teaches is an attitude of mind.

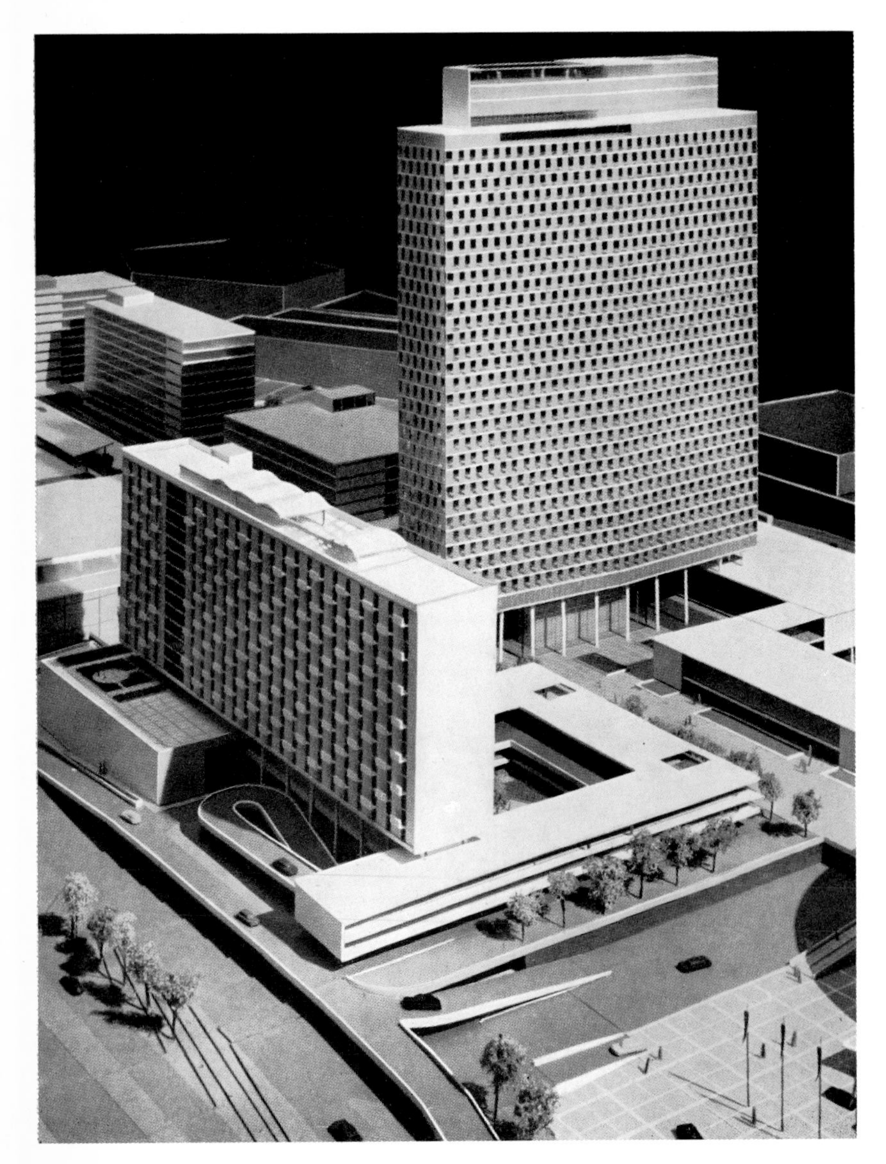

126. Boston Center. Architects: Walter Gropius, with The Architects' Collaborative, Pietro Belluschi, Walter F. Bogner, Carl Koch and Associates, Hugh Stubbins, Jr. New City Centre for Boston, 1953. Project for office buildings, shopping centre, convention hall and motel. Cars are parked in a three-storey underground garage. Free circulation for pedestrians amid the richly patterned groups of buildings.

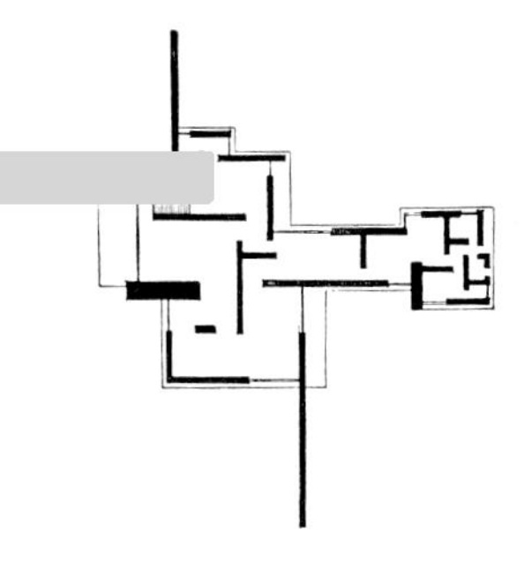

7a/127b. Mies van der Rohe. Brick country ouse; project, 1923. Floor plan and perspece. The walls, stretching out into the open, eak up the compact, self-contained impreson of the building.

Ludwig Mies van der Rohe

Mies van der Rohe[37], the son of a stonemason, was born in Aachen in 1886. Like Walter Gropius he was decisively influenced by Peter Behrens, whose drawing office he entered in 1908. By its collaboration with industry, which Behrens to a great extent succeeded in bringing about, his office exercised a strong attraction upon the rising generation of architects. Moreover his neo-classical trend, which developed after 1910, is clearly perceptible in the early designs and buildings of Mies van der Rohe [128, 129].

A change in the latter's outlook first became apparent about 1919. Mies van der Rohe devoted intensive study to problems of modern design. There were three particular themes around which his thoughts revolved: the effect of glass as a curved or flat architectural element, the composition of the building in horizontal layers as an expression of its inner structure and the house developed and organized according to its function. These were the principal tasks which Mies van der Rohe set himself, although he received no definite commission to carry them out. The arrangement of the ground plan was only outlined in the first two themes, and no more than the fringe of the town-planning problems was touched upon. But the absence of such factors enabled Mies to analyse exhaustively each question without being diverted from his purpose. It was, therefore, possible for him, with these studies – this word expresses the facts more clearly than the term "projects" – to clarify fundamental issues.

As his first exercise Mies tackled the problem of the curvilinear and obliquely angled, broken-up, glass surface on high buildings [130, 131]. This was followed by the study of a reinforced concrete office building [208]. If the relationship between structure and form in the glass studies was not the primary consideration, it forms in this instance the chief object of his investigation. The columns of reinforced concrete frame are set inside the building and the floor slabs are cantilevered outwards in both directions, so that the external wall has no supporting function. Continuous horizontal ribbon windows are the logical expression

28. Peter Behrens. Schröder (Country) house, lagen, 1911.

29. Mies van der Rohe. Perls House, Berlinehlendorf, 1911. Mies van der Rohe's early work ended towards the classicism of Karl Friedrich schinkel, which the buildings of Behrens (Mies's eacher) reflected at this period.

130. Mies van der Rohe. Competition design f a skyscraper at the Friedrichstrasse statio Berlin, 1919. Upon a prismatic plan a steel fram building with external walls of glass. Studies the reflective qualities of walls constructe entirely of glass. Vertical dominant.

131. Mies van der Rohe. Glass skyscraper. Pro ject, 1920–21. Model of a steel skeleton buildin entirely faced with glass. Free interpretation c curvilinear plan.

of this construction. A new form, to which the minds of modern architects were to turn again and again, has been logically worked out here. In its identification of structure and form this study is the first demonstration of a type of construction which was often to be used later.

In his third exercise, the project for a house (1923), Mies van der Rohe formulates a new conception of space [127a, 127b]. The wall is not treated as a subordinate element of the boxlike enclosed room, but is free-standing, reaching out beyond the frontiers of the interior of the house into the natural world around it – in short linking together indoor and outdoor space. Instead of windows set one by one in the walls, whole walls become glass and contrast with plain unbroken wall surfaces.

The splitting-up of the plan according to functional needs implied in this study – separation of living and service areas – is made a fundamental principle of form in a further project for a house in 1924. Unlike Le Corbusier, who starts from a basic geometrical shape, to which he subordinates function, Mies van der Rohe takes function as his point of departure and from it evolves the disposition and form of the different parts of the building. In this way an open unhampered layout is obtained.

Mies van der Rohe was fortunate in being able to demonstrate his architectural principles in their absolute purity with the German Pavilion at the International Exhibition at Barcelona in 1929 [133, 134]. Instead of a space to be filled with exhibits, he erected a building which, in clarity of form and beauty of materials – travertine, onyx and glass in various colours – was both an exhibition pavilion and an exhibit at the same time. Architecturally, it exemplifies a new conception: flowing space divided only by free-standing walls. The structural system rests on a clear distinction between supporting and non-supporting elements. The roof is carried on steel columns, which stand in the open, while the division of space is effected by partitions which have no load-bearing function and can, therefore, be made of glass or other thin materials. Mies van der Rohe differentiates logically between elements subject to structural laws (stanchions, roofslabs) and those to which such rules do not apply (free-standing partitions). The absence of any purely decorative treatment of the structural members is fundamental.

2. Mies van der Rohe, and Philip C. Johnson. eagram Building, New York, 1956–57. The most cent work of Mies van der Rohe and the ultiate logical development of the revolutionary eas which he evolved thirty-five years earlier. ain tower with projecting bronze fins and nber glass surfaces. Supreme eloquence in rmal expression achieved with absolute simicity of means.

The design of this pavilion brought world-wide fame to Mies van der Rohe. In 1930 he built the Tugendhat House in Brno, Czechoslovakia [135, 136, 202, 322]. What could be achieved in Barcelona by the interplay of surfaces and materials was applied here to a new conception of the house. The Tugendhat home stands on a sloping site and Mies uses its position to brilliant effect, arranging his spatial programme on two levels. On the upper floor the bedrooms are on one side of an open passage, with the garage and chauffeur's flat on the other. Even before the visitor has entered the house from the side of the hill, he has an immediate view through the open passage of the valley stretching away below. A shallow staircase leads to the lower floor, most of which is occupied by a living-room measuring 50 by 80 feet, which is divided by partitions into four functional areas – entrance, living room, study and dining room. By organizing space in this way Mies van der Rohe succeeded in accommodating systematically the particular needs of a superior type of house without destroying the scale of the existing living areas by cutting them up into small spatial units. In the manner in which inside and outside are equated, in its flexible adaption to the

133. Mies van der Rohe. German Pavilion, Barc lona, 1929. Partition walls in rich materia placed independently of the stanchions, crea an impression of flowing spatial movement.

4. German Pavilion, Barcelona. Floor plan.

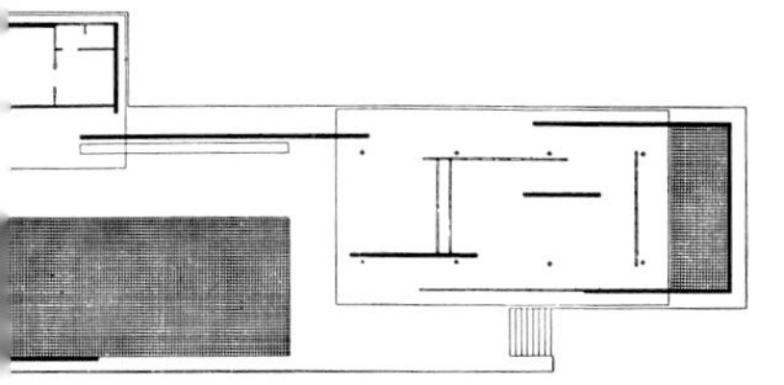

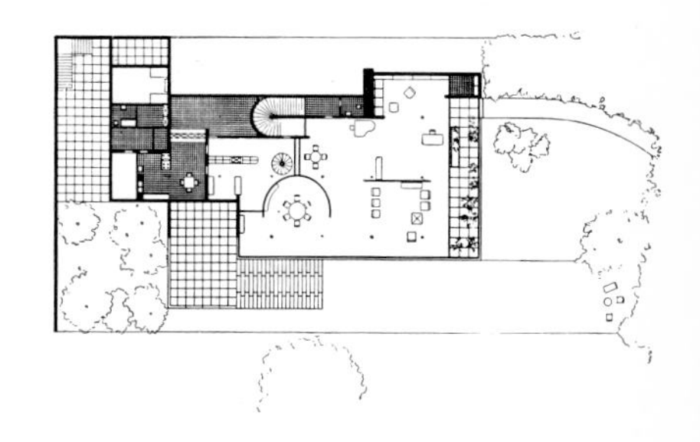

135. Mies van der Rohe. Tugendhat House, Brno, 1930. Ground-floor plan.

136. Tugendhat House, Brno. Large principal room divided into spaces for various activities by a flat-surfaced partition in onyx and by another, semi-circular, in ebony.

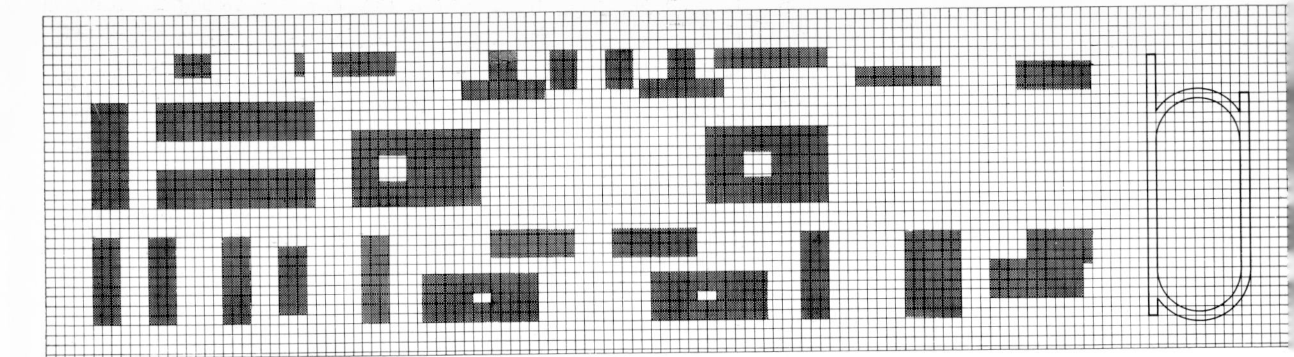

site, in its openness to natural surroundings, and above all in the harmony of its proportions, the Tugendhat house is one of the classic solutions of the modern house.

The idea of flexible space, which holds a predominant place in the aesthetic philosophy of Mies, also found practical application in an entirely different social context. In 1927 a large Werkbund exhibition took place in Stuttgart, to which leading architects from various countries were invited [72], each of whom had to design a house or a housing group. The chief artistic director and co-ordinator of the schemes was Mies van der Rohe, who himself built a multi-storey block of flats. This is a pure steel skeleton structure in which the staircase and the adjacent service rooms provide reinforcement.

The provision of the greatest possible freedom, which Mies achieved in the principal room of the Tugendhat House, was also his desire here. Every flat in this multi-storey block can be subdivided according to the wishes of the individual tenant, since the partition walls can be arranged without regard to structural needs.

When Mies van der Rohe went to America in 1938 the number of his executed works was not large, but the fascination of these few buildings and projects was all the greater. This was due above all to his capacity for analysing problems exhaustively. His inaugural address as Director of Architecture of Armour Institute (now the Illinois Institute of Technology) in Chicago in 1938 summarizes his

137. Mies van der Rohe. Illinois Institute of Technology, Chicago, 1940. Block plan. The group of buildings, which are planned upon a uniform system of proportions, include research institute, library, assembly hall, sports buildings (field house) and technical installations.

138. Illinois Institute of Technology, Chicago. From left to right: Alumni Memorial Hall, chemical engineering and metallurgy building, chemistry block. Meticulous detailing, subtle interplay of brick and glass surfaces, articulate and disciplined vocabulary of form, aesthetic clarity of structure.

9. Mies van der Rohe. Skyscraper apartments, ke Shore Drive, Chicago, 1951. Projecting steel ctions give a pattern in relief to the wall sur- ces. The siting of the slab-shaped blocks in ation to one another – narrow side facing oad side – reveals a new silhouette from every esh position.

attitude: "The long path from material through function to creative work has only a single goal: to create order out of the desperate confusion of our time. We must have order, allocating to each thing its proper place and giving to each thing its due according to its nature. We would do this so perfectly that the world of our creations will blossom from within"[38].

A year after his appointment he received the commission to plan and build the Illinois Institute of Technology in Chicago [137, 138, 142a, 142b]. In this scheme Mies tries with scrupulous exactitude to express unity of surface, space and volume by a uniform system of measurement, applied to the spatial content of the buildings, the distances between them and the size of the wall areas. Steel is used as structural material and the sections available to the architect are exclusively standard. Steel lends itself to simple rectangular forms, and Mies van der Rohe finds a way of creating an architectural element out of a featureless technical product. In the subtly contrived proportions, in the economy of means and structural clarity, the Illinois Institute of Technology is the culmination of his life's work.

In the last ten years Mies van der Rohe has been constantly concerned with two problems in particular: the skyscraper apartment house and the unsupported spanning of wide spaces. For both he seeks a solution which will symbolize the clear cut, sharply defined block, whether this is a soaring tower, or a recumbent cube. In his buildings Mies van der Rohe pursues the ultimate simplicity. "They should be simple, and they are simple. But this does not imply a primitive simplicity, but one that is noble, monumental even"[39]. Simplicity for him is not the blind simplicity of an inability to appreciate the problem, but the simplicity based on the knowledge of having solved the problem, which has therefore become simple again. Mies van der Rohe means just that.
In building the apartment houses on Lake Shore Drive in Chicago Mies van der Rohe has revived his theory of the glass skyscraper which he had projected in 1919 and 1921 [130, 131]. What was then only a vision has now been translated into a structural form of the highest significance. Glass and steel are the only architectural elements in this conception of his. In minimising the number of formal elements and in his search for an objective language of form, his architectural

141. Mies van der Rohe. National Theatre, Mannheim. Project 1953. Application of the "single enclosed space" to a building type to which one would not expect it to be appropriate.

axiom "less is more" is clearly exemplified. A similar simplicity is shown in the floor plans. The living and sleeping space is disposed about a central core comprising all the service installations.

The logic with which Mies van der Rohe strives for pure form has led him in certain buildings to a point where form begins to be dissociated from function. Thus the Farnsworth House (1950) is more a demonstration of an architectural idea than the solution of a building problem set by the practical needs of the owner [40, 140]. The compartments incorporating the service core are concentrated in a closed box, the walls of which are not carried up to the single-span ceiling. This box is placed right inside the cube without the balance of its spatial unity being upset. Earlier in the Tugendhat House Mies van der Rohe had organized the huge living room functionally with a few movable elements, accentuating its form and achieving the openness and sense of scale of flowing space.

Mies has carried this idea further in his latest buildings. The essential subdividing elements are so reduced in number that the surfaces defining the whole spatial content of the house remain always apparent. Here is the apotheosis of the "one room" theory, which is also what makes his project for the National Theatre at Mannheim [141] significant. Entrance hall, foyer and auditorium are so integrated with the internal space that they organize, without dismembering it. The Mannheim Theatre remains a project; but in his Crown Hall building which houses the Department of Architecture of the Illinois Institute of Technology, Mies van der Rohe has been able to realize his conception of the single room [142a]. Spatial continuity is achieved by suspending the ceiling from a frame, which – as in the Mannheim Theatre design – passes above the roof slab. By installing low partitions Mies succeeds in preserving spatial unity and in creating a rhythmic effect. To those who doubt whether the one room of Crown Hall is functionally right for students at all stages of their studies, Mies van der Rohe contends that the wide expanse of space with its abundance of light and air is more important than the absence of visual and acoustic separation. This interpretation of space, with its mingling of interior and exterior, was only possible, however, because all rooms which require subdividing – staff rooms, lecture rooms and studios – are on the ground floor. Many problems of detail which arise from this new attitude towards living space have still to be solved. But already it can be said that Mies

←

140. Mies van der Rohe. Dr. Edith Farnsworth House, Plano, Illinois, 1950. Reduced to its simplest elements, the cube-house is slung between eight stanchions. Sumptuous materials used for the interior.

142a. Mies van der Rohe. Crown Hall, Illino Institute of Technology, Chicago, 1956. Buildin of the Department of Architecture and Desigr The load-bearing frame passes above the roc and so permits the perfect "single enclose space", unobstructed by any columns.

van der Rohe has formulated here for the first time a new form of spatial expression, which will prove most important in the continuing evolution of modern architecture.

The dazzling brilliance of his ideas and his uncompromising vocabulary of form [132] have exercised a very strong influence on present-day architecture. Mies van der Rohe is one of the great creative minds of our time. With his austere steel structures he presents the greatest conceivable contrast to the plastic compositions of Nervi and Candela, which arise from a completely different interpretation of the possibilities of reinforced concrete [143a].

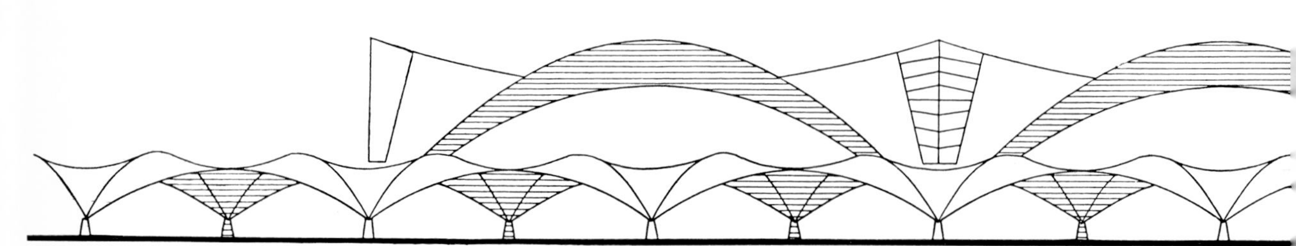

42b. Mies van der Rohe. Chapel, Illinois Institute
Technology, Chicago, 1952. The unobstructed
ngle space. External walls with steel frames
nd yellow brick infilling, flat roof of prefabricat-
d corrugated components carried on steel
eams.

143a. Félix Candela. Design for a market hall. The strictly rectangular forms of Mies van der Rohe developed from the steel skeleton frame, and the curvilinear shells in the shape of the parabola and hyperbola which reinforced concrete makes possible: contrasts inherent in modern architectural form.

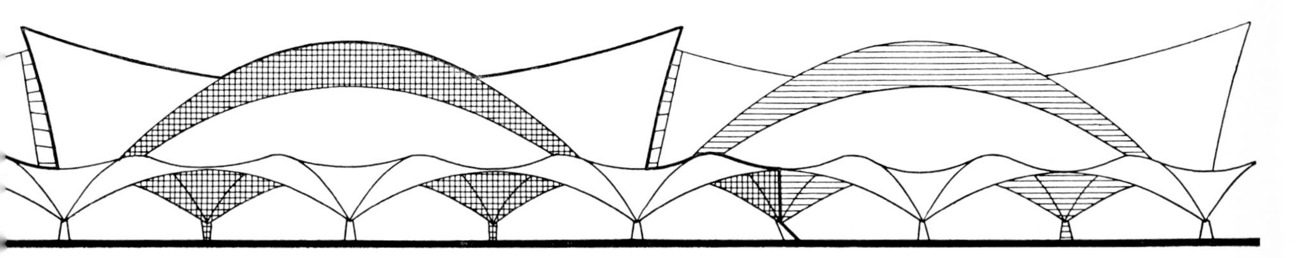

Le Corbusier's individuality can only be understood if one accepts his buildings not as isolated phenomena, but sees them against the background of a comprehensive architectural philosophy, which has been explained in a whole series of books and other writings[40]. Both a painter and a sculptor, he looks for a synthesis of the arts in architecture. It was characteristic of his attitude at the beginning of the twenties that he became better known for his ideas about an architecture of the future than for what he had built.

Le Corbusier was born in 1887 at La Chaux-de-Fonds in the West of Switzerland, but he has spent most of his life in Paris where he has been working since 1917. The public attitude to architecture in Paris at that time leaned towards tradition and outmoded forms – in contrast to the approach to painting and sculpture. Le Corbusier therefore found himself isolated and was obliged, in order to make himself heard, to clothe his utterances in less temperate terms than perhaps were essential to the expression of his views. This explains a great many over-emphatic statements of principle.

Le Corbusier is indebted to Auguste Perret, in whose office he worked in 1908–09, for his knowledge of the structural possibilities offered by reinforced concrete. This is the material which he uses to put his theories of form into practice. Instead of massive stone walls, which both support and enclose and cannot be varied in their arrangement, reinforced concrete enables him to use a skeleton frame in which the supporting members are confined to a few points. With this system the walls are relieved of their load-bearing function. Inside the building they can be disposed at will as partitions, and as external walls they can be pierced with openings of any size without the strength of the construction being impaired in the least.

Le Corbusier's grammar of form is markedly influenced by geometrical figures which emerge not only in his preference for clear, stereometric, forms like cubes and cylinders, but also in his geometrical organization of elevations. "Architects to-day", he asserts, "are afraid of the geometrical constituents of surfaces. The great problems of modern construction must have a geometrical solution"[41]. Thus Le Corbusier deliberately limits himself to one of the possibilities for creative design which can be developed out of the qualities of reinforced concrete. Within the restricted sphere of his geometrical conception he has none the less evolved a structural architecture that is admirably consistent and clear.

Le Corbusier's aesthetic philosophy, which he formulated early in the twenties, contains the following points[42]:

1. The separation of load-bearing construction from space-enclosing walls. Free-

43b. Le Corbusier. Law Courts, Chandigarh, 1951–56. In building the new Capital of the Punjab, Le Corbusier has been able to realize his town-planning dreams on a large scale. In the centre of this city for 500,000 inhabitants stands the Capitol with its government and parliament buildings and law courts. Square-mesh lattices of "brise-soleils", jutting galleries and projecting roofs reveal an increased concern for plastic expression in Le Corbusier's later work.

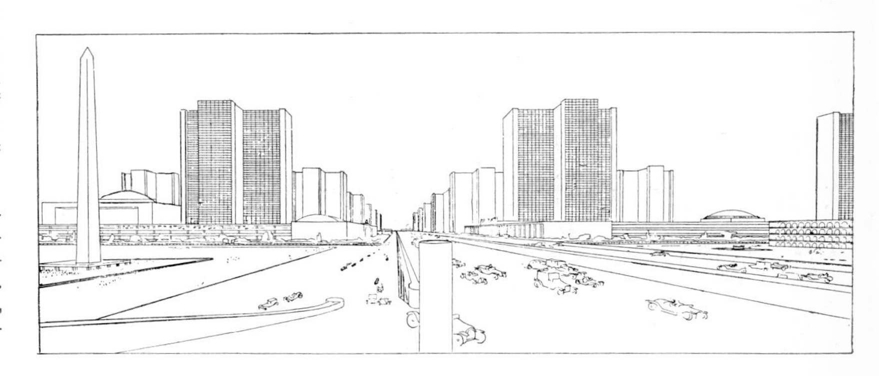

43c. Le Corbusier. Plan for "Une Ville Contemporaine", 1922. Thirty years before his development scheme for Chandigarh Le Corbusier evolved his first conception of the town of to-day. Close inter-related patterns of sky-scrapers, multi-storey blocks of lower heights, public buildings, green spaces and huge traffic arteries.

standing columns lift the first floor off the ground: "The house is suspended in the air, away from the ground, while the garden spreads under the house." Le Corbusier differentiates between the house and its surroundings, at the same time establishing a new relationship with nature by bringing green spaces under the building. A structure like Le Corbusier's Villa Savoye does not reach with outstretched wings into the open like Wright's houses or the early projects of Mies, but forms a compact cube [147].

2. The flat roof, appropriate to the idea of a house as a cube,since a pitched roof would spoil the desired unity of its rectangular shape. It has long been structurally possible, by the use of new materials, to protect the roof against damp and to carry rainwater away centrally. Le Corbusier takes advantage of the flat roof, using it as a terrace garden. By such means nature is introduced into man's living environment, without destroying the precision of stereometric form [146,148].

3. Freedom in planning the interior, made possible by frame construction, had already been demonstrated by Auguste Perret in his house in the Rue Franklin, Paris. In the floor plans of the Villa Savoye the "plan libre" is apparent. By con-

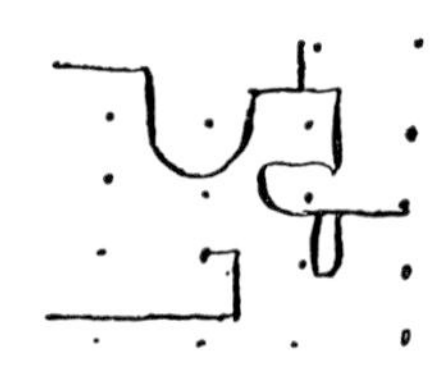

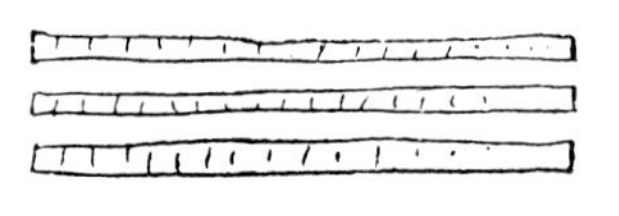

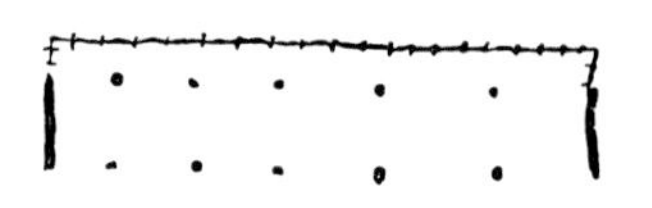

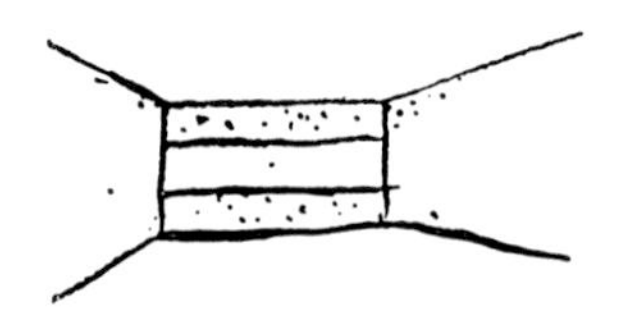

144. Le Corbusier. The five points of a new architecture. Sketches. Left, those proposed by Le Corbusier. Right, traditional solutions.

145/146. Le Corbusier and Pierre Jeanneret. Villa Savoye, Poissy, 1928-30. A house on stilts. On the top-floor, roof garden and solarium.

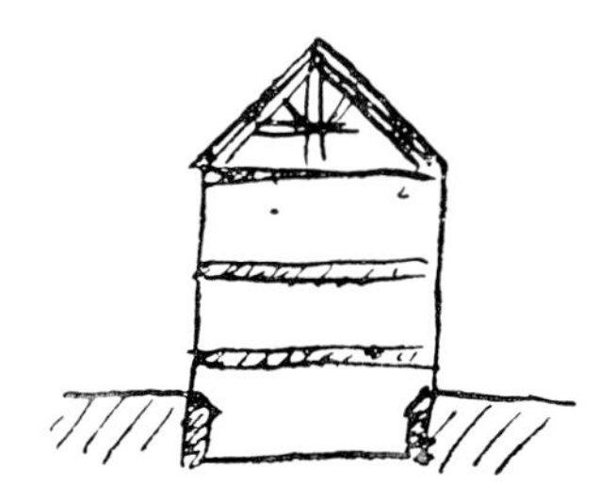

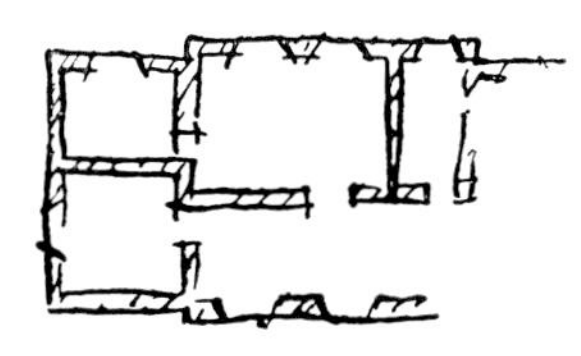

centrating the function of support entirely on the skeleton frame, it has been possible to place the walls in different positions on each floor. Their arrangement is exclusively determined by spatial requirements.

4. Freedom in designing the exterior – the load-bearing stanchions of the frame are inside the building – has a direct bearing on the flexible ground plan. The windows can run continuously round the house from one side to the other [150].

5. Horizontal ribbon windows enhance the unity of the external appearance and are a logical expression of the system of construction. Their use in buildings of vastly differing types and spatial needs (League of Nations Palace, project 1927; Villa Savoye, 1928–30) shows that at that time identity of internal space and external form was not so important to Le Corbusier as the application of particular kinds of geometrical figure. His emphasis on this aspect of design reveals a parallel with the forms which began to appear in the 1920s with the Dutch movement of "De Stijl" [147, 152].

Time and again Le Corbusier returns to the problem of a basis for a new kind of dwelling. He traces the shortcomings of domestic building to the fact that our

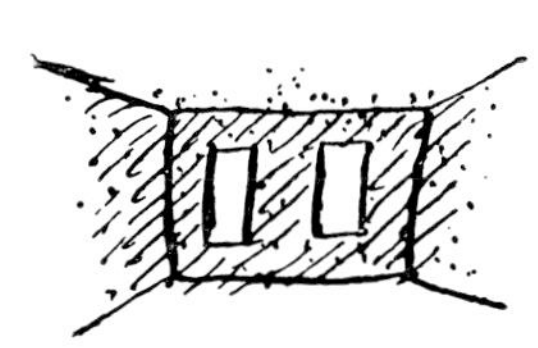

147/148. Villa Savoye, Poissy. Free handling of exterior, horizontal ribbon windows, plastic modelling of roof features. Terrace garden and large living-room on one-from-top storey. Interplay of solids and voids.

homes no longer satisfy modern needs. In order to make these needs understood, he demands a clear programme for the dwelling of the future. He instances products of the technological world, which completely fulfil their purpose and at the same time reveal a new beauty. He perceives that the development of ocean liners, aircrafts and cars was only possible because a clear, carefully considered, programme of requirements had been laid down first. "The lesson of the aeroplane is not primarily in the forms it has created...; the lesson... lies in the logic which governed the enunciation of the problem and which led to its successful realization. ... we must learn to see in an aeroplane not a bird or a dragon-fly, but a machine for flying"[43].

149a. Le Corbusier and Pierre Jeanneret. Pair of houses. Weissenhof housing scheme, Stuttgart, 1927. High and low blocks. Left, the house shown in plan below.

Then there occurs that portentous saying of his: "A house is a machine for living in", which was to become the catch-phrase of all critics of modern architecture. In its original context it simply means that the programme for a home should be set out with the same exactitude as the programme for building a machine. Exactitude in the programme means for Le Corbusier not only consideration for the immediate practical needs of living, but a concern for human problems in a much wider sense. When Le Corbusier, as a kind of extension to his definition of the house as a machine to live in, declares that "architecture has another meaning ... than ... responding to needs", he means to imply by this the linking of architecture with moral values like cleanliness and clear thinking, with freedom for individual self-expression and with the ability to educate the community, while establishing the status of architecture as an art.

"Responding to needs", or fulfilment of purpose, is obviously attained in the house (1927) in the Stuttgart Weissenhofsiedlung by a carefully considered plan, for example in the connection between kitchen and maid's room and in the spatial sequence of kitchen-dining-and-living-rooms [149a, 149b]. But Le Corbusier's inspiration did not end here. One of the most important elements is the two-storey living-room, into which the smaller adjoining rooms open. The theme of the two-storey room stems from a tradition of the Anglo-Saxon country-house, and Le Corbusier has always been deeply interested in it. The way from the low-ceilinged dining place into the open spaciousness of the living-room, the view of the principal room below from the gallery of the upper floor, the various directions in which the gaze is attracted in the large living room – downwards, upwards, and through the windows into the open air – induce a sense of spatial fantasy and are translated into a broader and richer feeling for life. The world outside spreads through the house, into the pillared patio at ground level and onto the terrace at the top, and by this fusion with nature refutes the reproach that Le Corbusier had reduced man's abode to a mere piece of machinery.

Only at the end of the twenties did Le Corbusier have an opportunity to put his architectural ideas into practice in a series of big projects and commissions.

His competition design for the Palace of the League of Nations at Geneva dates from 1927 [152, 154]: The building masses are no longer concentrated into a compact block, but grow out of their function. The wedge-shaped trapezoidal assembly hall with 2,600 seats stretches down to the lake, whilst the offices and smaller committee rooms are disposed in a rectangular building behind. The details of the office block display all the features of Le Corbusier's aesthetic philosophy: free-standing columns, freedom of planning and elevational treatment, roof gardens and horizontal emphasis of the façades. The hall tapers towards the speaker's dais, which is the principal feature of the room, and to which the paraboloidal roof also curves. The outstanding spatial and acoustic

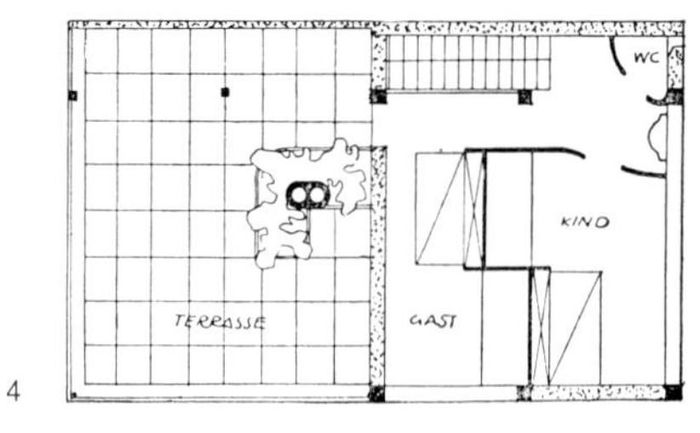

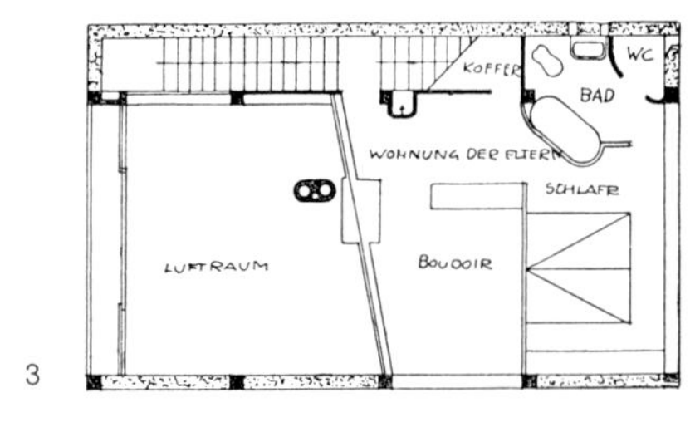

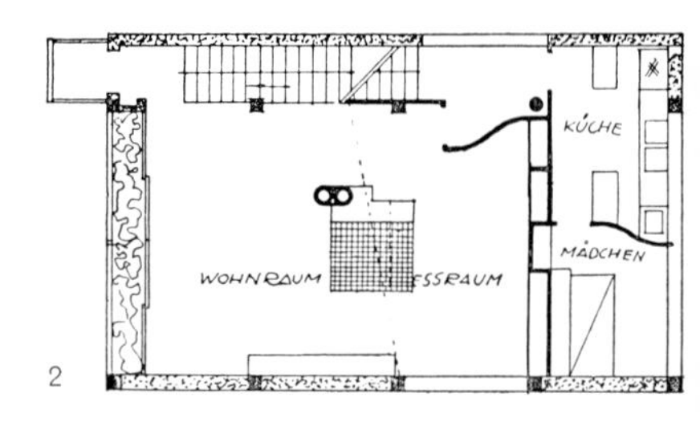

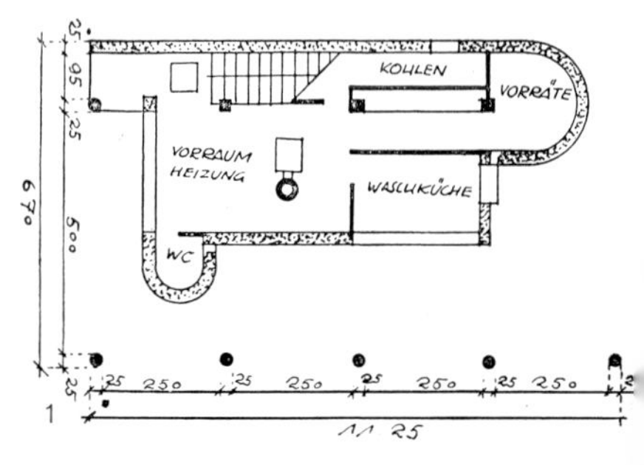

0. Le Corbusier and Pierre Jeanneret. Villa, arches, 1927. North front. The ground-floor conins hall, servant's flat, cloakroom and garage.

solution is achieved by orientating the structural system in the same direction: two main girders placed longitudinally carry the suspended ceiling of the hall. By this penetrating interpretation of function, structure and form, a new and original type of hall emerges, which is having a stimulating effect on the design of large concert and meeting halls generally.

Among a succession of executed works [288] the Swiss Students' Home (Pavillon Suisse) in Paris (1930–32) is outstanding [153]. The idea of buildings suspended above ground, which has always appealed to Le Corbusier, is here consistently worked out. To achieve this result, six massive stilts, upon which the building rests, are set in the middle of the ground floor area and linked by a huge longitudinal joist. Above this striking structural device rises the four-storeyed main block with its smooth outer skin of windows and concrete-slab cladding, which gives no indication of the method of construction. This dramatic contrast is the keynote of the whole design.

Faith in Le Corbusier's authority was already so firmly established in the 1930s that the Brazilian government, at the request of the responsible committee, invited

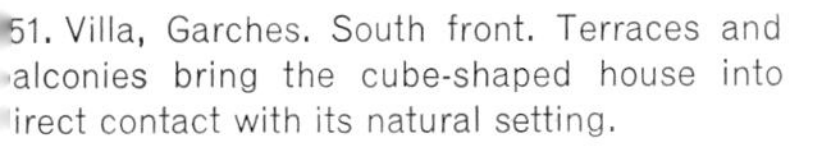

51. Villa, Garches. South front. Terraces and alconies bring the cube-shaped house into irect contact with its natural setting.

←

49b. Weissenhofsiedlung, Stuttgart. Floor plans of the smaller of the two houses (149a, left). Ground-floor (1), the two floors with the two-storeyed principal room (2, 3), roof storey (4).

Le Corbusier to be consultant for the Ministry of Education buildings at Rio de Janeiro [155, 156, 420, 421]. This commission not only influenced the manner in which the project was carried out, but at the same time introduced modern architecture into South America. As later happened with India [143b, 302], a young nation gave Le Corbusier the means to put his theories into practice on a large scale. During his stay in South America Le Corbusier prepared two plans, which decisively influenced the final execution of the scheme. The completed building shows the clear impress of Le Corbusier's ideas. It rises as a thin slab with a low connecting wing supplying a contrast in scale, and is carried on tall, round, slender columns, between which pedestrians can circulate. Because of the need to protect the North side from the sun, an earlier idea of Le Corbusier (cf. projects for Barcelona and Algiers) is applied [300]. The entire north front is faced with a network of brise-soleils, the surfaces of which are movable and provide an ever-changing rhythm.

In his designs of recent years Le Corbusier has abandoned his geometrical rectangular preoccupations and has arrived at a markedly plastic interpretation of form. In many earlier buildings this tendency can already be discerned. But it had never involved all the building, being confined, as in the case of the roof structures of the Villa Savoye or the internal walls of the Villa at Garches, to particular details, which contrast with the crystalline clarity of the building as a whole [146]. This kind of free handling of wall elements, his way of moulding them according to spatial needs, arose logically from the idea of freedom in planning, which was part of Le Corbusier's aesthetic philosophy. The step to sculptural form, not

152. Le Corbusier and Pierre Jeanneret. Palac of the League of Nations, Geneva. Project, 192 View from the lake, with secretariat and assemb ly hall.

153. Le Corbusier and Pierre Jeanneret. Swis Students' Pavilion, Paris, 1930–32. View fron south west. "Floating cube" building; unobstruct ed circulation for pedestrians.

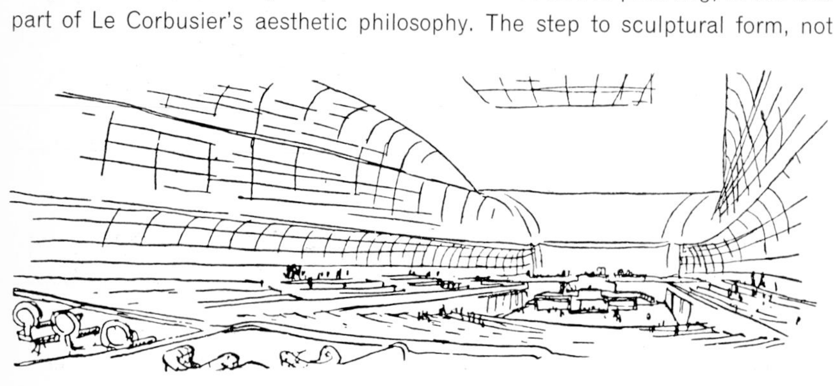

154. Palace of the League of Nations, Geneva Project. The curved ceiling is suspended fron invisible longitudinal beams. Acoustical advan tages, dynamic spatial effect.

merely of details, but of the whole building, becomes immediately feasible when Le Corbusier gives up his strict adherence to geometrical precision. The sculptural quality of his later buildings is not directly connected with their construction, but is the product of an uninhibited inventiveness.

Le Corbusier gave a plastic interpretation of an entire building for the first time in the Pilgrimage chapel of Ronchamp in 1950–53 [158, 159]. The exposed position of the chapel on the brow of a hill enables him to site the building in relation to the landscape. The interior is lit on the south side by deep-set windows, which with their small openings enhance the sculptural impression of the whole. The roof, supported at only a few points, appears to be detached from the body of the building and gives an effect of floating. The three towers are wholly manifestations of his sculptural conception of the general plan.

The town as a social and architectural entity has always held a particularly important place in Le Corbusier's mind. In a number of town-planning studies, such as the plan for "Une Ville Contemporaine" of 1922, the "Plan Voisin" of 1925 and the "Plan de Paris", 1937, he has expounded many new variants of his vision of

5. Lúcio Costa, Carlos Leão, Jorge Moreira, car Niemeyer, Affonso E. Reidy, Ernani Vasncelos. Consultant architect: Le Corbusier. nistry of Education, Rio de Janeiro, 1937–43. lumns of the main block, which support the rrow slab of the high building. The building no ger erects a barrier against free movement. ditional circulation space is obtained.

5. Ministry of Education, Rio de Janeiro. North e. The adjustable sun louvres ("brise-soleils") e lightness and variety to the façade.

157. Le Corbusier. Unité d'Habitation, Marseil
1947–52. Children's play space on the r
"Architecture is the exact and wonderful pla
forms in light" (Le Corbusier).

158. Le Corbusier. Chapel of Notre-Dame-
Haut, Ronchamp, 1950–55. View from south e
Chapels in the three towers. External altar
open-air services. The plastic conception of
individual parts embraces the entire mass of
building.

159. Chapel of Notre-Dame, Ronchamp. The south wall from inside. Shafts of light enter through deep-set windows, the proportions of which have been evolved from the "Modulor", Le Corbusier's system of measurement. The roof rests on slender stanchions hidden in the cavity wall, from which it is separated by a band of light.

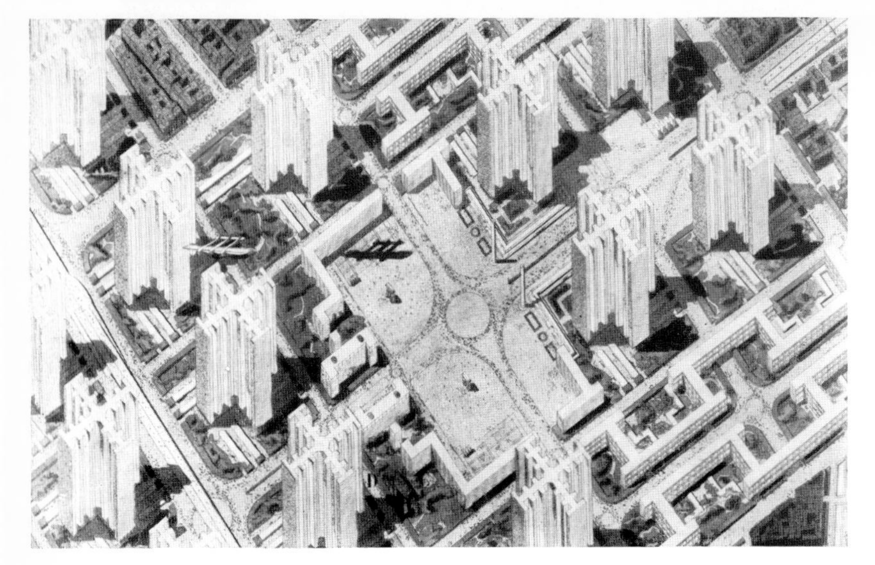

160. Le Corbusier and Pierre Jeanneret. Pla Voisin, 1925. New city centre for Paris on th right bank of the Seine, north of the Rue de Rivol At approximately four-hundred-yard intervals towering glass prisms, cruciform in plan, se well back from the streets. Le Corbusier's conten tion: by higher, but less concentrated, develop ment, greater population densities and increase value of land.

the town of to-day [160, 161]. Whether in the form of the "Ville Radieuse", with its serpentine rows of interconnecting blocks, or in loosely disposed groups of independent buildings, Le Corbusier tries to open up dense built-up areas by means of large vertical units of flats with wide green open spaces between. This parkland stretches right under the buildings which are carried on stilts, the ground being left free for the pedestrian, and for recreation and sports purposes. Factories are grouped in special industrial zones, while government, commercial and cultural establishments occupy separate precincts [289].

The "Ville Contemporaine" remains a dream, but Le Corbusier has been able to realise the basic element of this concept: the dwelling unit, the "Unité d'Habitation", first exemplified in Marseilles [157, 162, 163, 164]. This represents a little world in itself, provided with every necessity like shops, infants' schools, medical facilities and hotel accommodation. The individual dwellings are self-contained and two-storeyed, so that even here Le Corbusier has been able to preserve the dwelling on two floors. Each of the larger flats occupies the whole width of the block and therefore has direct cross-ventilation. The dimensions of the building are based

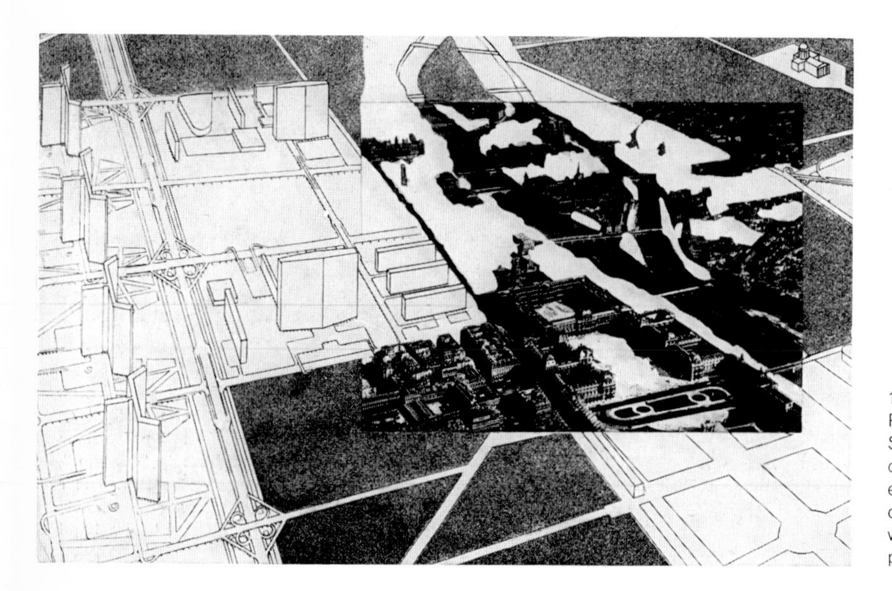

161. Le Corbusier and Pierre Jeanneret. Plan de Paris, 1937. Proposed for the right bank of the Seine, north of the Rue de Rivoli. High buildings of various shapes and heights, no longer arranged in strict symmetry. The contrast with districts containing buildings of historical importance which would be preserved, is introduced with particular ingenuity.

162. Le Corbusier. Unité d'Habitation, Marseilles, 1947–52. Air-extraction shaft, infants' school (behind). Installations with functional purposes handled freely as sculpture.

on the "Modulor" method evolved by Le Corbusier, which is an attempt to reconcile the abstract metric system by a "harmonious measure" of proportion "to the human scale".

As Max Bill once said, Le Corbusier is not an architect concerned solely with building in a conventional sense[44]. He is an artist who, looking far beyond what is practicable to-day, sees a vision of a new architecture in a new society. The logic of his vocabulary of form has from the outset exercised a compelling influence. Yet we misunderstand Le Corbusier if we forget that he himself, in his continuous search for an architecture appropriate to our age, frequently calls in question the very conclusions that he has already reached.

3. Unité d'Habitation, Marseilles. The first ·actical example of one of the dwelling units pon which Le Corbusier's town-planning con- ·ptions are based. Two-storey flats with two- oreyed principal living room. Five internal reets with all welfare services, shops, hotel; the roof-terrace – children's play area, swim- ing bath, gymnasium, sun-bathing, restaurant.

4. (page 98). Unité d'Habitation, Marseilles, outh elevation.

Accentuation of formal elements – De Stijl

5. Piet Mondrian. Large composition with red, ue and yellow, 1928.

6. Georges Vantongerloo. Composition, 1919.

The development of a new language of form is an all-embracing intellectual process, in which creative forces in the most varied fields fashion the elements of the coming style, often independently of one another. Thus it was that the fundamental inspiration in architecture at the beginning of the twentieth century came from painters and sculptors, a decisive factor being the emergence of a new vision which can be detected first in the work of Paul Cézanne. The representation of space in perspective is superseded by a way of looking at an object from, so to speak, different points at the same time. Cubism, as development by Picasso and Braque about 1908, dissected the outward semblance of nature into individual elements and represented them one after the other on a flat surface. "It goes round objects and penetrates into them; so, to the three dimensions which defined space for the Renaissance (length, breadth and height) is added in our century a fourth: time"[45].
Translated into architecture this means that the room, regarded uniquely from one point of view, as separated from the outside by walls, is replaced by a complex of interpenetrating masses. The room is no longer defined by its four walls but by the relationship of solid objects and free-standing dividing elements. The tacit agreement over the methods and purposes of our time is not least displayed in the opportunity offered on the structural side, by the introduction of the steel and reinforced concrete frame, to realise spatial forms of this sort.
Moreover, similarities of form can be recognized which are the expression of a similar desire to discover the elements of a new architecture by a reduction to the simplest essentials. As early as 1910 Adolf Loos built the Steiner house in Vienna [75], which in its exclusive concern for stereometric forms offers a parallel to contemporary movements in painting – in Cubism and especially in the activities of the "De Stijl" group in Holland later. "Cubes, cones, spheres, cylinders or pyramids", Le Corbusier expounds theories already laid down by Cézanne, "are the great primary forms .... The image of these is distinct and tangible within us and without ambiguity. It is for that reason that these are beautiful forms, the most beautiful forms"[46]. Similarly in the declarations of "De Stijl" the demand is constantly reiterated for architecture to free itself from the

condition of purely individual emotions and adopt instead "elementary means of expression" like cubes, surfaces and lines.
The Dutch "De Stijl" group[47], formed in 1917 by the painters Mondrian, van Doesburg, van der Leck and Huszar, the architects Oud, Wils, and van 't Hoff, the sculptor Vantongerloo and the poet Kok, not only pursued their aims with great consistency in painting, sculpture and architecture, but also strove to apply their theories in other fields of human expression like the theatre, dancing and films. Under the ethical and moral grounds of truth, objectivity, order, clarity and simplicity they were opposed to the social and economic situation of their time, striving always to move away from the hazards and accidents of individualism to a collective universal view, in which the "general consciousness of the age" – an often-used phrase of "De Stijl" – would find expression.
In painting "De Stijl" found its purest manifestation in the work of Piet Mondrian [165], who aimed at an art of absolute harmony. According to "De Stijl" theories, harmony can only be attained by a balance of contrasts. The right angle as the point of intersection of two lines provides the simplest form of contrast. Mondrian therefore composes his pictures with a pattern of intersecting right-angled lines, in which some of the spaces between are emphasized by colour. These principles were translated by Vantongerloo into his sculpture with its markedly structural characteristics of rectangular intersecting cubes, from which the step to architecture was obviously extremely short [166].
Kasimir Malewitsch, founder of the Russian "Suprematism", arrived at similar conceptions. His point of departure had also been painting [167], and as long ago as 1913, in search of a fundamental means of expression, he had adopted geometrical forms of the simplest kind, such as the square, rectangle, circle and triangle. He too sought a new architecture by transferring such forms, and the relationship between such forms, from the surface of the canvas to space[48] [168, 169].
Mutual influence between the arts, which was specially productive in "De Stijl", led to a particular manifestation of form in the widely differing fields of painting, applied art, sculpture and architecture. It also concealed the danger that to carry out a set programme without any concession to compromise can cause an over-emphasis of individual elements of form. When Theo van Doesburg, the

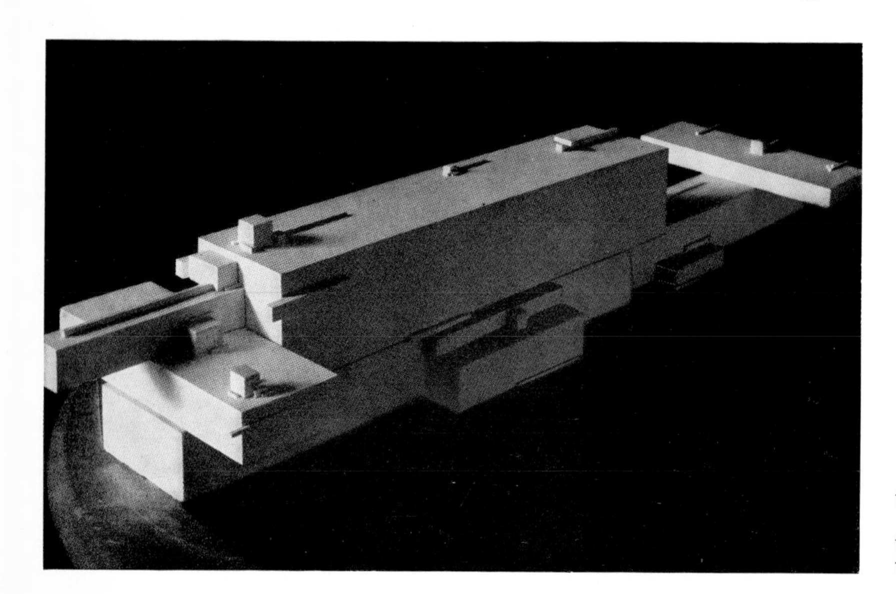

167. Kasimir Malevitsch. Composition, 1921.

168. Kasimir Malevitsch. Architectural Sculptur
1920–22.

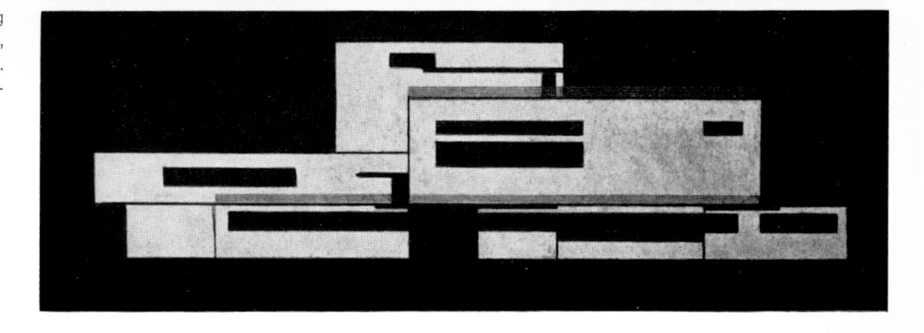

169. Kasimir Malevitsch. Design for a working men's club, about 1925. Use of surface elements, as first developed in painting and sculpture. Space and volume created out of simple contrasts of rectangular shapes.

spokesman of "De Stijl", defined architecture as "total expression of all physical and spiritual needs", embracing "every individual structural, artistic and economic problem"[49], these elements – in contrast to the declaration of principle – are not given equal weight in the projects and executed buildings of "De Stijl". Abstract geometrical forms predominate. The designs rely principally on the harmony of cubes, surfaces and lines, behind which the functional and structural composition of the building takes second place. The great importance of "De Stijl" in the historical evolution of the arts, however, will only be appreciated if one bears in mind that the projects have the character of manifestoes. It is thus essential for elements of form, which have a special place in the theory of "De Stijl", to be thrust strongly into the foreground.

The architecture of "De Stijl" bears the impress of van Doesburg's theories, but also of those of Berlage who was one of the first to stress the unadorned wall surface, and lastly of influences, which came from Frank Lloyd Wright through Berlage and Robert van't Hoff, who visited America before World War I and had been greatly inspired by Wright. His two houses at Huis ter Heide near Utrecht (1916) show, in the treatment of big surfaces and in the complete absence of any ornament, tendencies which could be seen in "De Stijl" architecture, although the accentuation of horizontals does not correspond with "De Stijl" theory with its insistence on harmony between the various elements of a building [171].

The influence of Frank Lloyd Wright can also be detected in J. J. P. Oud's design for a factory in 1919 [170]. In addition to its projecting roofs, heavily shading cornices and horizontal rows of windows which immediately recall Wright's Prairie houses, there are parts of the house like the middle section, in which the components of the building are organized in a harmonious pattern of horizontal and vertical cubes, planes and lines. Oud's lasting preference for the simple, undecorated, cube as a fundamental form is most clearly shown in the prominent block with the entrance gates.

In a series of projects in the following years the architectural ideas of "De Stijl" members found clarification, of which the studies deriving from the collabora-

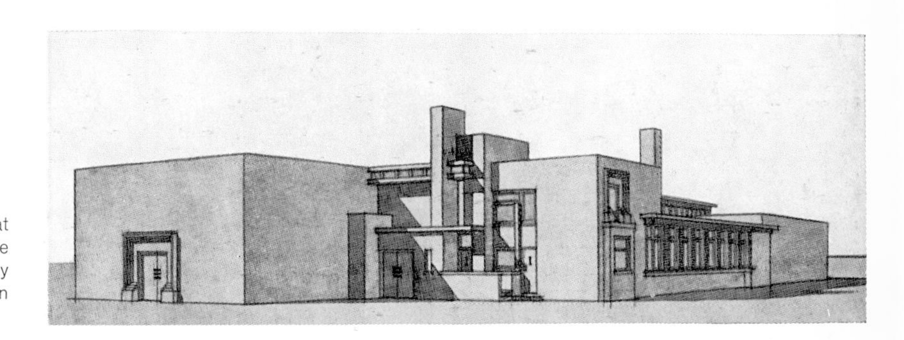

70. Jacobus Johannes Pieter Oud. Factory at urmerend, project, 1919. Application of "De tijl" principles to architecture. Note especially ıe contrast in harmonies in the middle section "De Stijl" manner.

171. Robert van 't Hoff. House at Huis ter Heid Utrecht, 1916; inspired by Frank Lloyd Wrig Vigorously emphasized horizontals and de shadowed silhouette. Rows of separate windov merging into one long window. Preference f the interplay of pure cubic forms already detec able.

tion of van Doesburg and van Eesteren afford examples [172]. "The house was dismembered", comments van Doesburg on these experiments, "and separated into its plastic elements . . . . , the house was an object which could be approached from every direction . . . . (it) rose unencumbered from the ground and the roof was a terrace, an open-air storey, so to speak"[50]. Basically this conception was very like the one expounded by Le Corbusier in his theory of modern building. The new vocabulary of form evolved simultaneously from many sources. The year 1924 saw the completion of two projects which reflect the architectural conception of "De Stijl": a house in Utrecht of Gerrit T. Rietveld and Oud's workers' housing scheme at the Hook of Holland [174, 173]. Oud indeed had left "De Stijl" in 1921, but his work developed on parallel lines in this early phase. His workers' houses are one of the first realizations of the new architectural principles achieved in a wider social context, while Rietveld's building is a typical example of the application of "De Stijl" theory to the private house.
By a dramatic juxtaposition of horizontal and vertical surfaces of different depths, by cubes and voids and by expanses of colour and whiteness, Rietveld achieves

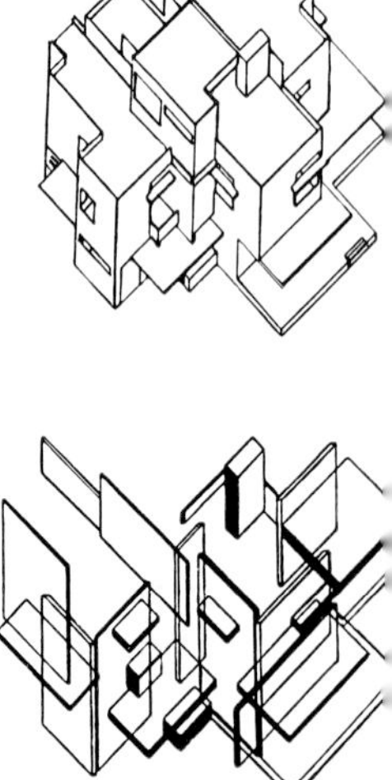

172. Theo van Doesburg and Cor van Eestere Studies for a house, 1923. Contrasting relatio ship of surfaces, the basis of "De Stijl" house

173. Jacobus Johannes Pieter Oud. Housin scheme, Hook of Holland, 1924. Two-store terrace houses. Each dwelling has large livin room on ground floor, bedroom and balcon above. Kitchen and further bedrooms face ga den behind. Rounded corners soften the shar rectangular outline.

74. Gerrit Thomas Rietveld. House at Utrecht, 924. Harmonious balance between verticals and orizontals. Line, surface and cube; wall pattern f solids and voids, catching light and casting hadow.

a dynamic balance of masses and planes. An emphasis on particular elements of form is apparent in this house in many features: in the parapet of the balcony which descends well below the floor level, or in the middle section of the façade which represents a vertical formal element, rising on its own above the upper limit of the cube of the house and thus offering a contrast to the horizontal line of the roof, which juts out prominently on one side only. This emphatic use of contrast as an element of architectural form – sometimes in the relationship of the different parts of the building and at others in the distribution of wall openings – is particularly characteristic of "De Stijl" architecture. As in earlier studies windows serve chiefly to break up surfaces and are not entirely connected with the spatial organization of the interior. The importance of the cube and the surface leads to the renunciation of the pitched roof, and from the desire for pure stereometric form even the projection of the roof is fairly often omitted.
To the architects of "De Stijl", particularly Oud and van Eesteren, there came early a conviction that it was more important to apply the theories which they had elaborated to town-planning schemes than to individual buildings [175, 176,

307, 308]. In their studies and projects, in which town-planning complexes and spaces were organized with the simplest elements, ideas were formulated which are used in town-planning to-day. Thus van Eesteren, in his prize-winning design for the reorganization of "Unter den Linden" in Berlin (1925), tried to achieve a new interpretation of the town by varied relationships of single- and multi-storey blocks, by the effect of grouping and of mass, by the creation of open forecourts and the dramatic siting of tall buildings [177].
The strong influence of stereometric forms and the pre-eminence of surface as a dominant principle mark a phase in the evolution of modern architecture which lasted from about 1917 to 1926. From this source came inspiration of the greatest importance in the period of quest and uncertainty which followed the upheavals of the first world war. The inclination towards simple basic forms necessarily caused the rejection of superficial ornament from the past. At the same time this overriding concern for simple shapes sharpened the feeling for clear proportions and encouraged an appreciation of the beauty of materials.
In the projects of "De Stijl" much is anticipated which was to prove its impor-

175/176. Jacobus Johannes Pieter Oud. Kiefho[illegible] housing scheme, Rotterdam, 1925–30. Garde[illegible] replace backyards. Small squares break t[illegible] parallel rows of houses and lend interest to t[illegible] scheme.

177. Cor van Eesteren. Redevelopment of Unter den Linden, competition design for Berlin, 1925. The organization of masses and a carefully studied variety become the corollaries of town-planning.

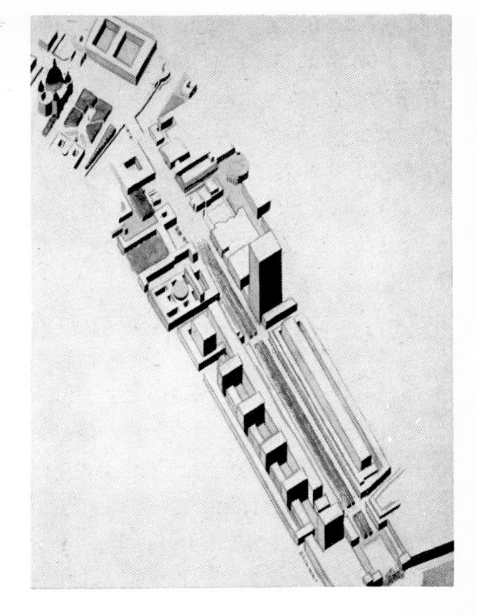

tance in future developments. The change in attitude towards the form and function of the house led to a less rigid conception of space sharply separated from the outside world, and to the establishment of the modern view of the close interrelationship of interior and exterior. In "De Stijl" studies this development indeed is only hinted at, Mies van der Rohe being the first to exemplify in his Tugendhat House of 1930 the new spatial order which was now taking shape. He released the surface from its isolation as an element of form and integrated it as a constituent part of the architectural whole [135, 136, 202].

The mellowing and refinement of form

By the middle of the twenties the techniques of the new architecture in the creation of form were beginning to be apparent, and a basis existed for their wider application. The problem now lay in fitting architectural forms, often independently developed by individual artists, into the practical realities of society in general. On the other hand the demand for purely functional excellence was often in apparent contradiction to the tendency to consider form alone, not least because such a request could rely on a quick response. A chair had first of all to be suited to its purpose. That was a straightforward requirement which could be understood and from which something new could emerge. Individual questions of form, construction and function were each an isolated concept, but at the end of the 1920s people began to appreciate the close mutual relationship of such problems of detail and worked to find a synthesis. In the language of form this respect for all factors meant that architecture was shedding its geometrical predilections[51], as well as those elements which were given exaggerated emphasis in "Expressionism", and also freeing itself from the tyranny of an all too narrowly defined conception of function.
The changed conditions of the post-war period set new tasks which reflected the pressing needs of society. Housing schemes, to meet the serious shortage of homes, and school buildings and hospitals were now problems as compelling as factories, which until now had been the only field in which the pace-makers of

modern architecture had been able to put their ideas into practice. The changed situation was also expressed in the type of client, who was now less and less frequently a private individual, but usually the representative of big interests in the form of the state, the local authority or large firm.

In September 1930 the Third Congress of CIAM, an international group of leading architects, took place in Brussels, at which a significant subject was chosen for discussion: "Rational Methods of Building". The intention was to examine the problems of planning modern housing schemes by a comparative study of international examples. In particular the "effectiveness of various building types – low, medium and high blocks – as well as mixed development" was investigated on the basis of an accurate statistical analysis of building densities, the number of dwellings and inhabitants and of floor space standards [52]. Gropius came to the conclusion that "low and high buildings ..... should be developed in close association according to particular needs. Low buildings, when possible as single-storey blocks in the outer areas of towns with lower population densities, multi-storey buildings of rational heights of ten to twelve floors ..... wherever

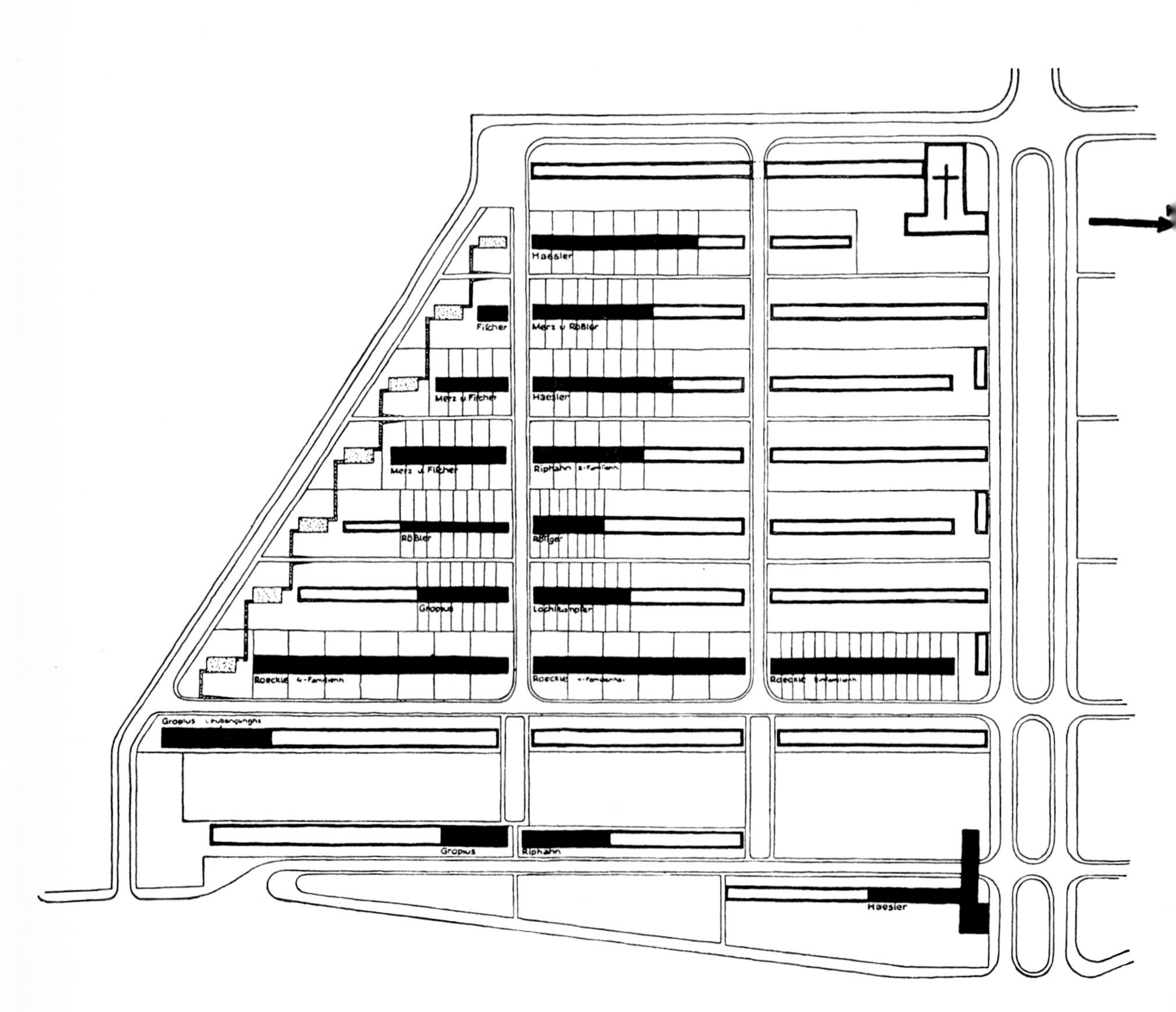

178. Walter Gropius and others. Dammerstock housing scheme, Karlsruhe, 1927–28. Terraces in north-south direction. Axial planning of blocks with due regard for all economic factors.

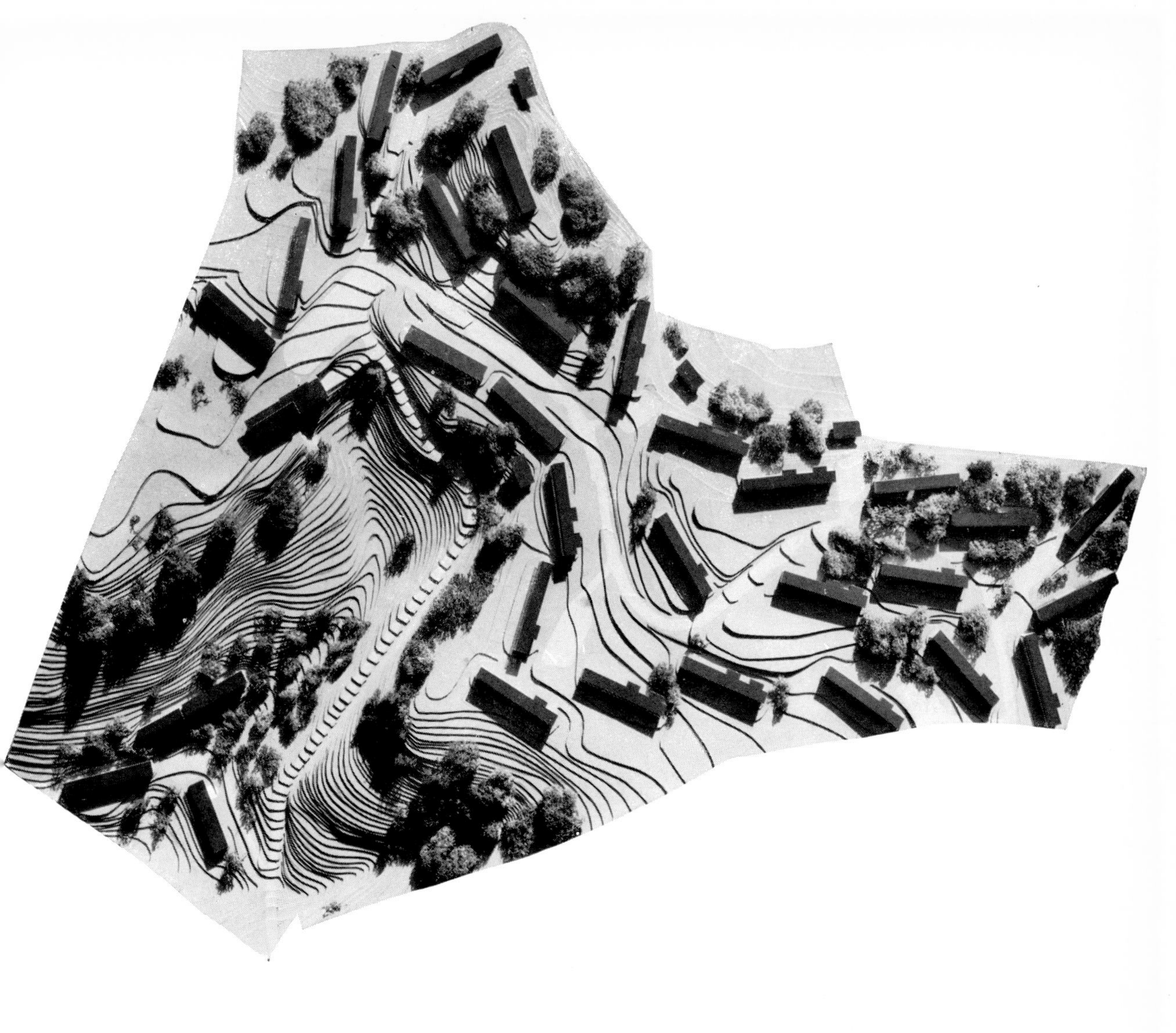

their value is proved . . . ." The blue print of the modern town of to-day was thus drawn up.

Rational methods of building? Did this mean that exclusively rational considerations were to decide the planning of a housing project? Undoubtedly there lay a danger of misinterpretation in this principle. Walter Gropius therefore particularly stressed that the term "rational" in this context must include above all, besides economic needs, psychological requirements as well. "Any form of rationalization is only worth while when it leads to an enrichment of life". It was recognised – although the need for a rational analysis was also urgent – that knowledge acquired in this way must never become an end itself.

Most of the schemes exhibited at this congress, chiefly products of the mid-twenties, were still predominantly characterized by the straightforward, objective, approach, but in the papers of the conference the need for a different attitude towards form was strongly emphasized. Much of what was then disclosed has preserved its value to this day. The experiment of the English garden cities had shown that a town-planning lay-out consisting entirely of "one-family houses"

79. Walter Gropius and Marcel Breuer. New Kensington housing scheme, Pa. Timber-built errace houses. Small units instead of long rows. The blocks follow the contours of the site. Free grouping of buildings which blend with their environment.

must lead to the breaking-down of the town as an entity. Bringing together, not breaking-down, therefore became the goal of modern urban planning.
In 1927–28 the Dammerstock housing scheme was carried out in Karlsruhe [178], for which Gropius had won first prize in the competition, eight other architects sharing in its execution under his leadership. The scheme, which is planned throughout with terrace houses, is bounded by a main traffic artery, from which the residential streets branch off. Paths for pedestrians connect the rows, the siting and organization of which ensure a quiet home for each tenant, and a sunny one, too, since the buildings are laid out strictly in a north-to-south direction. An economical use of the ground is achieved, the distance between rows being one-and-a-half times the height of the blocks in order to obtain good sunlight. Communal services like laundry, heating plant and shops are grouped centrally. The plan seems to be a practical solution to a clearly organized programme, which completely fulfils the economic requirements.
More than ten years later, in 1941, Gropius built the New Kensington housing group near Pittsburgh, this time in collaboration with Marcel Breuer [179]. This

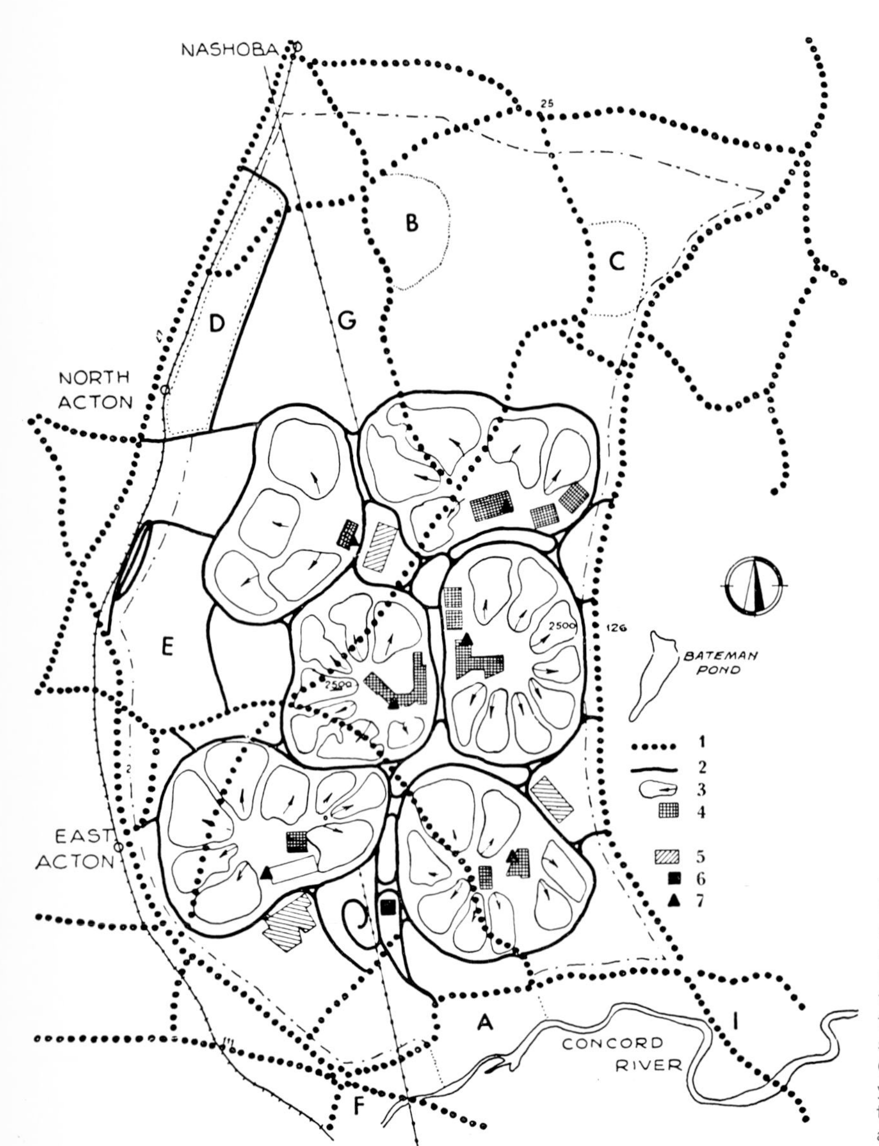

180. Walter Gropius, John Harkness, Marti
Wagner and students of Harvard Universit
Cambridge, Mass. Six townships in the vicinit
of Concord, nr. Boston. Mass., 1942. Study
1. Existing roads; 2. Projected roads; 3. Single
family houses; 4. Public buildings; 5. Blocks c
flats; 6. Central administration; 7. Communit
services; A. and B. Sewage and refuse disposal
C. Cemetery; D. Warehousing; E. Railway good
yard; F. and G. Access roads. Division of the
town into self-contained neighbourhoods, sep
arated from one another by green belts.

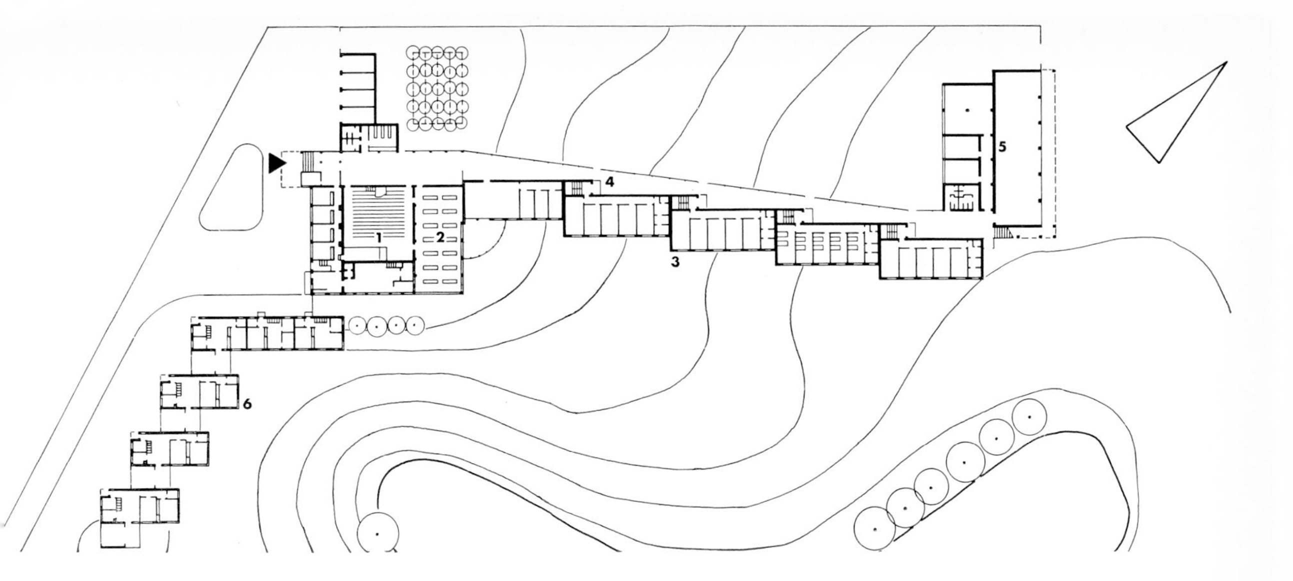

1. Hannes Meyer. School for the amalgamated ·rman Trades Unions, Bernau, nr. Berlin, 1928 1930. Ground-floor plan. The advanced cours of the trades unions required a school lay-out mbining simple straightforward form and onounced modernity. Meyer split up the buildg according to its functions. Open forecourt th side wings. 1. Hall; 2. Dining-room; 3. Reiential pavilions; 4. Glazed access corridor; Lecture and class rooms, gymnasium; 6. Acmmodation for teaching and administrative aff.

scheme also comprises short, detached terraces, each containing from six to eight dwellings. But the blocks are not, as in Karlsruhe, orientated in one direction but follow the contours of the site, with green areas woven into the plan. The open spaces around which the terraces are grouped and which they overlook create a friendly, intimate atmosphere. Topographically the site of the Dammerstock scheme was greatly inferior – although it was larger in extent – but that does not account for the difference. There has been a complete change in approach. The conception of a housing scheme has been developed and enriched, without – and this shows the continuity of the modern attitude – the fruits of earlier researches being rejected.

In housing projects on a larger scale, involving the accommodation of thousands, even tens of thousands of people – like the English satellite towns developed after World War II – came the need, not only for improved housing, but for cultural centres as fundamental elements in the spiritual and physical planning of towns. In 1942 Walter Gropius in a study of the structure of the town, in which he collaborated with John Harkness, Martin Wagner and students of Harvard University, divided the entire town into individual "neighbourhood units" of about 5,000 inhabitants [180].

Main traffic roads, located in green zones, ring each neighbourhood unit, and connecting roads branch off from them to the residential areas. The focal point is the community centre – the core of the city – which is both the cultural and business nucleus of the scheme.

Cheerfulness and variety of form also characterize the individual buildings. In 1928, at the same period as the building of the Dammerstock project, the Deutsche Gewerkschaftsbund (Trades Union Congress) held a competition for a Trades Union school near Bernau [181–183]. The school was to be built in the middle of woods, in gently undulating country, on the banks of a small lake. The programme included residential accommodation for students and staff, lecture rooms, a gymnasium and the necessary assembly and common rooms. The first prize was awarded to Hannes Meyer, who had taken charge of the Bauhaus after Gropius. Meyer worked on the principle that a school of this sort must be a living organism. He conceived the whole plan on a functional basis while exploiting the lakeside site. Placed in the middle and forming the principal feature of the

182. Trades Union School, Bernau. Natural se ting exploited, but without romanticism. Th group of buildings, situated in a clearing ar open on the lake side, climb the sloping site i steps.

scheme, stands the block containing the assembly hall and the main entrance. This is connected on one side to the students' dormitories comprising five three-storey buildings, which follow the slope of the ground. The gymnasium is sited at right angles to the residential wing, thus forming an open spatial group on the side away from the lake. A glass-walled corridor links the buildings with one another. The staff's homes spread out from the other side of the assembly block. Thanks to the variety in the architect's conception of form each individual building in the group derives its own inherent characteristic from its function.

A comparison with the other prize-winning designs reveals the significance of Meyer's scheme. They too were the work of architects who appreciated the creative possibilities of the new architecture. Max Taut proposed a Y-shaped building, the centre of which accommodated the assembly hall and common rooms [184]. This form has no relation to the landscape and seems out of place. On the other hand Max Berg, the architect of the daring reinforced concrete dome of the Century Hall at Breslau, tried to adapt his design to the site, the whole spatial programme being fitted into a long building, which follows the

183. Trades Union School, Bernau. Glaze access corridor, linking the living quarters. Eac pavilion has fifteen double rooms and forms small social group.

84. Max Taut. Model of Trades Union School, Bernau, 1928. One of six competition designs, Monumental solution despite comparatively small dimensions. Three-pointed star layout with hexagonal core, containing common rooms – hall, dining-room.

shore-line of the lake in a gentle curve. Whilst Meyer considered the function of each part of the scheme, rooms of various sizes and intended for different purposes are here compressed into one block.

In the contrast between the home for old people in Kassel by Otto Haesler (1930–31) and the tuberculosis sanatorium by Alvar Aalto in Paimio (1929–33) the change of attitude at the end of the twenties is apparent [185–187, 188–190]. Both buildings speak a similar language of form, but Aalto's has taken a significant step beyond a strictly practical matter-of-fact conception.

The home for the old in Kassel consists of two parallel wings, which contain the inmates' rooms, linked to a transverse block set at right angles, comprising common rooms and administration. An annexe houses staff and heating plant. Equally straightforward and practical, like the functional solution, is the elevational treatment. The bed-sitting rooms are completely glazed in front and open onto a continuous balcony. Between the double glazing there is a space of two feet for window boxes which soften the severe appearance. The backs of these wings, towards which the room entrances face, have narrow horizontal ribbon windows. Perpendicular bands of windows run up the staircases, giving a vertical emphasis to these parts of the building. A steel skeleton is used throughout, the stanchions rising in the partition walls of the rooms.

In Aalto's sanatorium the right angle is no longer fundamental to the plan. The grouping of the buildings follows a freer pattern without being shapeless. Aalto points the six-storey patients' block south-south-east, to form a slight angle with the solarium. The entrance is located in a block connecting the patients' rooms with the medical wing, which again swings away from the patients' area, although in a parallel direction to the solarium. Thus an entrance court enclosed on three sides is formed between the medical wing, administration and patients' blocks.

Aalto gave the same attention to detail in his treatment of the interior. By exhaustive studies the most advantageous type of equipment was provided for the patients' rooms. Aalto profited by the experience and knowledge accumulated in earlier developments, but he rejected the conception of a merely straightforward practical architecture. The slight bend in the principal elevation is as important in its effect on architectural form as the expanding forecourt. The buildings spring to life, embrace their natural setting, and no longer oppose it.

185. Otto Haesler. Old People's Home, Kassel, 1930–31. View from north-east. Rectangular layout, sharply defined cubic form. The passages and landings of the main buildings are lit by uniform horizontal (and the staircases by vertical) ribbon windows.

186. Old People's Home, Kassel. Glass-fronted south façade.

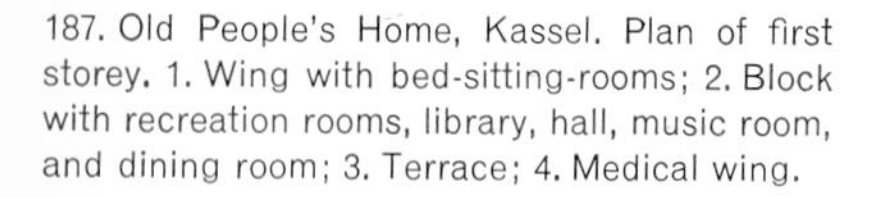

187. Old People's Home, Kassel. Plan of first storey. 1. Wing with bed-sitting-rooms; 2. Block with recreation rooms, library, hall, music room, and dining room; 3. Terrace; 4. Medical wing.

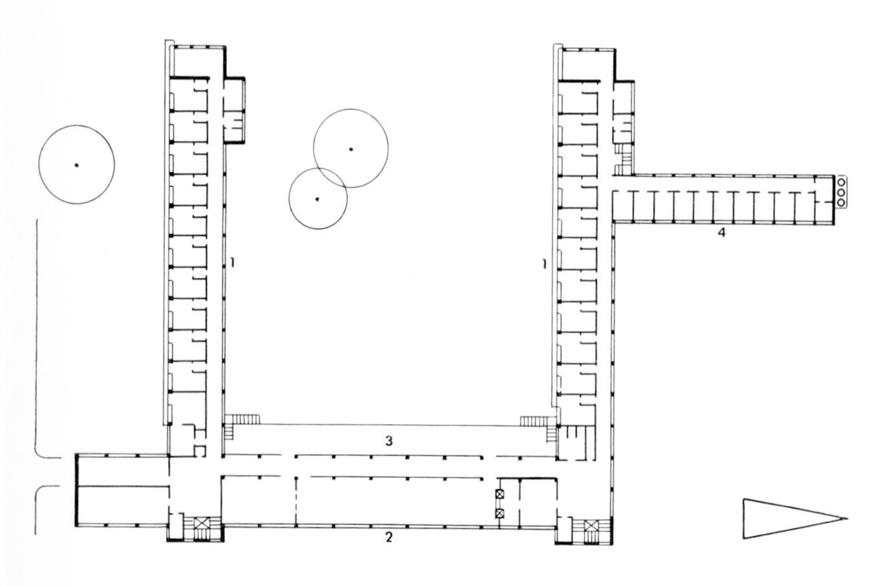

8. Alvar Aalto. Tuberculosis Sanatorium, Pai-io, 1929–33. View of main entrance. The fore-urt expands outwards. The buildings are no nger placed at right angles to one another. The inforced concrete construction permits deep ojecting balconies. Buildings closely related to eir environment.

39. Paimio Sanatorium. Rest room of the sola-um with view of patients' wing.

90. Paimio Sanatorium. Floor plan. 1. Main ntrance; 2. Patients' wing with double rooms; Solarium; 4. Treatment and common rooms. Additional sick rooms, kitchen, laundry. Heat-ıg plant, doctors' and employees, accommoda-on are in separate buildings.

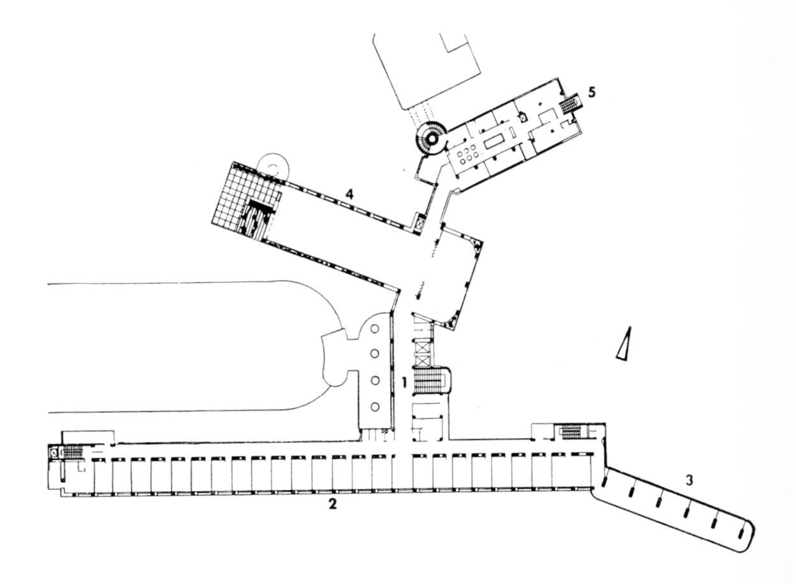

191. A. Aubert, J. C. Dondel, M. Dastugue, Viard. Museum of Modern Art, Paris, 1937. Ne classicism in France: monumentality of offic buildings. Gigantic plastic conception, althou livelier composition of masses and greater lig ness than in the buildings of the totalitari régimes.

Alvar Aalto

By 1930 modern architecture had reached the goals which had been sought and proclaimed in the course of the twenties. At the same time tendencies were already emerging which pointed to wider horizons, but the results so far attained were not bearing fruit in every country. The shadow of politics was partly responsible for this. National Socialism in Germany produced a sterile neoclassicism, intended to represent imperial magnificence [192] [53]. In Russia the competition for the Palace of the Soviets in 1931 marked the turning point away from the lively experimental phase of the 1920s to the regimented state architecture which followed. None of the designs entered by an international élite of architects like Gropius, Le Corbusier and Mendelsohn won prizes. In Italy, too, a monumental neo-classicism held sway in official architectural circles, although modern architecture, which was beginning to spread in Italy at this time, was tolerated.
But even nations whose artistic evolution was not hampered by political events, could not escape the unhappy experience of an inflated neo-classical architecture. The French contribution to the 1937 International Exhibition in Paris, comprising the Palais de Chaillot and the Musée d'Art Moderne with their gigantic colonnades, was not very far removed from the neo-classical pavilions erected by the totalitarian states [191].
For the same exhibition Alvar Aalto [54] built the Finnish pavilion, an eloquent antidote to pomposity [193, 194]. The modest scale of the building, shaded with high trees, is in sympathy with the psychology of the visitor. Instead of crushing him with new superlatives, it offers him a helping hand and puts him at ease with the exhibits.
At this period European countries like Switzerland, Denmark, Sweden and Finland had accepted the tradition of modern architecture and were carrying it on. In the work of Alvar Aalto in Finland an advance on current architectural thinking is apparent.
From the outset Aalto turned away from the cube-block, which contrasts so harshly with its environment. Vitality of form, conspicuous in the grouping of the buildings at Paimio, characterizes his interiors as well. The ceiling of the lecture room of the library at Viipuri (1927–34) is unusual in shape. It is not evenly

192. Paul Ludwig Troost. House of German A Munich, 1937. Neoclassicism in Germany; echoe of antiquity as an architectural expression political power. Lifeless rows of closely packe columns, blank wall surfaces. Proportio oblivious of human scale. The urge for "sho front" elevations produces inconvenient ex bition rooms.

193. Alvar Aalto. Finnish Pavilion, Paris International Exhibition, 1937. Internal court of the Social Services section. Instead of the neoclassical buildings like the Museum of Modern Art and show pieces of the dictatorship powers, Finland was represented at this exhibition by a building of modest scale in a park setting.

194. Finnish Pavilion, Paris. Main building, faced with birch.

constructed, but undulates like waves [195]. There is of course, a logical explanation for this. The undulations reflect the sound waves, so that every listener in the room can hear the speaker clearly. But this is only the obvious explanation. At the same time a considered interpretation of form has made its appearance, which reflects a new conception of spatial composition. The simple space enclosed by rectangular surfaces which dominated the architecture of the twenties is replaced by a dynamic spatial structure. This indeed had long been

195. Alvar Aalto. Library, Viipuri, 1927-34. Detail of suspended pine ceiling. The undulating shape offers acoustical advantages as well as introducing a new conception of form.

196. Alvar Aalto. Finnish Pavilion. World Exhib tion, New York, 1939. Curved and sloping wa "flowing space", excellent display condition

197. Alvar Aalto. Storage building for nitroge plant. Oulu, 1951. Roofs of varying pitch, irregul lines, jagged silhouette.

anticipated. The use of the reinforced concrete frame, making it possible to differentiate between bearing and non-bearing elements, permitted the unhampered positioning of walls, which had already persuaded Le Corbusier to make use of detached partitions moulded to various shapes [144, 146]. There were similar possibilities in the handling of the ceiling. Aalto separates his undulating ceiling from the structure of the building, which is a normal skeleton of vertical stanchions and horizontal beams. As the ceiling is suspended and, therefore, has no supporting function, it can be shaped at will.

Like the ceiling of the lecture room at Viipuri, the wall of the Finnish Pavilion at New York (1939), which is curved and leans inward, is in the first instance a purely functional statement. The curved surfaces allow more room for pictorial matter to be displayed, and the slope of the wall makes it easier for the visitor to examine the exhibits placed high up [196]. But at the same time a spatial pattern emerges, a structure defined in flowing movement – that organic movement, which is also imparted to Aalto's glass vases and wooden chairs.

In the same way as his interiors, Aalto can make a whole building undulate, like

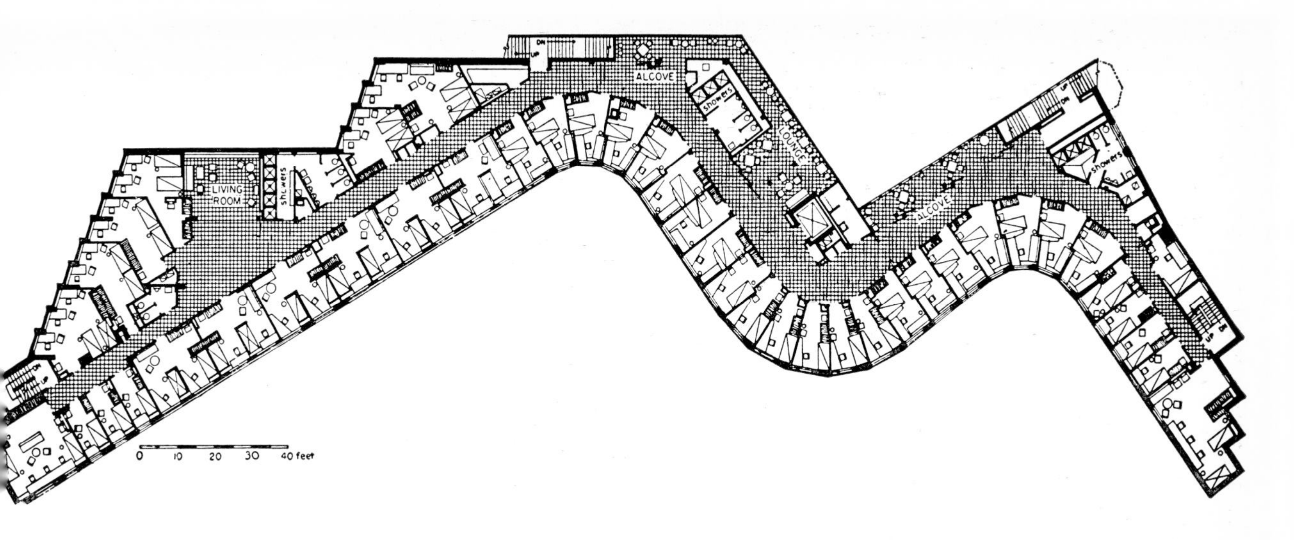

the dormitory at the Massachusetts Institute of Technology (1947). Every room in the building is thus offered a view of a different part of the landscape [198]. But Aalto also uses the jagged staccato silhouette, an effect obtained in the warehouse at Oulu from the varying angles of roof pitch and the straight surfaces of the narrow roof lights [197].

For Aalto the first consideration is an exact analysis of functional requirements, and from these he develops his interpretation of form. How much Aalto learned from the traditions of the twenties, whilst enriching and developing them further, is shown by a comparison between Mies van der Rohe's Tugendhat House in Brno (1930) and the Mairea House built by Aalto in 1938–39 [200–202]. Both designs are based on the fundamental conception of "flowing space". While Mies van der Rohe divides up the predominantly rectangular principal room according to the different functions of living-room, dining area and study, simply by means of partitions which can be placed as required, Aalto organizes the main room into interconnected spaces and thus achieves a more intimate relationship between the areas. Opposite the entrance is the dining space, which extends in front

3. Alvar Aalto. Students' dormitory, Massachu-ts Institute of Technology, Cambridge, Mass., 47. Typical floor plan. Curvilinear building ass, which avoids the monotony of the long, aight, block.

9. Alvar Aalto. Mairea (country) house, Norr-ark, nr. Björneborg, 1938–39. View from west. udio faced with timber battens. Carefully lculated effects with materials and colours: te plinth, fir shutters, balcony parapet of teak, ite-washed brick walls.

200. Mairea (country) house, Norrmark, nr. Björne
berg, 1938–39. Large living-room. Unity of natura
materials, ceiling of fir battens, steel tube star
chions with bast cladding. The principal room i
divided up according to its various functions int
different areas set apart from one another.

of the main room. On the left the living-room with its fire-place opens into the big music room. In the Tugendhat House – and earlier in the Barcelona Pavilion (1929) – Mies had been one of the first to use natural materials, but in sharp contrast to purely technical materials like chrome, steel and glass. Aalto, on the other hand, exploits the unifying effect of natural materials. Even the stanchions essential to the structure are not shown as technical elements, but are covered and become part of the atmosphere of the house. Aalto made the important discovery that each material is only suitable for one particular kind of task. Steel and reinforced concrete, if used visibly, must be given definite assignments.
Aalto's humane architecture carries a stage further developments which were already apparent in other large buildings of the late 1920s, like the school at Bernau. His buildings are organized according to their function and harmonize with their environment. In Aalto's work the building is sympathetic to nature and uses the opportunities which she offers, his vocabulary of form being a direct reflection of the characteristics of the landscape. This is even apparent in his factories, although they have no false romanticism about them.

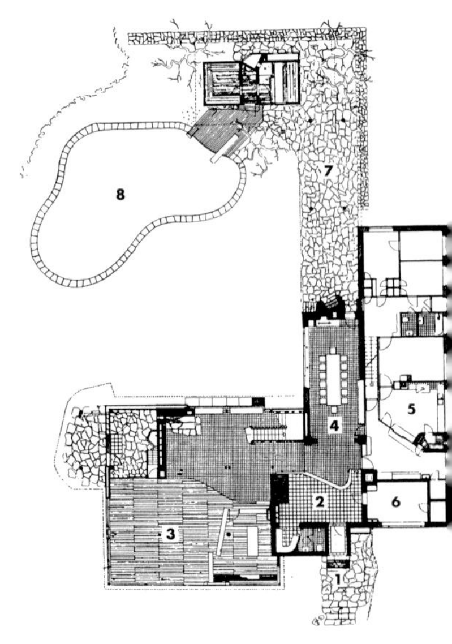

201. Mairea (country) house, Norrmark, nr. Björn
borg. Ground floor plan. 1. Entrance; 2. Ha
3. Principal living-room, with bedrooms ar
studio above; 4. Dining-room; 5. Kitchen; 6. St
dy; 7. Open corridor; 8. Sauna (bath house).

202. Mies van der Rohe. Tugendhat house, Brn
1930. Living-room and study. Contrast betwee
natural and artificial materials. Partitions do n
destroy the unity of the room.

)3. Alvar Aalto. Cellulose Factory, Sunila, 37–39. The group of buildings is as appropriate the landscape as to the needs of production ocesses.

4. Alvar Aalto. Housing, Sunila, 1937–39. Terce houses. Work space is provided by the ctory on the island, living space by homes in e forest.

The Sunila cellulose plant (1937–39) is conspicuous in every respect as an industrial work, but its design is related to the landscape [203]. The horizontal accent of the long, flat, warehouse is repeated in the mirror flatness of the lake, to which the vertical factory chimney provides a contrast. The contours of the granite rocks in front are brought into extraordinarily effective association with the elevational treatment of the building.

In Säynätsalo (1949–52) Aalto has provided a community centre for an industrial housing scheme. It lies on a hill in the inner part of an island and fits comfortably into its setting. The group of buildings, which includes town hall, library and a few small shops, is built about a courtyard, which can be entered at one side by a broad grass-clad flight of steps [206, 207] – symbol of the open countryside welcomed into this little man-made space. As with Frank Lloyd Wright, the buildings are sited high up, but do not obscure the top of the hill. If the block, which contains the community hall, gives an impression of a tower from the steps, the dimensions of the other buildings are so modest that from every side they appear lower than the tall trunks of the pine woods.

205. Alvar Aalto. Housing Scheme, Kauttua, 1938. Entrances at the side. The roof of one house serves as roof garden to the next.

Frequently Aalto's buildings conform to the geological pattern of the land. The terrace houses at Kauttua (1938) follow the contours of a hill, and are built on its slope [205]. The roof of each house lower down serves as a terrace to the one above. The combination of economical plan and imaginative solution, exemplified in this comparatively minor undertaking, indicates the wealth of possibilities latent in the tendencies of the late twenties and the importance of the rôle played by Aalto in the predominantly unproductive 1930s.

Aalto's architecture is always adjusted to the psychology of the people for whom he builds and to the needs of their particular situation. For him the yardstick is the individual person with his own special requirements, not the vision of a new society for which a new architecture would be appropriate.

206. Alvar Aalto. Community Centre, Säynätsal 1951–52, Comprises local council room and off ces, homes, library and shops. Grass spread over the flight of steps leading to the inner cour Nature becomes a partner in the scheme.

207. Community Centre, Säynätsalo, 1951–5 Council room. The warm tones of the brick wall and the wooden ceiling give the room a sens of intimacy despite its height.

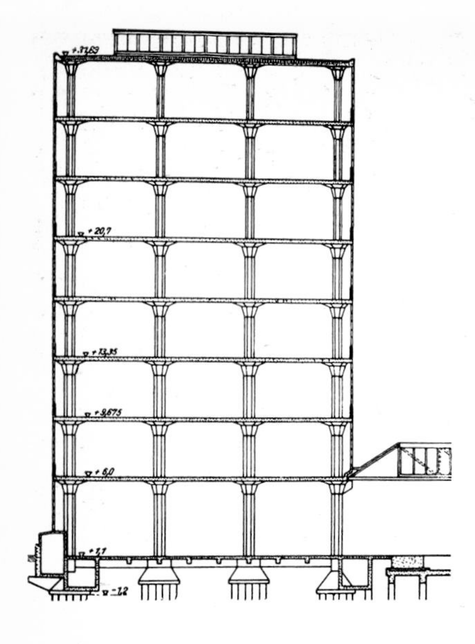

223. Johannes Andreas Brinkmann and L. C. van der Vlugt. Van Nelle Tobacco Factory, Rotterdam, 1928–30. Section. The walls consist of windows and panels with no load-bearing function; use of mushroom stanchions which splay outwards and form a monolith with the floor slabs, which have no supporting beams.

transparent curtain in front of the interior, interrupted only by the delicate articulation of the glazing bars. Again the stanchions are erected inside and no structural members are found in the external wall elements. Here for the first time – and not in the buildings using the continuous ribbon window – thanks to the fragility and transparency of the plain wall surface, is an absolutely logical illustration of the wall with no supporting function.
In the Dessau workshops Gropius developed, and gave expression to, tendencies earlier suggested in the Fagus works and the factory building of the Werkbund exhibition, which are to-day distinguishing marks of modern architecture: extreme lightness and transparency. Glass, as a material, implies a characteristic relationship between interior and exterior, between the building and its environment. The building indeed is wide open to the world about it; light streams in unhindered, and the unobstructed view of the surroundings outside determines the atmosphere of the interior. On the other hand the glazed cube is more obviously man-made than the building constructed with natural materials like stone and timber, and contrasts with its setting. Just as glass both reflects and

224. Van Nelle Tobacco Factory, Rotterdam. The low, curving, office block supplies a visual scale and contributes to the elegance of the solution

9. Network for shell dome of the planetarium the Zoological Gardens, Berlin, 1926. Zeiss-widag method. Latticed system of short rods fore covering with a layer of concrete.

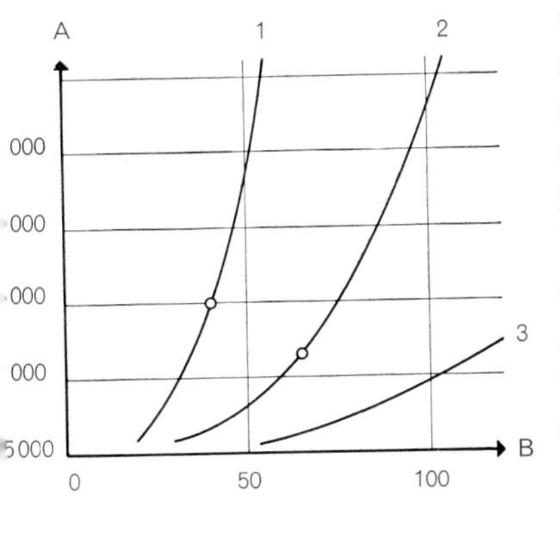

0. Graphic representation of the relationship etween width of span and weight. A: Weight of onstruction in tons. B: Width of span in metres. tructural principle of (1) a masonry dome (St. eter's, Rome); (2) a reinforced concrete ribbed ome (Century Hall, Breslau); (3) a curved rein-rced concrete space frame (Market Hall, Leip-g). Greater width of span demands stronger onstruction; increasing weight limits the pos-ble width of span.

with a minimum expenditure of material. Reinforced concrete, however, does not possess the high strength which steel – the material of the Machinery Hall – embodies. Halls in reinforced concrete were, therefore, more difficult to build until it was learnt how to progress from plane frame construction systems – beams, arches and simple frames – to space frames, the shell and the folded slab. It was only with these that a characteristic construction form for reinforced concrete was found. The Century Hall in Breslau (1912–13), by the architect Max Berg and the engineer Trauer [94, 238], shows with what determination new forms were worked out in the early days. The exterior of the hall, entirely built with reinforced concrete, reveals no trace of the structural daring of the interior, but inside the majesty of the conception is at once apparent. From a circular base of massive walls and huge elliptical arches, 32 slender ribs spring upwards and converge upon the compression ring of the dome, where a circle of brooding darkness contrasts with the light shining through the bands of windows, visible behind the diagonal braces. Countless patterns attract the eye and enhance the drama of this adventure in space.

Although lacking the emotional impact of the Century Hall, the works of the French engineer Eugène Freyssinet are clear and straightforward exercises in the creation of form. The airship hangar erected in 1916 at Orly near Paris exemplifies the parabolic arch [241]. In this form of construction the stresses are borne by the foundations without generating severe tension in the structure itself. The reinforcement of the concrete, which increases the tensile resistance, can therefore be kept to a minimum. Furthermore Freyssinet constructed the carcass, not, as was customary, as a thick vault, but as a thin skin, to which he gave the necessary strength by ribs. The structural theory on which the folded slab is based, and which was later to play an important rôle, is put into practice here for the first time.

The advances, which then took place at the beginning of the twenties, led to a completely new spatial form. Just as in the nineteenth century engineers had laid the foundations for the great developments in modern architecture at the turn of the century, so now, too, the new ideas were first worked out in the minds of engineers. Freyssinet was an engineer and so were the designers of a series of epoch-making buildings: Dischinger and Bauersfeld, Maillart, Nervi and Can-

41. Eugène Freyssinet. Airship hangar, Orly, nr. aris, 1916. Arched parabolic hall. The folds of e slender-sectioned barrel vault increase its rength.

242. Aircraft hangar constructed on the Zei Dywidag principle. In the mid-thirties ma barrel shells were built with slender ribs.

dela. A unity emerges, in which the differences between the analytical thinking of the engineers and the creative intuition of the architects disappear.
It was also the work of engineers which led to the discovery of a construction system, the importance of which cannot yet be estimated. In 1922 Walter Bauersfeld[57] needed a domed room in the mathematically exact form of a hemisphere in which to test optical equipment. After various experiments he decided to construct the dome with a network of short rods about two feet long. This lattice was covered with a layer of concrete about 1 ¼″ thick, which at this stage had no supporting function, but was merely intended to provide the covering surface [239]. Experiments revealed the enormous strength of this curved shell. Intensive collaboration between Dischinger and the firm of Dyckerhoff and Widmann followed. Dischinger suggested that their special case study of the dome shell should be extended to the barrel shell (vault). Their joint work led to the formulation of the shell theory, in which the load is borne by both the concrete and the reinforcement. The first large dome shells were used in the Planetarium building of Jena in 1925 and in the market halls of Leipzig and Basle. The space frame was a fact.

243. Eduardo Torroja. Race course, La Zarzue 1935. Boldly cantilevered stand roofs of curv segmental shells of reinforced concrete.

244. Hermann Brenner. German air experimen station, Berlin-Adlershof, 1932–36. Vertical wi tunnel for spin tests. Unusual building probler produce novel building forms.

5. Robert Maillart and Hans Leuzinger. Cement
ıll of the Swiss National Exhibition, Zürich,
38–39. Parabolic barrel vault, demonstrating by
lightness the possibilities of reinforced con-
ete as a building material.

The proportions of these buildings are astonishing. The market hall at Basle spans more than 200′ with a shell thickness of barely 3½″. These exceptional dimensions can only be realized because of the space-supporting effect of the curved surface. A simple example can explain the structural properties. A piece of paper, spread out flat, possesses no appreciable strength. The same sheet of paper, bent in the form of a barrel and firmly held at the straight edges, has surprising strength.

In the last twenty years shell construction, first developed for one specific purpose, has entered many fields of architectural design. In 1935 Eduardo Torroja built the wide jutting shell roofs of the Madrid race course, while in Germany a series of aircraft hangars were erected in the mid-thirties, which spanned large areas with great daring [243, 242]. A building developed entirely from its function like the wind tunnel at Berlin-Adlershof, constructed in 1932–36 by Hermann Brenner, shows new forms in embryo [244]. A softly rounded outline defines the thimble-shaped reinforced concrete structure, the stairs emphasise the curves of the building and the entrance is modelled out of its mass. The right

246. Pier Luigi Nervi. City Stadium, Florer 1930–32. Entrance to stands. The curved li of the stairs and the correspondingly cur beams essential to the construction reveal ingenious pattern of movement in the structu members.

247b/247c. Pier Luigi Nervi. Aircraft hangar reinforced concrete components, 1939–41. C struction of remarkable daring and simplicity. T roof of this type of hangar (erected on seve Italian airfields) rested on only six piers, wh spanning an area of approximately 330 × 135 fe The pre-cast reinforced concrete units used cover the barrel-vault roof are poured in situ simple wood moulds and assembled on lar skeleton frames. The tracery effect of the c struction can be clearly seen in the photogra of the carcase.

247a. City Stadium, Florence. Side view of sta The powerful, muscular form of the support frame is developed from the structural con tions.

angle, the straight line and the flat surface no longer occupy the front of the stage; the construction principle of the shell, which draws its strength from the three-dimensional curving of thin-walled surfaces, quickly adapted its structural characteristics to other forms.

The new forms, which were to be evolved from shell construction, were demonstrated by a building, of which the creator did not in the first place have to consider practical requirements. The Swiss engineer Robert Maillart (1872–1940), the builder of many bridges noteworthy for their audacious curves, designed in 1938 the Cement Hall [245] for the Swiss National Exhibition in Zurich. The parabolic barrel vault reveals a creative inspiration unsurpassed to-day in its imaginative power. While the shell domes were conceived as double curved – i. e. in two directions – supporting structures, the Cement Hall is constructed as a simple curved supporting structure.

The characteristics which emerged most clearly from shell construction influenced a considerable section of modern architectural opinion. Freer spatial conceptions took the place of the room enclosed by surfaces standing at right angles

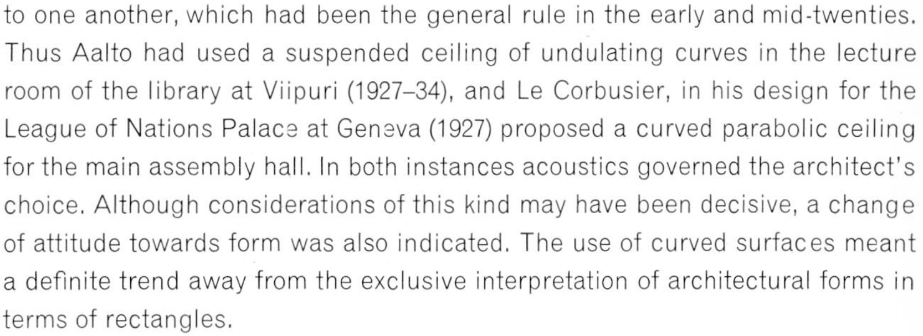

to one another, which had been the general rule in the early and mid-twenties. Thus Aalto had used a suspended ceiling of undulating curves in the lecture room of the library at Viipuri (1927–34), and Le Corbusier, in his design for the League of Nations Palace at Geneva (1927) proposed a curved parabolic ceiling for the main assembly hall. In both instances acoustics governed the architect's choice. Although considerations of this kind may have been decisive, a change of attitude towards form was also indicated. The use of curved surfaces meant a definite trend away from the exclusive interpretation of architectural forms in terms of rectangles.

The change of structural methods and conceptions of form can be seen very clearly in the work of Pier Luigi Nervi (born 1891) [58]. His stadium at Florence, built in 1930–32, exemplifies the slab and beam, which had already become the classic elements of reinforced concrete [246, 247a]. But in the ordering of the main horizontal members, in their flexible adaptation to the pattern of stresses and in the free handling of the building elements, a new sense of form is clearly detectable. Nervi is above all a creative artist in reinforced concrete. This mat-

1

erial, with its responsiveness to plastic forms, which until now had been subordinated almost exclusively to the right angle, is moulded into shapes which are as daring as they are novel.

In the building of the Exhibition Hall at Turin (1948–49) Nervi employed precast units of reinforced concrete for the barrel-shaped vault of the hall, their maximum thickness being scarcely 2″ [248a–249]. With these thin-sectioned components he bridges an area 240 feet long, an astonishing ratio between expenditure of material and performance. The corrugated arrangement of these pre-fabricated units forming the ribs of the roof gives them the necessary strength and at the same time solves most handsomely the problem of direct lighting, which enters through glass strips set in the sloping sides of the roof elements. Even more daring structurally were Nervi's aircraft hangars erected in 1939–41, their enormous roofs resting on only six piers. Modern architecture's endeavours to achieve lightness and to reduce supporting members to an absolute minimum are embodied in these buildings [247b, 247c].

Nervi's collaboration with Marcel Breuer and Bernard H. Zehrfuss in the Unesco

3b. Exhibition Hall, Turin. The pre-cast com-nents, corrugated in shape, were assembled steel scaffolding.

—

3a. Pier Luigi Nervi. Exhibition Hall, Turin, 48–49. The ribs of the shallow barrel vault nsist of prefabricated concrete components, ough the glass sides of which light is evenly read.

). Exhibition Hall, Turin. Fan-shaped members tribute the stresses from the ribs to the nchions. The pattern of forces is mirrored in s dynamic interpretation of form.

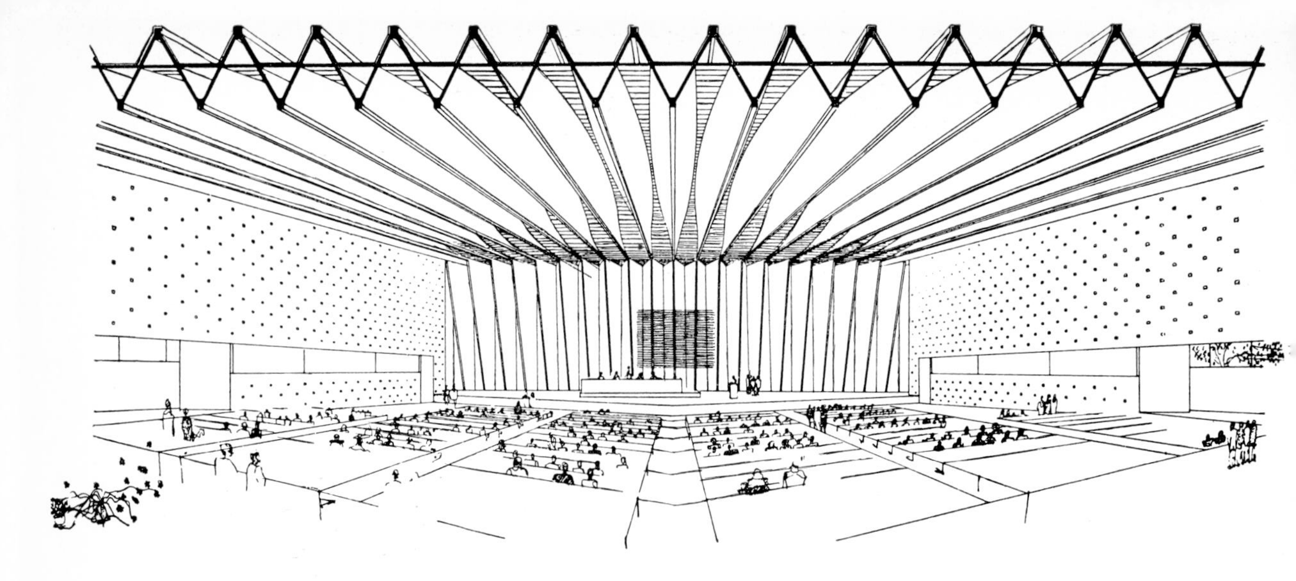

building (1953–58) in Paris [250] is a landmark in his career to date. The conference hall, connected to one side of the Y-shaped office building, has a folded-slab roof, the ribs of which are extended to the front of the hall. The emphasis thus given to the principal feature of the room, the speaker's dais, is underlined by the slab passing through the folds of the ceiling and rising towards the front. The position of this slab is determined by the distribution of the compression stresses in the construction. In the same way the folds which are also visible outside at the narrow ends serve a double purpose. They strengthen the building longitudinally against wind pressure and they enhance the unity of wall and roof; of interior and exterior. Aesthetic and structural considerations with Nervi are never treated separately.

Like Nervi, Felix Candela (born 1910)[59], a Spaniard by birth and to-day living in Mexico, has envolved an individual and novel vocabulary of form out of re-inforced concrete. Nervi's buildings are composed for the most part of prefabricated units and result in muscular, articulated, structures. Candela on the other hand constructs the shell as a monolith, which had already been realized in its

250. Marcel Breuer, Pier Luigi Nervi, Berna H. Zehrfuss. Unesco Building, Paris, 1953–5 The folds of the ceiling, which are also visib on the outside, are continued on the intern face of the wall at the narrow end of the wedg shaped hall, where they give additional emphas to the speaker's dais, the "spiritual centre" the room.

251/252. George Francis Hellmuth, Joseph Willia Leinweber and Minoru Yamasaki. Airport, S Louis, 1953–55. Reception building of intersecti barrel shells. Light enters through the gla spandrels and side walls.

INFORMATION
INSURANCE

early forms in the twenties, and of which Maillart had revealed the possibilities in his Zürich Cement Hall. Candela's compatriot Gaudí, half a century earlier, had anticipated hyperbolic parabaloidal shell forms in some of his buildings – if not in reinforced concrete.

Candela goes so far as to see in the application of reinforced concrete frame construction a misuse of the material in a structural process suited to timber and steel. All his efforts are devoted to furthering "the development of the structural form appropriate to the new material" (Candela). In this he is influenced by an urge to find a style which can be regarded as a protest against determining form exclusively in terms of the geometry of the right angle. To simple cylinder shells, and dome and barrel vaults, Candela adds highly complicated structures: folded-slab roofs and interpretations of hyperbolic curved surfaces of the most varied plan.

The Cosmic Ray Pavilion of the University of Mexico – in which a thin shell was required to admit cosmic rays – and the churches and factories which Candela has built, show both grace and daring [256, 257]. The complex structural proportions of these buildings, which often have the unaffectedness of natural forms, are not the result, in Candela's case, of analytical calculations alone. Rather does he defend the intuitive approach to each particular task, demanding from the architect an instinctive appreciation of the distribution of forces.

A method of building, in which the high tensile strength of thin steel cables is exploited in the construction of hanging roofs, illustrates a very different approach. These cables are strung from strong abutments and carry the thinnest possible

253. Jörn Utzon. Design for Opera House, Sydne 1956. East side. First Prize in International Com petition. The programme included two theatre Two series of interlocking shells like inflated sai cover the auditorium and scenery tower.

254/255. Design for Sydney Opera House. Si plan and longitudinal section. Access to th auditoria, which rise in steps as in an amph theatre, is past the scenery towers.

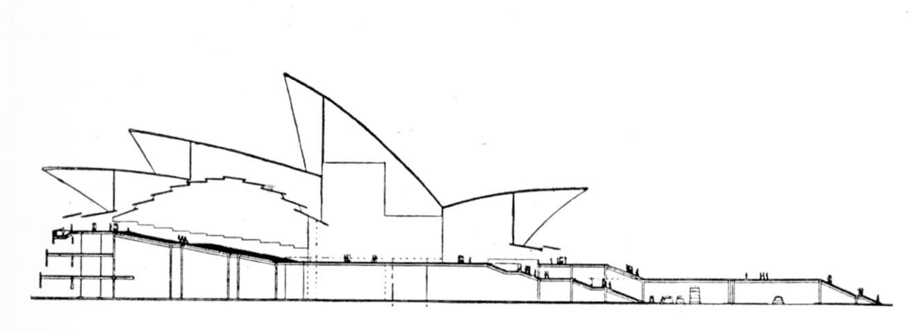

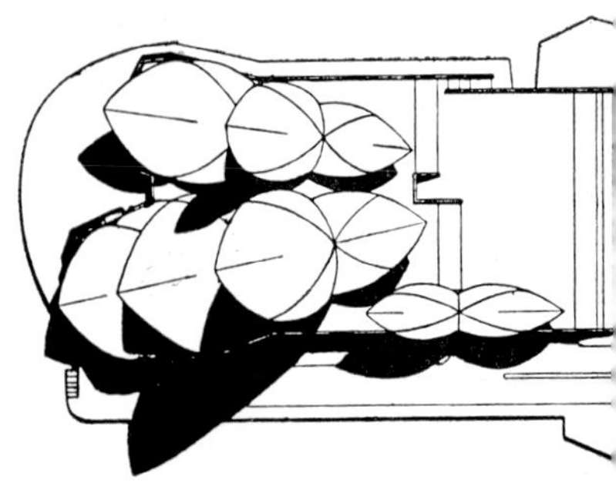

The Contributions of the Nations

Although so many lands nowadays acknowledge modern architecture, internationalism has not led to uniformity. The architecture of individual countries [61] has preserved original features in its outstanding architectural creations, deriving distinctive expression from regional and climatic conditions and the varying needs and emotions of mankind. Scandinavian architecture differs from Italian just as clearly as North-American from South-American.
Differing as much as form, the conception of the functions of buildings and the preference for particular building tasks have also provided opportunities for different countries to make their distinctive contributions. If development in one nation threatened to stagnate, in another it continued all the more impressively. In England iron was already used from the end of the eighteenth century as a new type of structural material, and Ruskin and Morris soon began their work which led to a renewal of the intellectual basis of architecture. At the same time building with iron was further developed in France, while Perret became in 1903 the first creative artist in reinforced concrete. A few years earlier Berlage commenced the Stock Exchange building in Amsterdam and so paved the way for the great advances in Dutch architecture. In the twenties the spread of the new architecture occurred not only in Holland, but above all in Germany, where Gropius founded the Bauhaus. After these endeavours had come to an end in Germany, the tradition of modern architecture was carried on in Switzerland during the thirties. Parallel with these activities developments started in Sweden and Denmark, inspired by Asplund's Stockholm exhibition of 1930, and at the same period Aalto erected his first buildings in Finland. Italian architecture looks back to the thirties for its beginnings, enjoying its brightest period to-day.
The continent of America received powerful inspiration from Europe, which led to the founding of modern Brazilian architecture in the mid-thirties. It also gave new life to the building arts of the United States which, by the end of the nineteenth century, had already contributed handsomely to the history of modern architecture.

Great Britain

The seeds of modern architecture were sown in England[62]. Morris, and later Voysey and Mackintosh, decisively influenced Art Nouveau, Jugendstil and the Vienna "Sezession". In architecture, as in the applied arts, England played a leading part at the end of the nineteenth century. Morris and his followers extended the architect's field of activity from houses through the applied arts and interior decoration to housing schemes, and were also the first to start organizing the home from a functional standpoint, no longer subordinating the interior to traditional conceptions of form, but giving every room the position, shape and size appropriate to its purpose [58–61, 264].
Morris's work was inspired by a protest against the negative results of industrialization, but he did not yet appreciate the opportunities which industry and industrial production offered in realizing new ideas. English engineers had performed the great service of applying iron as a typical industrial product to building. Since the end of the eighteenth century a series of daring iron bridges had been built, which revealed the structural possibilities of the new building materials [10–14]. Paxton's Crystal Palace in London (1851) illustrated the new tendencies in architectural style [19, 20, 263]. At the beginning of the century, however, progress came to an abrupt end, while on the continent the English theories were developed independently.
It was not until 1930 that an interest in modern architectural design was rekindled in England. The Mars group was founded in 1931, an association of young English architects linked with C.I.A.M. A few years later Walter Gropius came to England and, like Erich Mendelsohn and Marcel Breuer, who also saw no more chances of work in the Germany of rising National Socialism, influenced the younger generation of English architects. Of the projects which German architects succeeded in carrying out after their emigration to England, two were particularly important in their results: the De la Warr Pavilion in Bexhill by Erich Mendelsohn and Serge Chermayeff (1935) and the school at Impington by Walter Gropius in collaboration with Maxwell Fry (1935) [267, 120, 121, 265]. The effect of Le Corbusier was also enduring.
In the first buildings of modern English architecture a strong continental in-

263. Joseph Paxton, Crystal Palace, London, 1851

264. Philip Webb, Red House, Bexley Heath, Kent, 1859.

265. Walter Gropius and Maxwell Fry, Impington College, Cambridgeshire, 1936. This school type – a combination of secondary school with accommodation for adult education and social gatherings – proved equally important for England as an example of the group of buildings with single-storey classroom blocks.

66. E. Owen Williams. Chemical plant for Boots, Beeston, 1930–32. Mushroom construction, and therefore no supporting beams for the floors. Completely glazed walls which derive a sense of movement from the horizontal bands of the floor slabs. The division of the building into five transverse blocks above a ground floor covering the whole area, produces excellent natural lighting and counteracts the monotonous tendency of a large factory layout.

267. Erich Mendelsohn and Serge Chermayeff. De La Warr Pavilion, Bexhill, 1935. Assembly rooms of English seaside resort, with restaurant, library and concert hall. The horizontal emphasis – like the rounded projecting staircase, a favourite Mendelsohn feature – reflects the level character of the sea.

fluence predominated. It is clearly apparent in the early work of Maxwell Fry who in 1935 built the Sunhouse in Hampstead and the Sassoon House in Peckham. In 1935 Tecton erected the charming Penguin Pool at the London Zoo and in 1938–39 the strictly functional Health Centre in Finsbury [268], while in 1938 Crabtree, Slater and Moberly, and C. H. Reilly, built the Peter Jones Store in London [269]. A personality in his own right is Sir Owen Williams – "the Perret of Great Britain" – who erected the Boots' factory at Beeston in 1930 [266].
By the end of the thirties the threat of war overshadowed building activities, which came to a complete standstill while hostilities lasted. But even during these years there began an intensive study of questions which awaited solution when peace returned: in particular, the reconstruction of destroyed towns. Architects, public authorities, sociologists and politicians collaborated in preparing programmes, which are models of their kind. If, with exceptions such as Coventry and Canterbury, the execution of these schemes hardly attained the hoped-for architectural quality, England none the less produced far-reaching practical examples of the principles of her town and regional planning.

268. Tecton. Finsbury Health Centre, London, 1938, Symmetrical plan, determined by the functional needs of the building. The ground floor contains clinics; the upper storey holds offices. Entrance hall, treatment rooms and lecture hall are in the central block. The forecourts, despite the narrowness of the site, give an impression of spaciousness. Le Corbusier's influence is apparent.

In the new conception of satellite towns, which have been established particularly in Southern England, it was laid down as a principle that dormitories were not to be created for people working in neighbouring cities like London, but self-contained organisms containing everything which modern man needs for town life: homes and facilities for work, green spaces for recreation, schools and cultural centres [270, 271]. At the same time the social structure would represent a cross-section of that of the whole country; the inhabitants of the town were therefore to be not only workers in a few large firms, but employees of both small and big concerns, as well as craftsmen, clerical workers, teachers and professional men.

In one field especially, school building, modern English architecture occupies a leading position in the world [275–278]. School building is seen in England primarily as an educational problem and not so much as one of architectural form. English architects show a preference for the simple pavilion type of school; multi-storey buildings are not desired. The advantages of the pavilion, according to English ideas, lie in the opportunity of being able to combine classroom work

269. William Crabtree, in association with Slater and Moberly and C. H. Reilly. Peter Jones store, London, 1938. Modern retail shops require unobstructed sales areas and stock rooms. Structural frame placed inside; non-bearing walls of transparent and coloured glass. Gently curving outline.

70. Hubert Bennett and J. L. Martin; R. H. Mat-
hew and H. J. Whitfield Lewis. Alton Estate, Vandsworth, 1954–56. Mixed two- and four-torey groups, with point blocks following the ontours of the plateau. Advantage is taken of he wooded nature of the site.

71. Frederick Gibberd. Harlow New Town, plan-ed 1947. Neighbourhood unit. Houses with own arden. Each neighbourhood (unit), divided from he next by a green belt, has a row of shops and a rimary school. Three to four neighbourhoods re grouped about a small shopping centre, hurch, library and health centre. Large retail tores, administrative offices and cultural build-ngs occupy a town centre, which is common to ll neighbourhoods.

272. Architects' Co-operative Partnership. Brynmawr Rubber Factory, South Wales, 1945–51. Production areas are covered by shallow shell domes.

with study in the open air. The higher costs due, for example, to the amount of ground space used are trifling, since the increased size of the site area required in a pavilion system is insignificant compared with the expenditure of space needed for play and sports grounds without such a system. In these school buildings prefabricated units are principally used, which are standardized to provide a wide variety of combinations.

In 1951, a hundred years after the Great Exhibition in London, the "Festival of Britain" took place. This was not a world exhibition, but an attempt to take artistic stock of the achievements of one nation. Two buildings were of outstanding interest: the Dome of Discovery by Ralph Tubbs and the new concert hall, the Royal Festival Hall, by Robert H. Matthew and J. L. Martin [280, 281]. From the first the concert hall was planned not merely for the exhibition. It stands to-day, and – in the somewhat drawer-like form of the boxes – has greatly influenced European architecture in this field.

A spirit of experiment, of searching for new possibilities, is beginning in England to supersede the former strongly conservative attitude. It is above all the young

273. Alexander Gibson. House, Cannon Lane, Hampstead, 1955. Plain brick surfaces, relieved by verandahs. The horizontals of the roof are extended as beams, which preserve the unity of the rectangular cube.

274. Brynmawr Rubber Factory, South Wales. Light enters through round skylights and glazed spandrels.

75. Richard Sheppard. Churchfields School,
Vest Bromwich, begun 1954-55. Block for tech-
ical classes and library. Comprehensive School
or boys and girls from the seventh school year
ncludes general education, and trade and craft
chools. The separate, openly sited blocks, are
rouped about grass courts and playgrounds.

76. Churchfields School, West Bromwich. 1: Assembly hall, library with large reading room,
dministrative offices grouped round an internal
ourt. 2: Science block. 3: Gymnasium. Block for
raft school with workshop annexe. The remain-
ng buildings house the ordinary classes.

277. C. H. Aslin, County Architect. Junior School,
Croxley Green, Hertfordshire, 1947-49. Wide use
of prefabricated components is made in English
school buildings. An experiment of great interest
has been applied to fifty school buildings in the
County of Hertfordshire, where a standard grid
of 8 ft. 3 in. is used, divided into three to provide
a convenient size for window casements.

278. C. H. Aslin, County Architect. Pentley Park
Primary School, Welwyn Garden City, Hertfordshire, 1948-50. An intimate scale is preserved,
comparable to that of the children's own homes.
Projecting roof slabs stress the independence of
the separate pavilions.

279. Basil Spence. Cathedral of St. Michael, Coventry. Under construction. The tower and ruined nave of the war-destroyed church have been preserved. The new long structure is at right angles to the traditional east-west orientation. A monumental, richly decorated, building.

architects who are seeking new ways: Ralph Tubbs, with the daring aluminium construction of the Dome of Discovery, the team of the Architects' Co-partnership with the rubber factory in Brynmawr (1945–51) [272, 274], and Hubert Bennett with the design for a great exhibition and sports stadium in London (1956), which is to replace the Crystal Palace burnt out in 1936. Modern architecture is winning general acceptance in a country which, in past decades, adopted a conservative attitude with a leaning towards eclecticism.

280. Ralph Tubbs. Dome of Discovery, London, 1951. Modern English architecture at the Festival of Britain. Shallow aluminium dome, 365 ft. in diameter, on a steel ring girder supported by a welded tubular steel structure.

281. Robert H. Matthew and J. L. Martin. Royal Festival Hall, London, 1951. Holds audience of 3,000. The foyers are placed at half the height of the auditorium, so that the public can be quickly directed to entrances at various levels. Lively handling of the partly symmetrical, and partly asymmetrical, elevations.

France

As in England, the first contribution by architects and engineers in France[63] towards the establishment of a contemporary architecture was made in the nineteenth century. Of course one cannot yet speak of a broad front of sympathetically disposed architects, such as the twentieth century knows. The nineteenth century is a time of preparation, in which only the first components were evolved that were to form the foundations of modern architecture in the next century. Here France played a rôle of great importance. Iron and steel, of which the methods of production had been steadily improved since the end of the eighteenth century, particularly in England, were used by French engineers in increasingly bold constructions for bridges, department stores and exhibition halls [24–26]. The consistent study of structural laws was already leading to a point where the rules which governed form in later architecture become visible (Machinery Hall, Paris International Exhibition, 1889) [28, 282].

On the whole, French architecture, during the period when the engineers were achieving such remarkable work, was as much dominated by eclecticism as that of her neighbours. Voices were, however, raised in protest. Henri Labrouste, who used iron both in the construction and the formal conception of his library buildings, was by the middle of the nineteenth century already formulating his demand for functional integrity [22, 23]. His pupil Anatole de Baudot continued his work, and was one of the first to introduce reinforced concrete into architecture, using it before 1900 in the church of St. Jean de Montmartre (begun 1894) [82]. De Baudot was able to rely in this venture upon the knowledge and capabilities of French engineers, who had developed reinforced concrete – in addition to steel, the other basic material of our present-day architecture – as a structural material for building. To Lambot, Coignet, Monier, Hennebique and later Freyssinet belongs the distinction of having laid the foundations for the reinforced concrete buildings of to-day. The creative possibilities offered to architecture by this new material were revealed by Auguste Perret in his house in the Rue Franklin and the garage in the Rue de Ponthieu [86–88].

In later years Perret, one of the great pioneers of modern architecture, came ever more strongly under the influence of an architectural conception guided by

2. Ferdinand Dutert and Contamin. Machinery all of the Paris International Exhibition, 1889.

3. Auguste Perret. Notre Dame, Le Raincy, 22. Chancel elevation. Pre-cast concrete components of the non-bearing wall arranged ornamentally in the symbol of the cross.

284. Auguste Perret, Chief Architect. Flats in t
Rue Victor Hugo, Le Havre, begun 1947. Perre
extraordinary prestige in France led to his a
pointment at the age of seventy-three as ch
architect for the completely destroyed seap
town of Le Havre.

classical precedents. His late work exemplifies a monumental architecture in concrete, as is shown in the new residential quarters of Le Havre built after the destruction of World War II [284, 286]. Perret's great influence has left its mark on French architecture of the last decades, and this explains the long isolation of one of his pupils, Le Corbusier, who in the twenties shared with Gropius and Mies van der Rohe in the great advance towards a modern architecture. In the fairly recent past Le Corbusier's views and those of official France were very far from identical. Not until after the second world war did a change appear, when Claudius Petit, the French Minister for Reconstruction, supported Le Corbusier in face of every form of opposition in the building of the Unité d'Habitation at Marseilles [157, 162, 163, 164].

Le Corbusier's atelier in Paris was, like the Bauhaus, one of the key sources from which the modern movement took shape. Its influence inspired the architecture of many countries, but at first had no great effect in France. Among the few French architects whose work was stimulated by Le Corbusier were André Lurçat – school at Villejuif, 1931–33 [290] –, and Eugène Beaudouin and Marcel

285. Auguste Perret. Flats in the Rue Raynouar
Paris, 1930. Like the earlier house in the Ru
Franklin [88], surfaces broken up into bays. Dr
matic effect of strongly emphasised moulding
rhythmic patterns of balustrades and recesse
upper storeys.

286. Auguste Perret, Chief Architect. Flats in th
Place de l'Hôtel de Ville, Le Havre, begun 194
Mixture of massive high and low blocks, flat wa
surfaces often with dummy windows, and,
many instances, continuous balconies unde
lining the unity and monumentality of the bloc
without regard for the functional nature of th
buildings.

37. Le Corbusier and Pierre Jeanneret. Pavillon e l'Esprit Nouveau, 1925. Demonstration of a ew approach to living. At the International Exibition of Decorative Arts Le Corbusier showed two-storey dwelling, representing one "cell" f a projected larger block. This idea was later ealized in the Unité d'Habitation [163].

88. Le Corbusier and Pierre Jeanneret. Cité de Réfuge, Paris, 1929–33. Completely glazed south ront, nearly 250 feet long. The building, comissioned by the Salvation Army, provides sleepng accommodation for 500 people, dining and ommon rooms, library, administrative offices nd terraces.

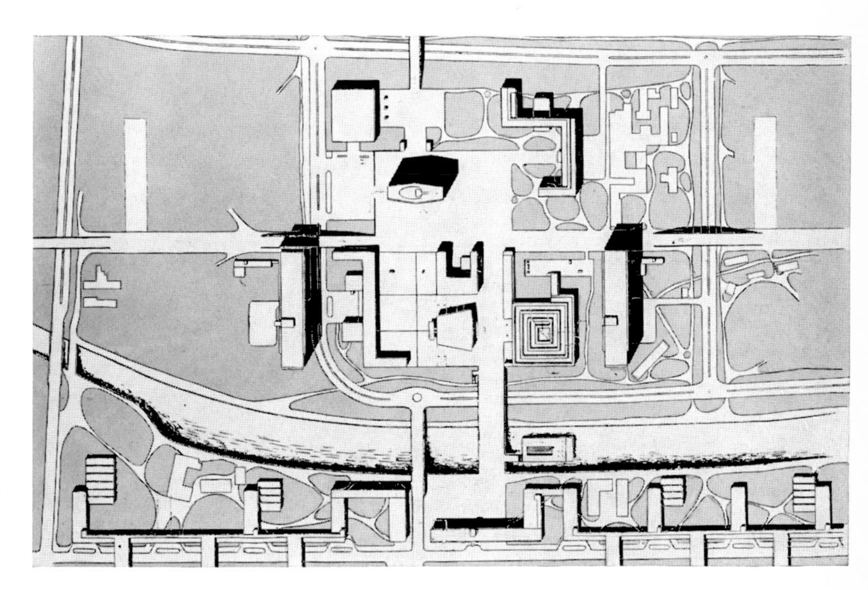

39. Le Corbusier. Town plan for Saint-Dié, 1945. reen-spaced, but concentrated, town "core" ith administrative and community centres, nops, cafés and museum in the form of a maze. eparation of pedestrians from fast, and commeral, road traffic; streets partly elevated. The plan as not carried out.

290. André Lurçat. School, Villejuif, 1931–33. Com
pact layout in the strict rectangular manner o
the twenties. The three-storey block containin
class rooms opens on to a playground on th
south side. An infants' school is located at th
west end.

291. Eugène Beaudouin and Marcel Lods. Open-air school, Suresnes, 1935–36. Pavilion for handicapped children. Two twin-storeyed wings with supervision rooms, play and dining-rooms, showers, accessible from the pavilion. The remaining class rooms are grouped independently about an internal court and connected by a covered way. Ramps replace stairs in all buildings.

292. Eugène Beaudouin and Marcel Lods. Cité de la Muette, Drancy, 1933. Both architects were early devotees of prefabrication. Point blocks, in which prefabricated components were widely used, are placed at the end of courtyards set between lower buildings.

93. Eugène Beaudouin. Cité Rotterdam, Stras-urg, 1951–53. Residential quarter of eight hun-red dwellings. Prefabricated elements, one torey in height. The danger of monotony has not een completely avoided in details. The group of uildings faces south, higher blocks providing rotection against the prevailing wind on the orth-west side.

94. Jean Dubuisson. Résidence du Parc, Croix, 955–56. Flats in parkland, rectangular in con-eption, but rich variety given to elevations by tepping and recessing. Sensitive use of trees.

95. Jean Dubuisson and Félix Dumail. Flats or SHAPE staff, Saint-Germain-en-Laye, 1952. -shaped precast concrete components.

Lods – open-air school at Suresnes, 1935–36 [291]; Maison du Peuple, Clichy, 1939. The rebuilding of towns and of housing destroyed in World War II has followed retrograde tendencies more noticeably than in other European countries. Nevertheless there stand to-day beside Le Corbusier, whose plan for Saint-Dié has not been carried out, a number of gifted architects who are slowly beginning to transform the picture of French architecture which has existed hitherto. Pierre Vago, in his house erected for Berlin "Interbau 1957" [296], alters Le Corbusier's two-storey living-room to a height of one and a half floors and thus reduces the sharp contrasts in spatial expression whilst preserving a clear differentiation between internal areas. Beaudouin designed the "Cité Rotterdam" at Strasbourg [293]; Dubuisson planned the "Résidence du Parc" housing group at Croix [294]; Pierre Vivien with André Sive and others was responsible for the reconstruction of Boulogne-sur-Mer. Sive himself, like Jean and Henri Prouvé, is an architect acutely concerned with rationalization – e. g., experimental houses at Meudon –, a problem which has become important to young French architects for the logical and practical questions which it poses [299].

296. Pierre Vago. Flats, Interbau Exhibition, Berlin, 1957. Dining and living-room. Vago varies the two-storey living-room of Le Corbusier by altering the floor, the ceiling in other flats, to only half the height of the second part of the room.

298. Courtois, Ch. Ferret and Salier. Firemen's quarters, Bordeaux, 1952-53. Block of forty flats. Attempt at achieving a rhythmic effect by variations in wall depths and a contrasting pattern of balconies.

←

297. Raymond Gravereaux, Raymond Lopez, Jean Prouvé. Offices of the Fédération Nationale du Bâtiment, Paris, 1951. Glass and aluminium panels are suspended between the projecting floor and roof slabs. The ground floor is entirely glass and offers those entering an uninterrupted view of an older building behind.

9. Jean and Henri Prouvé, André Sive. Experiental houses, Meudon, 1954. Combination of asonry construction and prefabricated components.

The creative powers of French architects have found freest expression when prejudices and susceptibilities did not need to be considered. In North Africa architects like Camelot, Delaporte and Emery have developed an architecture suited to the regional conditions of this territory.

Le Corbusier, too, has undertaken a commission outside France which in its size and importance represents the culmination of his life work. Since 1951 he has been building in India in collaboration with Pierre Jeanneret, Maxwell Fry and Jane Drew, the new capital of the Punjab, Chandigarh, the first stage of which provides living accommodation for 150,000 inhabitants [143b, 302]. A land of age-old culture embraced his ideas on a scale impossible in Europe. Le Corbusier has deliberately avoided translating to India architectural forms appropriate to the West. The special climatic and sociological circumstances have inspired him to create an architecture which suggests a synthesis of Indian sensibility and European imagination. Here, as in Brazil in 1936, the resourcefulness of his architectural ideas is shown. To-day Le Corbusier is still France's most significant architect, an ambassador of his country's high cultural tradition.

00. Le Corbusier. Cité d'Affaires, Algiers, proect 1938–42. Five-hundred-foot skyscraper conaining administrative offices and a hotel on the ıpper storeys. The balcony "cells" offer protecion from the reflections of the near-by sea and rom sun glare in summer, whilst allowing the gentler winter sunshine to penetrate.

301. Vladimir Bodiansky, Georges Candilis, Henri Piot and Shadrach Woods. Flats, Casablanca, 1952–54. The climatic conditions of North Africa and the different living conventions of the Mohammedans have produced an unusual honeycomb type of building. Each dwelling has two rooms and a patio two storeys high which cannot be overlooked. Access is by means of balconies and the flats have cross-ventilation.

302. Le Corbusier. Law courts, Chandigarh, 1951 t
1956. A curved projecting roof acts as a sunshade
An open space between the roof and the ceilin
slab of the top storey serves to cool the building
The roofs and the square-lattice work brise
soleils also reflect Le Corbusier's increasing con
cern for plastic forms. In association with Le Co
busier, who is building the government centre
Jane Drew, Maxwell Fry and Pierre Jeanneret ar
designing the new capital of the Punjab, whic
will have 500,000 inhabitants.

303. H. P. Berlage. Stock Exchange, Amsterdam, 1898–1903.

Holland

H. P. Berlage's masterpiece marks the beginning of modern architecture in Holland [64]; the Amsterdam Stock Exchange, erected between 1898 and 1903 [76, 77, 303]. With this building Berlage turned his back on style imitations and brought back a feeling of respect for materials, integrity and simplicity, while indicating at the same time the value of stereometric shapes. His great influence on the next generation is indisputable, although Berlage himself took no further part in the movement towards the architecture of the twenties.

In reaction against Berlage's strict rationalism, but influenced by him in details, especially in the courageous rejection of eclecticism which he first made possible, the school of Amsterdam was formed about 1910, with Michel de Klerk, Pieter Kramer and J. M. van der Mey prominent members. Emphasis was laid upon the invention of new and extravagant forms. Traces of a connection with German Expressionism, as it appeared in Fritz Hoeger's buildings, but also in the early work of Mendelsohn, are noticeable. The individuality of the school's vocabulary was so marked that in it the first signs of a modern architecture could easily be imagined [110, 305, 306].

In the work of "De Stijl", founded in 1917, extravagances of form are also visible, but they were conditioned by historical development and necessary; for it was essential first to isolate certain problems in order to understand them with absolute clarity. In contrast to the virtuosity in handling forms often shown by the School of Amsterdam, "De Stijl" tried to find objective elements of a new architectural language [170–177]. Its goal was the exclusion of arbitrary individualism, uniqueness. "De Stijl" was actuated by a new conception of space which rejected the boxlike enclosed area and substituted a free interrelationship of different spatial volumes.

At this period Holland was an experimental field for modern architecture and she spread her influence wide. As early as 1916 Robert van 't Hoff built houses at Huis ter Heide near Utrecht which in their horizontal emphasis and in the arrangement of the windows reveal the influence of Frank Lloyd Wright [171]. In 1918–21 Oud erected large blocks of flats in Rotterdam, designed a housing scheme in 1924 for the Hook of Holland and in 1930 carried out the Kiefhoek

304. W. M. Dudok. Vondelschool, Hilversum, 1928. Solid brick walls in a composition of surfaces and cubes.

305. Michel de Klerk. Eigen Haand flats, Amster-dam, 1921. Dutch development of the second and third decades was characterized by the contrast between "De Stijl" and Wendingen, between the Rotterdam and Amsterdam schools. Both stemmed from Berlage, the Amsterdam school in its feeling for the structure of the wall, the preference for brick and the imaginative masonry technique. Links with German Expressionism and Mendelsohn. Pointed forms and rounded lines: dynamic architecture, but a stronger tendency towards picturesqueness.

housing scheme in Rotterdam, which had been projected in 1925 [173, 175, 176, 307, 308]. The architectural theories of "De Stijl" were exemplified in their purest form in the house at Utrecht (1924) by Rietveld [174]. It was a time of great creative activity. J. B. van Loghem had begun his career with a house at Haarlem (1922), expressed in simple stereometric forms. B. Bijvoet and J. Duiker built the Zonnestraal Sanatorium at Hilversum in 1928 [313, 314], and Brinkmann and van der Vlugt (1928–30) the Van Nelle factory in Rotterdam [223–225]. A special place is held by W. M. Dudok, whose architecture exhibits influences of the School of Amsterdam and "De Stijl". The effect of his work (Hilversum Town Hall, built 1928–30), however, is confined to Holland, whilst the buildings of Oud, Rietveld, van der Vlugt and Duiker are part of the international movement and give it a vital impetus.

The social conditions which characterize life in Holland are also mirrored in her architecture. Housing and town-planning play a dominant rôle. Comprehensive housing schemes were completed immediately after the first world war in Rotterdam and Amsterdam, while the master plan for Amsterdam dates from the mid-

306. Michel de Klerk. Flats on the Henriette Ronnerplein, Amsterdam, 1920–22. Amsterdam School. Individuality applied to the problem of the terrace house: shallow hip roofs; chimneys as free-standing vertical features. Bow-fronted bays and traditional brick are used to suggest protection and safety.

)7. Jacobus Johannes Pieter Oud. Parish room
›r Apostolic Church, Kiefhoek housing scheme,
otterdam, 1929. An attempt to give a homelike
ppearance to an ecclesiastical building.

)8. Jacobus Johannes Pieter Oud. Kiefhoek
ousing scheme, Rotterdam, 1925–30. "De Stijl"
ıfluence. Strict interpretation of the row house;
iscipline and logic of the right angle. No orna-
ıentation, rendered walls instead of brick. Sober,
lean lines. In stressing the flat surface and the
ght angle, Oud and "De Stijl" reflect the views
f Berlage.

thirties, and controls the development of the city in logical ten-yearly stages. New dwelling types, too, have been tried out in Holland. W. van Tijen, in association with Brinkmann and van der Vlugt, built the slab-shaped "Bergpolder" block of flats (1933–34) in Rotterdam [311] and in 1938 the "Plaslaan" building in collaboration with Maaskant. These dwellings were intended primarily for single people and married couples without children, but the high blocks, associated with low buildings for families with children, give a distinctive character to the city plan. Every tenant can be said to have the chance of the home which he wants and at the same time the townscape is enriched by variety. The high regard which Dutch architecture enjoys was not least displayed in the nomination of Cor van Eesteren as President of C.I.A.M.
During World War II and afterwards a certain indecisiveness was detectable in the architectural field. Even architects like J. J. P. Oud lost the clarity of line of their earlier buildings. The isolation of this small country in a war-torn Europe the lack of contact with centres of modern architecture, which had shifted to America, and the heavy economic losses may have contributed to this decline

9. Gerrit Thomas Rietveld. Flats, Utrecht, 1928. fter the restless spatial patterns with their differ- nt "stepped" planes [174], Rietveld arrived at more placid conception of form.

0. Gerrit Thomas Rietveld. Bioscoop (Cinema) uildings, Utrecht. "De Stijl" echoes in the bal- nced effect of the two wide bands in relief and e introduction of lettering.

1. Johannes Andreas Brinkmann, W. van Tijen nd L. C. van der Vlugt. High flats, Bergpolder, otterdam, 1933–34. View from the West. Early xample of the balcony access block. The flats e accessible on the east side by means of open orridors. At the south end there is an open emer- ency stair. At the north end a glass-fronted aircase, its vertical glazing bars contrasting th the horizontal balconies and parapets of the oad front of the building. Lightness of form; eel skeleton construction.

2. H. A. Maaskant and W. van Tijen. High flats, uidplein, Rotterdam, 1949. Compact building th markedly rhythmical elevations, partly due the combination of different types of dwelling a single block. Imposing form. Reinforced con- ete construction, brick cladding.

313/314. B. Bijvoet and J. Duiker. Zonnestraal Sanatorium, Hilversum, 1928. Overall glass cladding, made possible by reinforced concrete construction, had been exemplified in the workshop building of the Dessau Bauhaus [222] and was most widely used in schools and hospitals. The brightening and sun-lighting of rooms – the problem of sun protection was not tackled until the thirties – proved as important for children and invalids as the feeling of not being cut off from the outside world.

315. S. Duiker. Open-air school, Amsterdam, 1930–32. Transparency of the entire building except for traffic ways and service core. Each floor contains two completely glazed classrooms, and a terrace for open-air teaching. The conspicuous structural frame enhances the cubic form.

The rebuilding of destroyed areas started on a big scale in 1948. More than a quarter of the homes had been destroyed or damaged as a result of the war. The housing shortage was accentuated by the steady increase in the number of births, which was higher than in neighbouring countries. The building of dwellings was thus a pressing task, which sometimes resulted in excellent solutions, such as the Frankendael housing scheme (1949–51) by architects Merkelbach and Elling.

In particular, the reconstruction of the completely destroyed inner town of Rotterdam offered a chance of realizing new ideas. The combination of handicrafts and small industries led to the erection of flatted factories which can be rented in small or large units. The tenants find workshops and office space with all essential connections for electricity, gas and water. The principal feature of the new plan for Rotterdam is the "Lijnbaan", a shopping centre in the heart of the city accessible only to pedestrians [318, 319]. It is the work of the Dutch architects J. H. van den Broek and J. B. Bakema, who have once more spread the fame of Netherlands architecture beyond the borders of their country. The idiom of their designs, stemming from the grand period of Dutch architecture from 1917 to 1938, is uncompromisingly masculine in its details, austere and incisive, without harshness, and with a sensitive understanding of materials. Their buildings (Department store in Rotterdam 1949–50, van Houten office and storage group 1952, also in Rotterdam) show how distinguished present-day architecture can be when expressed in simple stereometric forms [317].

316. Marcel Breuer and A. Elzas. Bijenkorf de partment store, Rotterdam, 1956–57. Sales area artificially lit; in consequence, windowless wall which can therefore be used exclusively for dis play and stock. Daylight enters the restaurar and offices, however, by ribbon windows. Th narrow slits, like the honeycomb pattern cladd ing, give decorative interest to the elevations.

317. J. B. Bakema and J. H. van den Broek. Va Houten office and storage building, Rotterdam 1952. The lower floor of mushroom constructio contains storerooms, the upper storey ha offices.

318/319. J. B. Bakema and J. H. van den Broek. The Lijnbaan, Rotterdam, 1953. After the second world war powerful influences came from Rotterdam, which had been the centre of "De Stijl" in the twenties. The 700-yard-long Lijnbaan with 85 shops, entirely reserved for pedestrians, connects the railway station district with the city's centre. Its double purpose of pedestrian way and shopping centre led to its development in continuous terrace form with projecting canopies and connecting bridges and divided into separate courts: a bazaar and street at the same time. The shops, with access for vehicular traffic at the back, are sometimes two-storeyed and at others have a third (lower) floor. Reinforced concrete construction and prefabricated facing components. The covered crossings afford weather protection, enabling the pedestrian to pass from one side of the thoroughfare to the other in the dry on wet days. Green spaces arranged informally, free-standing display windows, garden cafés.

Germany

The decisive phase in the evolution of the new architecture took place in Holland and Germany[65] in the period between 1918 and 1930, while in France the work of Le Corbusier stood alone. The origins in Germany go back to the last decade of the nineteenth century, to "Jugendstil". One of the first important events was the foundation of the Werkbund in 1907, in which architects like Hermann Muthesius, Theodor Fischer and Fritz Schumacher, Henry van de Velde, Peter Behrens and Walter Gropius found a common forum. In 1911–16 Gropius built the Fagus plant in Alfeld, which pointed to a new road for architecture [113, 114].

The end of the first world war completely changed Germany's position, intellectually as well as economically. The deeply rooted belief in permanent, stable conditions disappeared with the Kaiser's empire. The mistrust of traditional conventions offered undreamed-of possibilities to the new ideas. A strong current of optimism inspired new artistic endeavours in all cultural fields and especially in architecture.

In the brief space of seven years – during the transition period of 1918–23 growing inflation did not permit building activities – there occurred the profoundly stirring process of the development of a new architecture which owed much to "De Stijl" and to Le Corbusier. The centre of German architecture was Berlin and in its stimulating intellectual atmosphere Mies van der Rohe, Erich Mendelsohn, Hugo Häring, Hans Poelzig, Bruno and Max Taut and Walter Gropius were active. The Bauhaus at Weimar, founded through the initiative and courage of Walter Gropius, attracted young architects from all over Europe as the first school for modern design. In 1927 the Weissenhof housing scheme was carried out at Stuttgart on the occasion of the Werkbund Exhibition. It provided a review of achievements up to that time in the sphere of home planning and housing and also signified the end of the first revolutionary phase in modern architecture [72, 149a, 149b].

The new architecture in the twenties embraced all building types. Ernst May in Frankfurt, Gropius in Berlin and Karlsruhe, Bruno and Max Taut, Wagner and Mies van der Rohe in Berlin undertook housing projects, especially for the underprivileged sections of society [327, 4, 119, 178 and 326]. New types of school

320. Peter Behrens. AEG Turbine Factory, Berlin, 1909.

321. Walter Gropius and Adolf Meyer. Werkbund Exhibition, Cologne, 1914.

322. Mies van der Rohe. Tugendhat house, Brno, 1930. View from the garden. The cube as a principal element of form. Behind the ribbon windows of the ground floor is the main living-room [136], the bedrooms being above. The building exploits the sloping site and is entered from the road on the top storey.

35. Harald Deilmann, Max von Hausen, Ortwin Rave, Werner Ruhnau. Town theatre, Münster, 1954-56. The building was developed diagonally to the line of the site; a fresh conception producing an effect of gaiety. The façade of a destroyed classical building was introduced as monumental sculpture and surrounded by the theatre restaurant and the glass wing of the foyer.

36. Hans Scharoun. Philharmonia, project, Berlin, 1957. The "arena" stage enters the Concert Hall. A centralizing, asymmetrical space, which makes the orchestra and audience one. Canopy-like reflectors ensure even diffusion of sound.

337. Günter Wilhelm. School group on the Gäns- berg, Stuttgart-Zuffenhausen, 1952–53. North side of main building. The whole scheme includes primary school, school of domestic science and school for handicapped children.

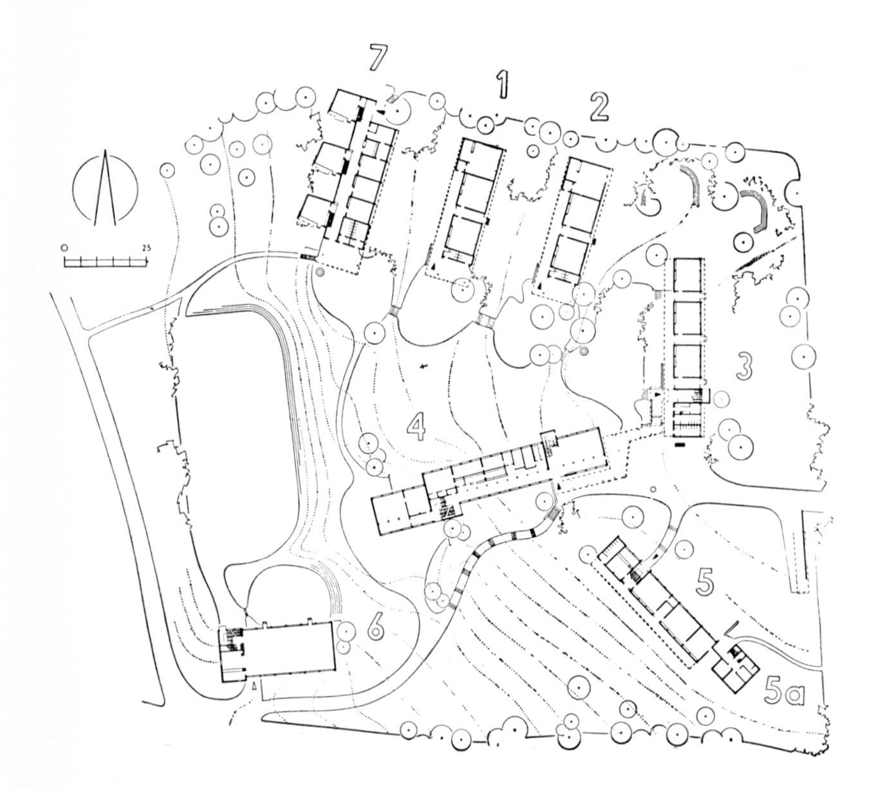

338. Günter Wilhelm. School Group on the Gänsberg, Stuttgart-Zuffenhausen. Site plan. Mixed single- and multi-storey class-room blocks. The classrooms of the younger children are at ground level. Small open spaces, intimate in scale, connected to a large grass court. 1 and 2: Single-storey classroom building. 3: Two-storey class-room building. 4: Main building. 5: Trade school. 5a: House. 6: Gymnasium. 7: School for handicapped children.

339. Johannes Krahn. French School, Saarburg, 1953–54. Connecting passage with view of "break" room. The school consists of a row of nine single-storeyed classrooms linked by a covered passage.

40. Otto Apel. Residential and commercial build-g, Berliner Strasse, Frankfurt, 1954–55. As this the north side the glass wall needs no sun pro-ection. Rhythm is given to the façade by varying e position of the mullions on the second floor. n the top floor the flats do not look on to the usy street, but open into an internal roof garden.

particular from Switzerland, Scandinavia and the United States, have contributed to its development, and important things have been achieved especially in school building, in which Günter Wilhelm, Paul Seitz, F. W. Kraemer and Johannes Krahn have made reputations [337–339]. In industrial building the linen mill in Blumberg by Egon Eiermann stands out. Influenced by Mies van der Rohe, Eiermann is one of the most distinguished representatives of German post-war architecture [342]. In his austerity and simplicity he offers the greatest conceivable contrast to Hans Scharoun who now has an opportunity for the first time of realizing his fantastic spatial conceptions in large schemes. His design for the Berlin Philharmonia (1957) sees the orchestra as an asymmetrically placed central feature surrounded by the audience [336].

The situation in Germany to-day is characterized by a very wide application of modern principles of design. If there is nothing comparable with the best American work, German architecture reaches a relatively high average standard. But the speed with which modern architecture reasserted itself after 1945 has also brought the dangers implicit in overhastily copying fashionable forms.

1. Friedrich Wilhelm Kraemer. Voets service ation and car repairs, Brunswick, 1956. Admin-trative building. Light (slender) steel construc-on.

2. Egon Eiermann. Linen mill, Blumberg, 1951. oiler house. Compact, clearly defined form, areful detailing. The asymmetrical features in e exterior reflect the planning of internal space. he free-standing chimneys are set behind the uilding.

Switzerland

It was especially in the perimeter states of Europe like Finland, Denmark and Sweden, but also in Switzerland [66], that modern architecture was able to evolve after 1930. Its development in these countries was based upon the experience of the twenties, while adapting itself to local conditions, and striving for refinement in the vocabulary of form, but at first – with the exception of Alvar Aalto's work – inspiring no fundamentally new conceptions.
Switzerland entered the field of contemporary architecture at the stage when the revolutionary phase was over. The Swiss mentality is cautious of anything uncommon, of the rebel genius disturbing the tenor of normality. Le Corbusier, a Swiss by birth, did not find in his homeland, but in France, the room he needed to expand his theories, although even there he was bitterly opposed. In the end, however, the step from dreams to reality was taken and Switzerland began to accept the new ideas with increasing enthusiasm. The achievement of Swiss architects rests less upon pioneering work in the field of structure and form than

343. Karl Moser. St. Antonius, Basle, 1925–2 Reinforced concrete construction as in Perret' church at Le Raincy [89], applied to a lofty angu lar spatial form. Rectangular choir, diminishe significance of the narrow side aisles. Four-side pillars instead of rounded columns; rectangul rib pattern under the vault.

on the love of perfection and quality, in the painstaking execution of details and in a highly developed sense of social responsibility.
A project like the Neubühl housing scheme at Zurich (1930–32) shows the particular capacity of Swiss architects to think out problems thoroughly and arrive at solutions which best serve the common good (architects Artaria and Schmidt, Haefeli, Hubacher and Steiger, Moser and Emil Roth) [347]. What had been in the Stuttgart Weissenhof housing scheme only an exhibition of the work of important personalities in architecture, a signpost to the future, but an essentially experimental signpost, has now reached the stage of community planning which takes into account the differing wishes of tenants and the particular characteristics of the site, without losing track of the architectural conception.
The Church of St. Anthony at Basle by Karl Moser (1926–27); the two blocks of flats, which Marcel Breuer built with Alfred and Emil Roth in the Doldertal at Zurich (1935–36); the administrative building for the Hoffmann-La Roche Company at Basle by O. R. Salvisberg; Hans Brechbühler's trades school in Berne (1937–39), in which the organization of the main building shows Le Corbusier's influence; Hermann Baur's pavilion school on the Bruderholz at Basle (1938–39) –

344. Hermann Baur. School on the Bruderholz, Basle, 1938-39. Pavilion-type buildings with provision for open-air teaching.

345. Hans Brechbühler. Trades School, Berne, 1937-39. The central block is raised on stilts and suspended between the two staircase towers. The glass-fronted floor below contains students' workshops.

346. Marcel Breuer, Alfred and Emil Roth. Flats in the Doldertal, Zürich, 1935-36. Advantages o the single-family house applied to the flat. Sur terraces open on to the landscape; tenants enjoy exceptional privacy. Obliquely placed walls make for flexibility in planning internal space.

347. Paul Artaria, Max E. Haefeli, Carl Hubacher Werner M. Moser, Emil Roth, Hans Schmidt Rudolf Steiger. Werkbund housing scheme, Neu-bühl, Zürich, 1930–32. Low parallel rows of houses stepped up three sides of a sloping site. From the gardens there is a view of both the lake and the mountainside.

all these buildings absorbed the traditions of the twenties, adding and subtracting features from them, so that they seem to us nowadays like a late flowering of the revolutionary period [343–346].

On the other hand the really memorable things in Switzerland are not to be found among traditional buildings types, but wrapped in the functional austerities of civil engineering. Robert Maillart's (1872–1940) undeviating attention to economic structural forms and his supreme mastery of reinforced concrete as a material place his designs on a level with the most important works of our time [245, 354]. Calculations alone do not produce such results. An intuitive feeling, akin to that of the artist, is needed, which instinctively grasps the essence of a problem.

During the war it was possible to continue building activities in Switzerland within certain limitations. Werner M. Moser built (1938–41) the Reformed Church at Zürich-Altstetten, which in its system of natural lighting – light concentrated upon the area round the altar, and the brightening of the nave by means of a narrow strip of windows placed high up – and in the separation of nave and belfry tower influenced many post-war buildings in Germany [350, 351]. Changes

48. Carlo and Rino Tami. Canton Library, Lugano, 940–41. Book stack. The articulation of the north ont, in which glass bricks were used, is deterined by the disposition of the book-shelves. The all presents a woven effect. The rounded extreities of the building contain spiral staircases.

349. Max E. Haefeli, Werner M. Moser, Rudolf Steiger. Prilly housing scheme, near Lausanne. Carefully planned mixed development, with low houses at the bottom of the valley, point blocks in the centre, slab-shaped buildings on the further side of the scheme.

350. Werner M. Moser. Reformed Church, Z rich-Altstetten, 1938–41. Sensitive respect for t reconstructed older church; the new nave, clo tower and parish meeting rooms, covered wi single-span sloping roofs, are grouped about common central space.

of architectural conception are revealed in buildings like the Canton Library at Lugano by C. and R. Tami (1940–41) [348], and the office building of the Adolf Saurer Company at Arbon by G. P. Dubois and J. Eschenmoser (1942–43). The charm of the materials and the use of contrasting forms extend the possibilities for expression available until now. During the forties neither Swiss nor Swedish architecture succeeded in escaping entirely the danger of sacrificing clarity of form to love of detail and of enlivening abstract compositions by a new romanticism.

During the post-war period housing schemes have been carried out in large numbers, which are models of landscaping and sensitive siting. The concern for humanity characterizing these schemes is shown in school building, which has at all times been important in the motherland of Pestalozzi. The class room, and indeed the layout of the entire school, must be intimate in scale. Large schemes are, therefore, avoided, the school buildings being decentralized into small units graded according to the age of the children. It says much for the perception of Swiss architects that plan types, which were beginning to paralyse pro-

351. Reformed Church, Zürich-Altstetten. Nave In its concentration of light round the altar, th building has served as a model for post-wa churches, particularly in Germany.

352. Max Bill. Swiss pavilion at the Triennale, Milan, 1936. Exhibits and exhibition linked in a single spatial and plastic composition.

353. Max Bill. High School for Design, Ulm, 1953 to 1956. The grouping of the building masses conforms to the contours of the site and to the functional plan. Concrete is left in its natural state even on the inside.

4. Robert Maillart. Schwandbach bridge, nr. hwarzenburg, 1933. Maillart's bridges, evolv- g out of their function and built in reinforced ncrete, combine economy with the beauty of ld plastic forms.

355. Ernst Gisel. Park Theatre, Grenchen, 1954. Auditorium with 600 seats. Folding partitions allow the incorporation of a side extension or of the foyer. Daylight enters through strip windows. Seating easily dismantled, so that the auditorium can be used for receptions or, with the help of the high plain walls, as exhibition space.

gress – like the stereotyped use of "packaged", multi-purpose, layouts – have been abandoned.
In other fields of architecture too, enterprising developments are apparent to-day. The single building for cultural purposes no longer stands alone, but as one of a group forming a representative town centre. A competition design by Otto Senn reveals an interesting interpretation: municipal theatre, art gallery, shops and restaurants are reached from an open space accessible only to pedestrians. At Grenchen Ernst Gisel has found an extraordinarily successful solution, both in form and plan, to the problem of the community centre for the small town [355, 356].
Owing to her geographical situation Switzerland has been fated to play a part of mediation and compromise. Moreover, thanks to her various territorial differences of language, she has close contact with her neighbours, Italy, France and Germany. But, however clearly these associations may emerge from her architecture, the inherent qualities of Switzerland, expressed in logic, practical sense and impeccable quality, are equally noticeable.

356. Park Theatre, Grenchen, 1954. Entran court and theatre building. Cultural centre fo small town: theatre wing, and block with resta rant, council room and hotel. The unequal-sid triangle is the dominant formal feature. T warm tonal effects of brick walls and copp cladding, the asymmetrical grouping, and t sense of scale imparted to a building of sm dimensions recall Finnish work.

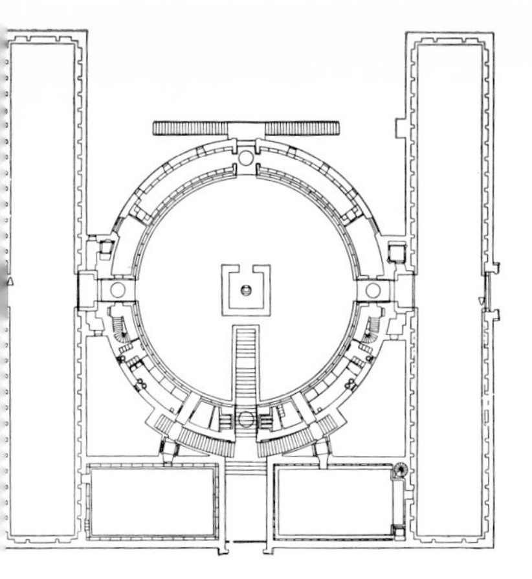

7. Erik Gunnar Asplund. City Library, Stock-
lm, 1920–28. Floor plan. The large reading room
the rotunda. Symmetry demanded the repe-
ion of the massive entrance doors at the sides.
ly from the front does the entrance lead
aight to the centre of the building, the reading
om.

8. City Library, Stockholm. Impressive effect of
adorned stereometric masses: a huge cylinder
rmounting a cube.

Sweden

The outstanding personality of Swedish architecture [67] is Erik Gunnar Asplund (1885–1940), in whose work in Sweden the transition from neo-classicism to modern architecture was accomplished. In 1930 he built the steel and glass halls of the great Stockholm Arts and Crafts Exhibition [361, 362]. The impression made by these buildings spread far beyond the frontiers of Sweden into Denmark and Finland. In Asplund's design for the Stockholm City Library (1920–28) the trend away from the classicism of the early twenties is already visible [357, 358]. The main block still displays all the elements of monumental classicism, but in the buildings in front containing the stack rooms a modern conception of style is apparent. The design also makes it abundantly clear that the new problems in building can no longer be solved within the resources of the traditional styles. The laws of symmetry require a repetition of the archaistic entrance feature on the two other long sides of the building. As these are only side entrances, there is inevitably a startling conflict between external form and internal spatial arrangement.

In his later designs Asplund logically developed the modern architectural theories introduced in his buildings for the Stockholm Exhibition – even in extensions to historical buildings. One of the happiest examples of adding an additional wing to an existing building is to be seen in Gothenburg Town Hall (1934–37) [359, 360]. The delicate pattern in low relief of the steel skeleton visible on the face of the extension is particularly effective next to the strong plastic modelling of the old building. Inside, Asplund grouped all the rooms round a central hall – a feature often used afterwards in Sweden and Denmark. Among his later works, the entrance portico to the Woodland Crematorium near Stockholm (1940) is especially noteworthy, a building of majestic simplicity and dignity [363].

The strong influence of the modern architecture of the twenties is more clearly reflected in the early work of Sven Markelius (born 1889) than in Asplund. In 1932 he built the Concert Hall at Hälsingborg, starkly cubic in its external conception. In its ingenious adaptability to functional needs, in the placing of exits and entrances, and in the general spatial effect, the concert hall displays the vigour and originality of his gifts [364]. These gained world-wide recognition when Markelius built the Swedish pavilion for the New York International Exhibition of 1939. In its external form, the Gothenburg Concert Hall of Nils Einar Eriksson (1935) [365] is not quite of the quality of the Hälsingborg hall, but impressive in the organization of the auditorium, the unity of wall and ceiling and the pattern of the side walls, which are stepped on plan. The foyer is disposed round the auditorium, which is conceived for acoustic reasons like a wooden mussel shell.

Right from the start modern architecture in Sweden did not have to rely solely on the interest of a certain section of society, but was popular in the best sense of the word, thereby offering a means of raising the living standards of the population. Its aspirations were matched by the similar ideals of the Svenska Slöjdföreningen (Swedish Society of Arts and Crafts), which demanded household equipment beautiful in form and suited to its purpose at prices within the reach of the man in the street. Modern architecture was, therefore, at no time entirely concerned with problems of form, but was regarded far more from a sociological standpoint. After Asplund and Markelius had shown their worth, an abundance of buildings followed which embraced every building type, private and public: theatres, concert halls, law courts, schools, hospitals, museums, flats and hous-

359. Erik Gunnar Asplund. Extension to the Town Hall, Gothenburg, 1934–37. Prolonged study of the problem dissuaded Asplund from copying the classical features of the older building and led him to a solution in which modern forms blend tactfully with the earlier work. Exemplary economy of means, restrained pattern in relief. The classical portico remains the main entrance.

360. Extension to Town Hall, Gothenburg. Multi-storey central hall. Galleries serve committee rooms and offices. A glass wall, two floors high faces the older courtyard. The emphatic, strongly defined, forms of a pioneer work are apparent in details.

→

362. Stockholm Exhibition, 1930. Light, pavilion-like buildings resulting from the use of steel and glass. Novel interpretations of form – as with the Paris Machinery Hall of 1889 or Mies van der Rohe's Barcelona Pavilion – developed for the purpose of exhibition architecture.

361. Erik Gunnar Asplund. Stockholm Exhibition, 1930. Main entrance. Wide-spanned roof slab without visible beams carried on slender steel stanchions, which at night served as lamp standards. The lightness, elegance and gaiety of this architecture without frills had a strong influence on modern building in Scandinavia.

FRANSKA AVDELNIN

363. Erik Gunnar Asplund. Woodland cremator um, Stockholm, 1940. Commanding site on a gen ly rising hill. The simplest elements combine produce a quiet unsentimental dignity, neve attained by the monumental architecture of Eu ropean neo-classicism [191, 192].

ing schemes. Swedish architecture, which up till now had followed in the wake of other European countries, acquired a standing of its own.

Certain peculiarities of present-day Swedish architecture are conditioned by climate, but they also reflect tendencies which operated during the forties in Switzerland as well, and later in Finland. The reaction against the extreme plainness of the twenties encourages a bias in the other direction, a manneristic inclination towards an architecture of heavily stressed features, a use of small window openings to break up plain wall surfaces, an intricate interweaving of buildings masses and a liking for rough-surfaced natural materials.

In Swedish architecture housing enjoys pride of place. Besides the high slab used especially in South Sweden by Jaenecke and Samuelson, the "point" block, which possesses advantages over the long low building on irregular sites, has been developed. Another Swedish building type, the "star" block – which architects Backström and Reinius introduced for the Gröndal housing scheme in Stockholm (1944–45) –, originated from the need to make the best possible use of land [369]. The "star" block, superior in this respect to the terrace house,

4. Sven Markelius. Concert Hall, Hälsingborg, 1932. Plain, but sympathetic, spatial form. Stalls curving sharply upwards at the back replace the circle. Access from below instead of from the sides.

also permits spatial grouping in small units, which was accomplished with particular skill in the Örebro housing scheme (1948–50) [366, 367]. Open spaces formed between the blocks, which enclose them on three sides, have free access on one side and connect with each other. Similar theories are often found in new housing projects, notably in the Baronbackarna scheme at Örebro (architects P. A. Ekholm and S. White), where the intimate feeling obtained by groups of small dwellings is associated with large green spaces.

Sweden recognized very early the cardinal factor in town planning control: the concentration of land ownership in a single body. Thanks to remarkable foresight the City of Stockholm is to-day the principal landowner and can steer future development along rational paths. In order to provide urgently needed living space, satellite towns have been built, among which Vällingby is particularly well known [370, 371]. Here the attempt was also made to give the new town an independent life of its own by providing cultural and commercial buildings. Swedish architecture is playing its part in the struggle to solve one of the most compelling problems of our time: the creation and organization of cultural centres which will truly be focal points in the lives of our new towns.

5. Nils Einar Eriksson. Concert Hall, Gothenburg, 1935. Wall and ceiling form a single unit. Access and indirect lighting from the side wings of the fan-shaped auditorium, which is faced with maple.

367. Örebro housing scheme. View into one of t
forecourts. Sharp differences in colour treatme
emphasise the individuality of the various dw
ling units.

366. Sven Backström and Leif Reinius. Örebro housing scheme 1948–50. Star-shaped blocks of dwellings in freely arranged rows. The green forecourts open onto larger stretches of grass with space for games. A point block supplies a vertical feature and gives coherence.

368. Sven Backström and Leif Reinius. High flats, Danviksklippen, Stockholm, 1945. Housing scheme of point blocks set on a high rocky site. Comparatively small window openings.

369. Sven Backström and Leif Reinius. Gröndal housing scheme, Stockholm, 1944–45. Blocks arranged upon a star-shaped plan, the three points of which are reached by a central staircase. The flats – one- and two-storeyed – occupy the entire depth of the wing, thus providing sunshine from both sides. The internal courts of the honeycomb-shaped blocks are protected from the wind and give an impression of intimacy and shelter. More economical use of land than with terrace houses.

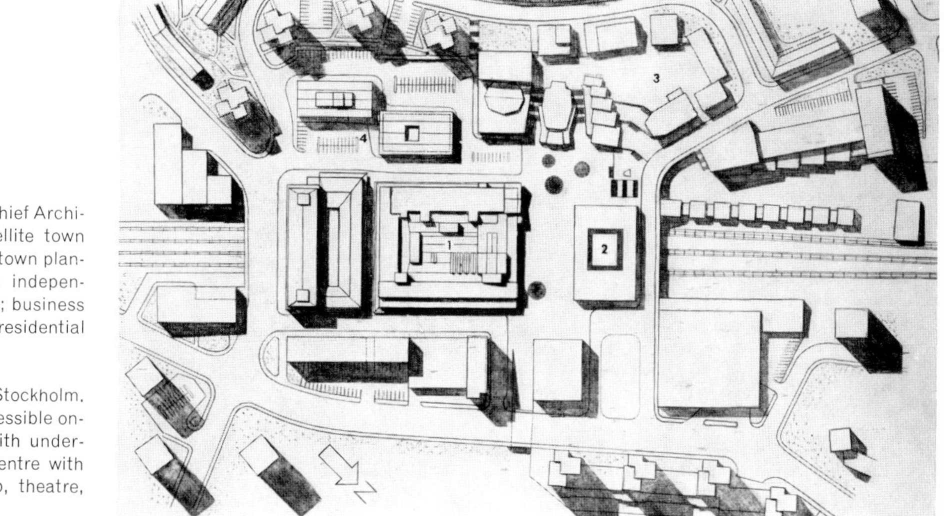

0. Stockholm City Planning Office; Chief Archi-
ct Sven Markelius. Vällingby satellite town
ar Stockholm, begun 1953. Centre of town plan-
d for 25,000 inhabitants. Relative indepen-
nce from the capital 12 miles away; business
d industrial quarters as well as residential
eas.

. Vällingby satellite town near Stockholm.
Business and shopping centre, accessible onto pedestrians. 2. Traffic centre with under-
ound railway station. 3. Cultural centre with
urch, assembly rooms, youth club, theatre,
ema. 4. Social and health centres.

Denmark

In Denmark[68] modern architectural development ran a totally different course from that of its Central European counterpart, but one parallel to that of Sweden. While the crucial changes were taking place in Central Europe between 1917 and 1930, Denmark was under the sway of a restrained post-classicism. But during this period the tradition of Danish brick-building was alive and even in blocks of city flats like the Hornbaekhus in Copenhagen (architect Kay Fisker, 1923) the green spaces of the large internal courts formed part of the design. By the end of the twenties modern architecture, represented in particular by the building magazine "Kritisk Revy", was gradually strengthening its hold, and the effect of Asplund's exhibition buildings (1930) finally swung Denmark into line. Two currents in her now rapidly developing architecture are clearly distinguishable, one directly stemming from the work of Le Corbusier, using reinforced concrete and favouring cubic forms, the other preserving the link with Danish tradition and employing natural materials like wood and brick. To-day, as in the past,

372. Kay Gottlob. School on the Sound, Cope hagen, 1938. "Hall" type. The classrooms a reached from the galleries. Light enters throu ribbon windows instead of a glass roof, to av the effect of a shaft of light.

373. Kay Fisker, C. F. Møller and Povl Stegma University, Aarhus, begun 1932. Assembly h Majestic spatial conception in warm colou yellow brick, wood, exposed concrete. The arc tects preferred to open the room wide onto surrounding landscape, although this makes c tact between speaker and audience more di cult in a hall by no means free from dazzle.

75. University, Aarhus. View of Assembly hall block. Both bricks and roof tiles are yellow. The University buildings embrace a gently-falling valley in a wide arc.

brick is preferred for building, since stucco – as in Holland – is not weatherproof in damp, maritime, climates. An unbroken tradition is revealed not only in the continued use of traditional materials, but also in the retention of a particular form of spatial composition. The Danish landscape, with its broad plains, compels people to seek seclusion in intimate groups of enclosing buildings. Thus the four-sided yard, the inner space completely surrounded by buildings, is a typical form of the Danish farm. This tradition is preserved in the Danish "Hall" schools [372], and in the multi-storey halls of municipal buildings, in which galleries lead to the individual offices.

Open spatial composition characterizes the design of the University of Aarhus, the buildings of which stretch in a wide arc about a green space which is left undisturbed (Architects Kay Fisker, C. F. Møller, Povl Stegmann, begun 1932) [373–375]. The effect is of sternness and severity. Yellow brick is the principal material, even the tiled roofs having the same yellow tones as the brick walls. The supreme mastery of the materials and an unerring sense of proportion give these buildings life. Wood is much used for the interior and with its warm colours

74. University, Aarhus. Corridor. Unity of interior and exterior. Brick walls left unplastered on the inside. The floors are also brick. A timber ceiling is used to deaden sound.

376. C.F. Møller. Savings bank, Aarhus, 1949–50. Effective use of materials in the interior. Sound absorbent perforated brick walls, reinforced concrete and wood ceiling. Every detail of the design is worked out with clarity and precision. Danish architecture exemplifies a highly devel oped feeling for structural and colour values in materials.

377. Knud Krøll. The architect's house, Aarhus 1947. Effective use of materials in a small build ing. Meticulous brick technique and good pro portions.

378. Povl Ernst Hoff and Bennet Windinge. Flat Høje Søborg, Copenhagen, 1949–51. Brightly de fined window surrounds and balconies se against a dark red brick background. Maximu service for tenants: restaurant with room servic reception rooms for hire, laundry, infants' schoo roof terraces.

379. Vilhelm Lauritzen. State Broadcasting House, Copenhagen, 1938–45. This building represents the international contribution to Danish architecture. Sharply defined cubes in reinforced concrete, differentiated according to their functions.

offers an exciting contrast to the brickwork which is left visible on the inside. Whilst the Aarhus university buildings represent a conscious perpetuation of Danish tradition, the Copenhagen Broadcasting House (Architect V. Lauritzen, 1938–45) is based upon the aesthetic philosophies of Le Corbusier and Gropius [379, 380]. Here too one can see, in the majestic handling of the staircases leading to the large concert room and in the sequence of entrance hall, cloak room, stairs and foyer, the talent of Danish architects for spatial composition. The building is an example of pure functional architecture; the meaning and purpose of each of its various parts determines the form and plan. Concert hall and administration building form a spatial group which shuts out the street and protects the studios behind from noise. The roof of the wedge-shaped auditorium – an idea of Le Corbusier – is vaulted; it enhances the sense of movement conveyed in the plan.
The most significant Danish architect at the present time is Arne Jacobsen (born 1902), in whose early work strong influences from Le Corbusier can be detected. But in the way his buildings blend with the landscape and in his utilization of regional characteristics Jacobsen follows his own line. The "Bellavista" group of

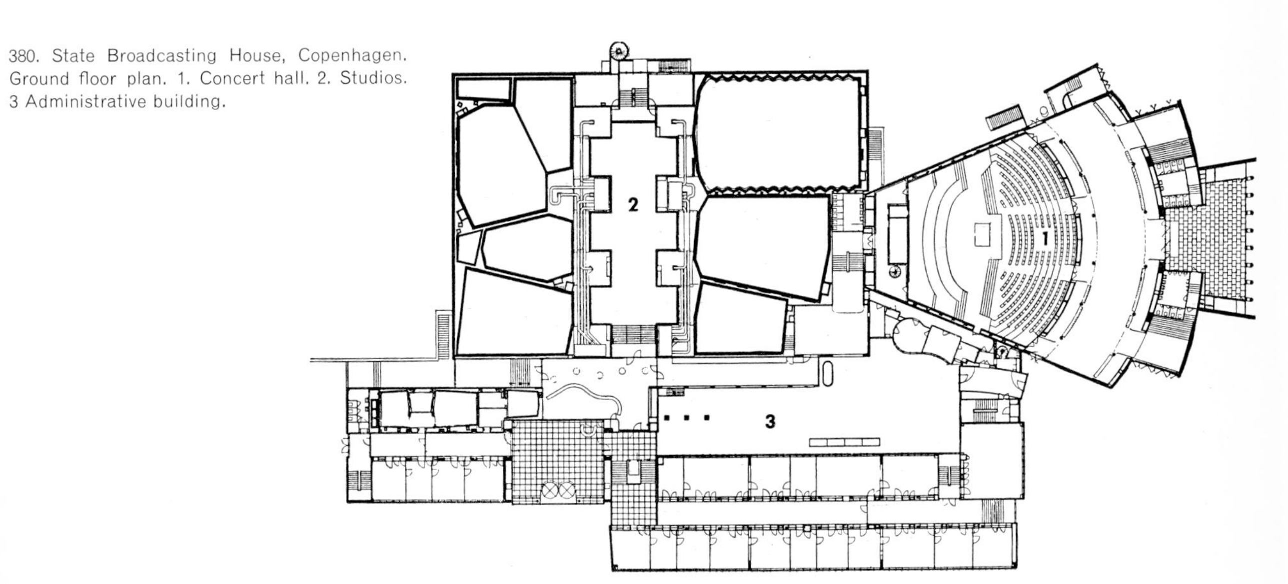

380. State Broadcasting House, Copenhagen. Ground floor plan. 1. Concert hall. 2. Studios. 3 Administrative building.

381. Arne Jacobsen. Bellavista flats, Klampenborg, 1933. Vocabulary of form typical of the late twenties, but a break away from the strict row. The dwelling units are stepped on plan, so that each flat has a view of the near-by sea.

flats at Klampenborg near Copenhagen (1933) is U-shaped, so that it is possible for each dwelling to have a view of the near-by sea [381]. While "Bellavista" still exemplifies the white stucco cube, with continuous ribbon windows, typical of the 1920s, the adjacent Søholm scheme, built in 1950, speaks an entirely different architectural language [382, 383]. The cubic form has gone and a markedly individual elevational treatment with its contrasting roof angles has been evolved out of a particular layout and floor plan. A flight of stairs, its slope reflecting the pitch of the roof, links the ground floor to the living room on the upper storey. The material is yellow brick. Noteworthy at this period in Jacobsen's work is the combination of freedom and originality of form with the strictest adherence to the qualities of his material, for the use of masonry construction and the consideration of a scale appropriate to brick demand a form analysed to the last detail. The design of the office block for Jespersen & Son in Copenhagen (1956) [384], which is supported on only two columns, also displays a masterly handling of detail and an infallible sense of proportion. Jacobsen was now turning again to more marked international tendencies. His town hall at Rødovre [385], impressive

382/383. Arne Jacobsen. "Chain" houses, Søholm, 1950. The unusual silhouette created by the denticulated pattern of the sloping roofs is the result of the internal plan. Under the low pitched roof a staircase leads to the upper storey, which consists of a large living-room with natural lighting from two sides and of a terrace overlooking the sea.

384. Arne Jacobsen. Jespersen Office building, Copenhagen, 1956. No stanchions behind the cladding. Cantilevered floors. Glass curtain wall with glazing bars in delicate relief, which cast no shadow, whatever the angle of light. The lightness of the glass skin is emphasized by the stripes of the wall panels.

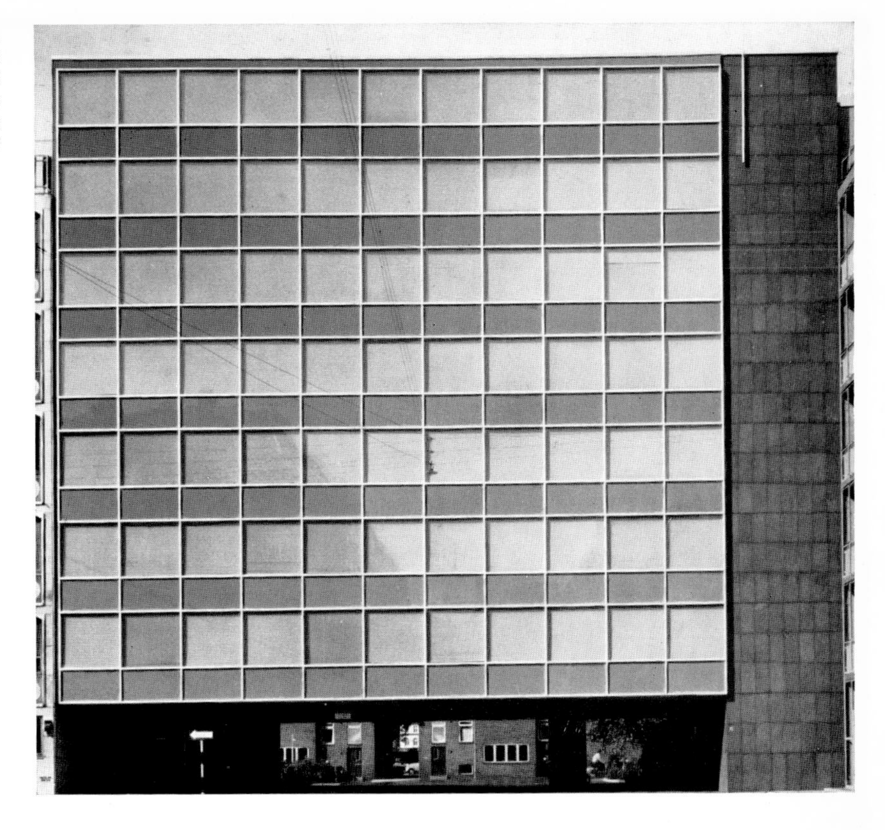

in its simple plan and structural clarity, would have been unthinkable without the precedent of the General Motors Research centre at Detroit. Jacobsen's work typifies the high level of Danish architecture. The sense of proportion, expressed also in the preference for brick, reflects the Danish temperament, which dislikes exaggeration. Danish architecture to-day, in the even quality of its output, occupies a position scarcely matched elsewhere. At the same time there is no lack of enthusiasm for the unusual, for the opportunity which opens up new prospects, without making premature claims for the latest achievement, like the scheme by Jörn Utzon for the Opera House in Sidney (1957) [253–255].

185. Arne Jacobsen. Town Hall, Rødovre, 1954 to 1956. Long, narrow, cube with transparent and grey glass cladding, the extension containing the council chamber faced with black granite panels. Jacobsen's most recent administrative buildings, in contrast to his domestic work, are linked with an international tradition represented in America by Eero Saarinen [463].

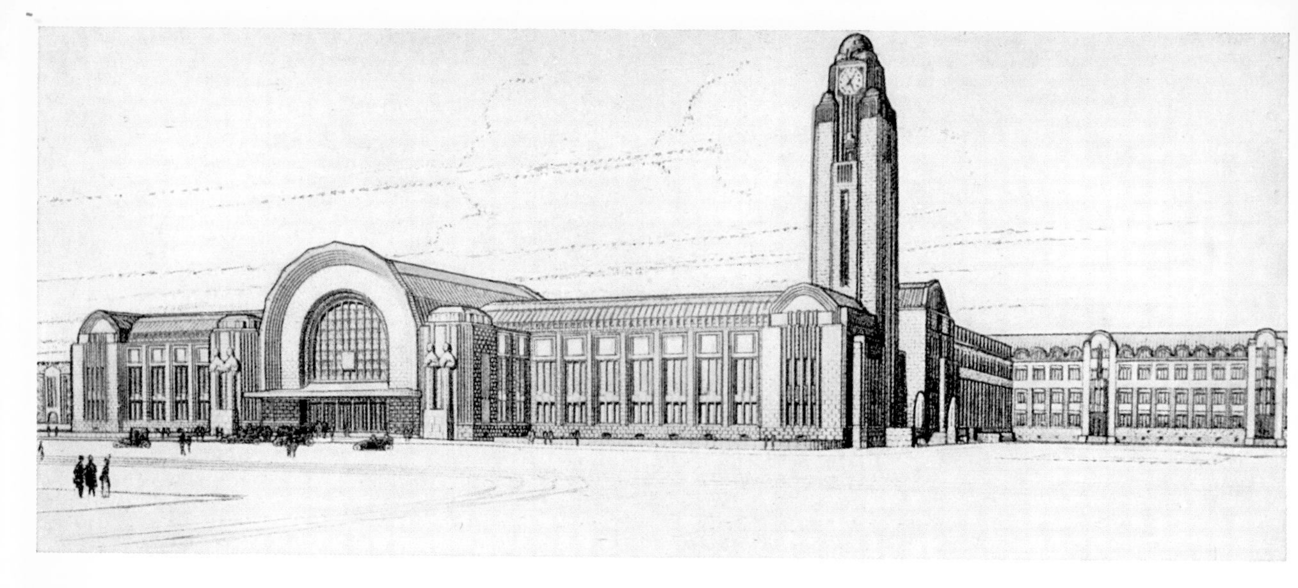

Finland

When Eliel Saarinen built the main railway station at Helsinki (1906–1916), Europe became aware for the first time of the architecture of a country which lies on the furthest frontiers of her civilization [386][69]. Saarinen, long regarded outside Finland as the artistic interpreter of his nation, won second prize in the "Chicago Tribune" Competition in 1922 and was invited in the following year to North America, where – after a short period at the University of Michigan – he became Professor of Architecture at Cranbrook Academy. In his most important work, Helsinki railway station, and also in the Finnish Pavilion for the Paris International Exhibition of 1900, which he designed in association with Gesellius and Lindgren, there already clearly emerges a quality exemplified most strongly in Finnish architecture to-day: an infallible sense of the fundamental value of natural materials. In Saarinen, however, this is combined with a vocabulary of form expressed in conservative terms, as is shown in the group of buildings for

386. Eliel Saarinen. Main Railway Station, Helsinki, 1906–16. Springboard of modern Finnish architecture; majestic handling of masses; the imposing entrances, flanked with massive pylons, give coherence to the scheme. Red granite blocks and copper roofing.

387. Alvar Aalto. Library, Viipuri, 1927–34. Eloquent conception of space, interpreted in the lecture hall by the curved ceiling [195], is achieved in the library by intermediate floors and ceilings of varying heights. Roof lighting permits the greatest possible wall space for book shelves and insulates the reader's attention from the outside world.

388. Alvar Aalto. Flats, Interbau Exhibition, Berlin, 1957. Aalto's later work tends towards a compact, smooth, rectangular form. The balconies do not project, the parapets being a horizontal extension of the cladding panels of the building proper. The flats are planned around a central living-room.

389. Alvar Aalto. Rautatalo Office building, Helsinki, 1954. Round ceiling lights as at Viipuri; the handrails of the gallery, in place of light bars, are now parapets faced with white marble, which fit like a clasp round the room.

390/391. Toivo Jäntti and Yrjö Lindegren. Olympic stadium, Helsinki 1940, enlarged 1952. Exterior, also view of structural system. The capacity of the reinforced concrete stands is increased by using wood construction at higher levels. The broken silhouette of the timber batten walls preserves the stadium from the monotonous effect of large plain surfaces.

Cranbrook Academy at Bloomfield Hills, Michigan, erected from 1925 to 1941. It was a rare piece of good fortune in the history of modern architecture that the career of Alvar Aalto, the greatest Finnish architect of our day, coincided with the movement away from strict functionalism to liveliness and variety of form [387–389]. Aalto combined the legacy of Finnish architecture, its natural richness in expressive values, with the clarity of form developed by Mies van der Rohe, Walter Gropius and Le Corbusier. His example prevented a possible halt in progress, even a period of retrogression, such as actually began to occur at the end of the thirties in Sweden and Switzerland, even if short lived. His buildings of the thirties form landmarks in a logical extension of ideas developed in the twenties: Paimio Sanatorium, 1929–33; Viipuri Library, 1927–34; Mairea house, 1938–39; Finnish Pavilion at the New York World Exhibition, 1939 [188–190, 193–201, 203–207]. Besides Aalto, Erik Bryggman (Turku cemetery chapel, 1940), and Yrjö Lindegren and Toivo Jäntti (Helsinki Olympic Stadium, 1940) [390,391] should be noted.

As an advanced outpost of Europe, Finland was drawn into the vortex of the

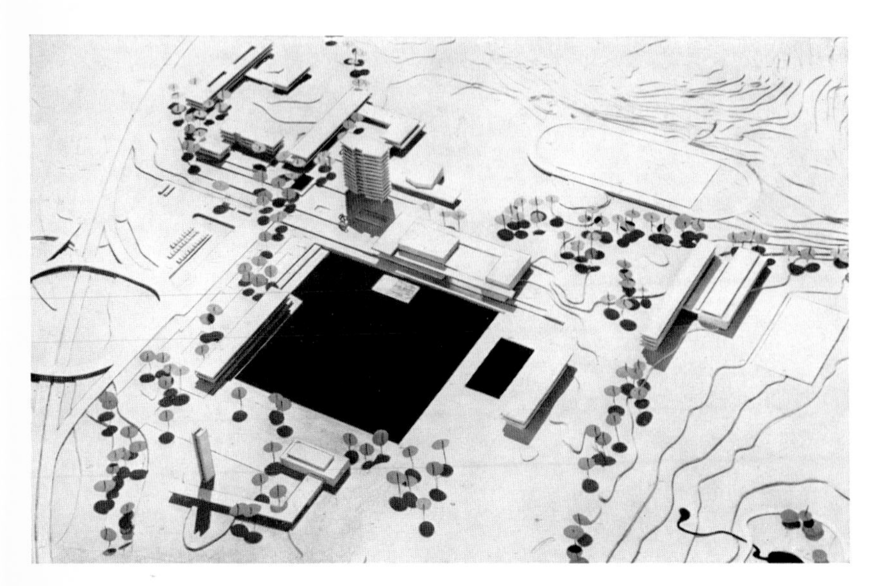

392. Aarne Ervi. Community Centre for the garden city of Tapiola, nr. Helsinki, 1955. Photo of model. Planned for about 15,000 inhabitants with church, theatre, shopping centre, tall office block and sports buildings. A large gravel pit in the middle of the site is converted into a sheet of water.

393. Keijo Petäjä and Viljo Rewell. Office building and hotel, Helsinki, 1952. Two mutually corres-ponding blocks connected by a central core con-aining traffic ways. The skeleton frame is placed nside and permits uninterrupted ribbon windows.

394. Viljo Rewell. Flats, Vaasa, 1952.

395. Erik Bryggman. Housing, Pansio. Recon-truction in Finland is often marked in housing chemes by a return to traditional timber build-ng types.

second world war and only succeeded by supreme efforts in preserving her independence from Russia. The price was heavy reparations and the loss of a region in which an eighth of her population lived. More than 400,000 people fled from the lost provinces.

In the process, most energetically pursued, of providing new homes for those driven from their old ones, Finnish architecture has not been spared the experiences which have been general during the reconstruction of Europe. The quantity of buildings bears no relation to their quality. An exception is the Tapiola garden city, 5½ miles from Helsinki, which is to house 12,000 to 15,000 inhabitants. Here a new architectural generation can be seen at work, whose leading representatives are Aarne Ervi, Jorma Järvi, Viljo Rewell and Heikki Siren. With them an important change is taking place in Finnish architecture. Alvar Aalto's genius is finding the necessary fresh inspiration from the work of these younger architects, who maintain their own individuality by the side of his work.

Ervi has designed the community centre for the Tapiola Garden City [392]. Church, theatre and shopping centre are grouped about an artificial stretch of

96. Kaija and Heikki Siren. "Little House" of the ational Theatre, Helsinki, 1954. The organiza-on of the interior is reflected on the face of the uilding; auditorium and scenery tower behind eramic panel cladding; entrance hall, foyer and, n the top floor, dramatic school behind the ansparent glazed parts of the façade. For the mall stage the dressing rooms and workshops f the old theatre at the back are used.

water, with a sky-scraper block to provide a vertical feature. The free massing of the various buildings is also reflected in the plan of the Otaniemi Clubhouse (1950–51), the central meeting place of a holiday camp for employees of a Finnish Bank. In 1954 Heikki Siren, in collaboration with Kaija Siren, built the "Little House" of the Finnish National Theatre, which is connected to the older building [396]. The exposed pattern of the façade shows the internal construction on the outside; behind unbroken wall surfaces of ceramic panels are the auditorium and scenery tower. The use of the surface as an element of form can be traced back to the beginnings of modern architecture. Siren has found an impressive solution to this problem. He handles with similar mastery the age-old material, wood. The roof construction of the restaurant consists of nailed timber trusses; pure structural engineering becomes architecture in his hands [397]. Timber and brickwork, natural materials, are adapted in a completely straightforward manner to the needs of our time.

The same attitude to materials and construction can also be seen in Jorma Järvi, whose principal work is the school at Kulosaari (1955) [398]. Viljo Rewell and Keijo

397. Kaija and Heikki Siren. Students' refector Otaniemi, 1952. Massive construction with timb stanchions and trusses. The V-shaped suppor provide cross-bracing.

398. Jorma Järvi. School, Helsinki, Kulosaari, 1955. Assembly Hall and Theatre, also contains staircases giving access to class rooms. The slope of the room follows the natural slope of the rocky site.

Petäjä, in their office building in Helsinki (1952), revive the idea prevalent in the twenties, of stressing the horizontality of the building mass, but giving it a fresh emphasis in the surface treatment of the elevation [393]. Aalto's saying: "Our job is to humanize the mechanical nature of materials" not only defines the importance of his own work since the thirties, but distinguishes present-day Finnish architecture as well.

Italy

No European country was ever so heavily overshadowed by her artistic past as Italy[70]. Since the eighteenth century time seemed to have stood still and Italy to have become a Museum. The search for a new art of her own was, therefore, bound to take the form of a violent protest against the enveloping mantle of history.

In 1909 Futurism, the movement with which Italy established her connection with European "modernism", demanded this break with the past in uncompromising terms. It glorified a new beauty in the machine. Its utopian claims were formulated by the poet Filippo Tommaso Marinetti, the painters Carlo Carrà and Gino Severini, the sculptor Umberto Boccioni and the architect Antonio Sant' Elia. The latter, influenced in certain details by Otto Wagner, strove to translate the feeling of movement which Futurist paintings and sculpture tried to convey, to architecture [111, 399]. His designs for a futuristic town stressed therefore those elements which represent movement and traffic: streets, laid out on different levels, determine the town plan. The architecture of the residential buildings is characterized by conspicuous lift towers. In this one-sided emphasis on particular elements of form a parallel can be seen with manifestations in Holland and Germany about 1920. Futurism's influence in Italy remained slight and had no direct descendants. Its most important personalities, Sant' Elia and Boccioni, were victims of the first world war.

In 1927 the "Gruppo 7" (Libera, Figini, Frette, Larco, Pollini, Rava and Terragni) emerged with ideas far removed from the utopian visions of Futurism. Demanding functional building, they made use of the knowledge and discoveries of modern architecture, but with a due regard for the special conditions of their country. In contrast to Germany, where National Socialism suppressed all activities of this kind, modern architecture in Italy was tolerated by Fascist officialdom.

Italian architecture in the thirties came under the influence of the first phase of modern architecture in Central Europe. But it soon showed in the work of Giuseppe Terragni tendencies of an essentially Italian kind, which found notable expression in the Casa del Pòpolo at Como (1932–36) [400]. At this period, too, can already be seen the outstanding gift of the Italians for developing structural

399. Antonio Sant'Elia. Project for a "Futurist" town, 1913–14.

400. Giuseppe Terragni, Casa del Pòpolo, Como, 1932–36.

401. Matté Trucco. Fiat Works, Turin, 1927. Ramp up which cars are driven to test-track on roof of works building. The curved line of the structural components and the exposed floor members give an impression of organic movement to a conception of form developed from the purpose and construction of the building.

402. Luciano Baldessari. Factory building, Milan, 1934.

forms. In 1927 Matté Trucco built the Fiat Works at Turin [214, 401], a skeleton frame building, in which the construction is strikingly used as a visible element, while Pier Luigi Nervi, to-day one of the most significant engineer-architects in the world, was beginning his career with the boldly cantilevered roofs for the stands of the Florence sports stadium (1930–32) [246, 247a]. Structural forms were designed with an instinctively correct grasp of the distribution of stresses; intuition and formulae complemented each other.

Even if, as a general rule, the years before the second world war still brought no individuality to Italian architecture, they were none the less of great importance as a period of preparation. The particular quality of present-day Italian architecture lies in the combination of prosaic calculation and exuberant fantasy, in the blend of sound economy and creative inspiration. Unlike Brazil, where – especially in Oscar Niemeyer's work – structural forms too often owe their appearance to superb showmanship, with Italian architects and engineers they are associated in an almost classical manner with the method of construction, without destroying the freshness of inspiration.

403. Luciano Baldessari. Exhibition Pavilion, Milan, 1952. The same architect turns away from the rectangular cube to moulded plastic forms. Freedom from all structural considerations, which in other building types might mean the risk of playing to the gallery.

404. Pier Luigi Nervi and Annibale Vitellozzi. Palazzetto dello Sport, Rome, 1957. Circular domed building of precast components assembled in forty days. The design of the slanting Y-shaped piers is dictated by the compression stresses of the roof. The stadium holds four to five thousand spectators and was built with an eye to the Olympic Games of 1960.

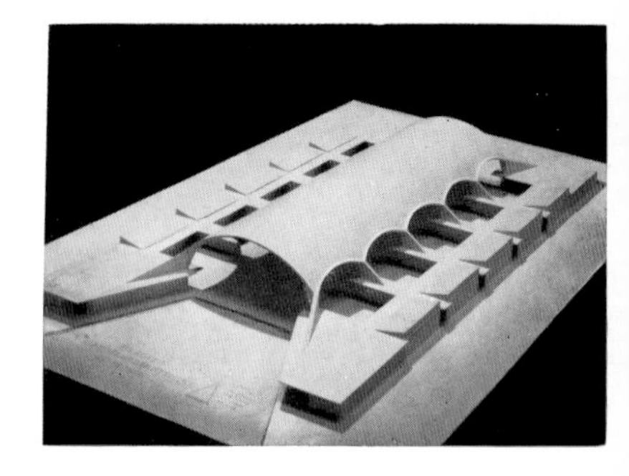

405. Emilio Brizzi, Enzo and Giuseppe Gori, Leonardo Ricci, Leonardo Savioli. Covered flower market, Pescia, 1951. Photo of model. Reinforced concrete barrel vault, supported on segmental arches.

406. Flower Market, Pescia. The narrow sides and the areas between the columns are left open. The market is the centre for the carnation trade of Tuscany.

407. Gio Ponti, in association with Arturo Danusso, Antonio Fornaroli, Pier Luigi Nervi, Egidio dell' Orto, Alberto Rosselli, Giuseppe Valtolina. Pirelli Tower, Milan, 1955–58. Photo of Model. Instead of the flat slab, a plastically moulded composition on a boat-shaped plan. As the working load increases, the internal space diminishes from the middle, where the lifts are located, to the sides. Triangular end sections house emergency stairs and services. The 420-foot building relieves the monotonous symmetry of the station square.

408. Pirelli Tower, Milan. Section through the transversal supporting columns. In contrast to the traditional structural system with stanchions placed close together, the wide-span floor construction is carried on two composite tapering piers.

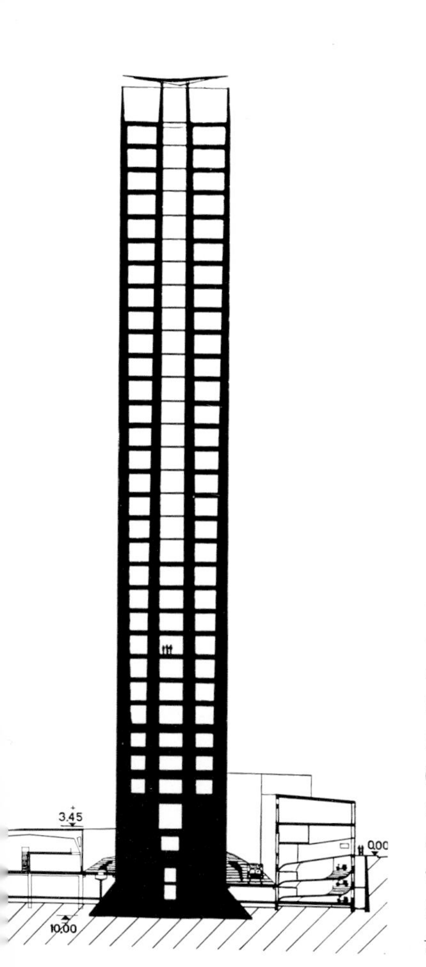

The concourse of the main railway station at Rome (architects Calini, Castellazzi, Fadigati, Montuori, Pintonello and Vitellozzi), built in 1948–50, is spanned by beams of daring design resting upon slender stanchions [412, 413]. Each of the forms used is the product of structural considerations, whilst also fulfilling its purpose as an interpreter of architectural expression. The same thing is applicable to the Pescia flower-market hall, erected by architects Gori, Gori, Ricci and Savioli and engineer Brizzi [405, 406]. This association of form with construction does not imply a system suitable for particular types of building, but simply illustrates a method of working, which sees its object achieved when construction and form are identical. In the competition designs for Naples railway station (1954), one can see the variety of possibilities presented in the basic architectural conceptions of individual authors. Nervi proposes a hall which is a simple spatial composition, while Castiglioni, Bongioanni and Sianesi foresee a space filled with dynamic movement [414, 415, 417].

In North Italy modern architecture has gained the support of large firms anxious to have their products, like their factories and employees' homes, designed ac-

409. Gian Antonio Bernasconi, Annibale Fiocchi and Marzello Nizzoli. Olivetti Headquarters, Milan, 1954. View of annexe from north west. Restraint and plainness in contradistinction to the lively movement of the main building [237].

410. Luigi Figini, Annibale Fiocchi and Gino Pollini. Olivetti administrative and factory building, Ivrea, 1948–50. The north front is faced with a glass curtain, the west and south sides being provided with sun protection devices. Like the Pirelli and Fiat firms, the Olivetti Company is one of the chief patrons of modern architecture in Italy.

411. Vincenzo Pantano. Exhibition building, Messina, 1952. The effect of the façade depends upon the contrast between the conspicuously displayed horizontal lines of the floors and the stanchions visible behind the glass skin.

cording to present-day ideas. No matter what architect may have been commissioned for a particular job, the buildings of the Olivetti Company speak a common language which expresses the decided wishes of the clients. One of the most attractive buildings which have been erected by this firm in recent years, is the administration building in Milan (Architects Bernasconi, Fiocchi and Nizzoli, 1954) [237, 409]. Another big company, the Pirelli Works, also offers practical opportunities to architects with creative ability. Its new headquarters building in Milan, which Nervi has designed with several other architects, rejects the conventional concept of the reinforced concrete frame building and opens up new possibilities for expression [407, 408].
The resourcefulness of the Italians in devising forms is also still apparent when they come perilously near to the verge of modishness, if not of overstepping it Moreover, certain fields of Italian architecture are to-day still stamped with a theatrical monumentality which awakens memories of the official buildings of Mussolini's era. Yet there is undoubtedly tremendous creative originality in Italian architecture to-day, which gives it high standing.

412. Leo Calini, Massimo Castellazzi, Vasco Fadigati, Eugenio Montuori, Achille Pintonello, Annibale Vitellozzi. Termini railway station, Rome, 1950. The unusual form of the members supporting the ceiling reflects the pattern of stresses in the construction. Cantilevered roof and completely glazed walls. The concrete columns are faced with brownish red granite, the ceiling members with white glass mosaic.

413. Termini Station, Rome. Boldly rhythmical articulation of the concourse and booking hall; emphatic horizontal elongated effect of the office block and of the gallery behind serving the platforms. The various parts of the station buildings are asymmetrically arranged in deference to town planning considerations. The ruins of the Agger Serviano are incorporated in the composition.

414/415. Pier Luigi Nervi, Mario Campanella, Giuseppe Vaccaro. Main station, Naples. Project, 1954. Concourse and booking hall. The diagonal cross-members of the reinforced concrete frame form on the inside a rhomboidal network which supports the ceiling. All the prize-winning designs, in contrast to the station at Rome abandon the idea of placing the booking hall immediately next to a massive office building.

416. Enrico Castiglioni. Pilgrimage Church, Syracuse. Project, 1957. Free plastic conception translated into architecture. Irregular hexagonal plan; outside walls of masonry. Reinforced concrete shell roof resting on three free-standing piers and on six supports set in the outside walls. Indirect lighting through slits in the "worm-like" sides of the dome.

417. Bongioanni, Enrico Castiglioni, Sianesi. Main station, Naples. Project, 1954. The original construction of the concourse and booking hall offers a fantastic, irrational, impression of space. Thin reinforced concrete shell domes are carried on three-armed stanchions. Light enters through openings between the shells.

Brazil

Between 1937 and 1943 the Ministry of Education and Health, now counted among the classic masterpieces of modern architecture, was built in Rio de Janeiro [155, 156, 419-421]. This achievement, inspired by one of the supreme exponents of modern European architecture, Le Corbusier, and realized by a group of young architects, is all the more astonishing since it occurred in a country which until then had played no part whatsoever in modern architecture. In Europe the phase of trial and experiment was over by the second half of the twenties, and the natural result of this consolidation was an increasingly wide extension of the new ideas into those fields of architecture which still clung to sterile academic ways. The position of maturity, which modern architecture had reached in Europe, provided young architects in countries like Brazil[71] with an opportunity of building upon firmly based principles of form and design. This sudden arrival of modern architecture, however, was perhaps hastened by a secret bond of sympathy between Le Corbusier's world of form and the desires and needs of a country which was still, architecturally speaking, uninitiated.
The modern movement was enthusiastically encouraged in Brazil by a large number of exceptionally gifted young architects. After its first stirrings in the twenties had been suppressed by unfavourable political conditions, support came from a source which would certainly have startled Europeans. In 1935 the Minister of Education, Gustavo Capanema, commissioned a young architect, Lúcio Costa, to prepare a new design for his Ministry, since the prizewinning academic projects in the competition did not satisfy him. Costa formed a co-partnership with Carlos A. Leão, Jorge Moreira, Affonso Eduardo Reidy and, later, Oscar Niemeyer and Ernani Vasconcelos, who submitted new proposals in 1936. In the same year Le Corbusier was invited to advise on the scheme for the Ministry and on the building of the projected University City in Rio de Janeiro. He accepted the invitation and in the summer of 1936 went to Rio de Janeiro, where he worked with Lúcio Costa and his collaborators on the project for the Ministry of Education and also gave a series of public lectures, in which he expounded his views on modern architecture.
Le Corbusier's personality and the force of his ideas had a great effect on young

418. Gregori Warchavchik. House in the Rua Thomé de Souza, São Paulo, 1929. Warchavchik's buildings (influenced by the early work of Le Corbusier and "De Stijl") and his active publicity prepared the ground for Le Corbusier's arrival in Brazil.

419. Roberto Burle Marx. Roof garden on the south annexe of the Ministry of Education building, Rio de Janeiro. A garden architecture of flowing rhythm and arabesque.

420/421. Lúcio Costa, Carlos A. Leão, Jorge Moreira, Affonso E. Reidy, Oscar Niemeyer, Ernani Vasconcelos. Consultant architect: Le Corbusier. Ministry of Education, Rio de Janeiro, 1937–43. South front. Le Corbusier prepared schemes for two different sites. The confined nature of the building plot decided the narrow high slab of the executed design. Le Corbusier's thirty-day collaboration with a group of leading young architects marked the beginning of modern Brazilian architecture.

Brazilian architects. His influence permeated the whole of Brazilian architecture and can be seen in many characteristic features: in the free handling of plan and elevations; in the conspicuously cubic form of the building mass; in the use of the top storey as a roof-garden, the effectiveness of which is enhanced by the plastic modelling of certain elements of the building; in the provision of ramps instead of stairs, and especially in the application of ingeniously designed sun louvers (the brise-soleil or quebra-sol).

However strong the influence of Le Corbusier and of European architecture may have been, Brazilian architects were not content to copy these forms. They succeeded in erecting on this foundation an architecture of strongly marked individuality, which to-day stands high in international esteem.

One of the particular characteristics of Brazilian architecture – freely curving, often plastically modelled, architectural forms – is especially apparent in the work of Oscar Niemeyer, the Brazilian architect best known abroad. To the familiar theme of modern architecture, the lifting of the building off the ground, he adds a novel variant by carrying the load of the upper storeys upon plastically

422. Zenon Lotufo, Eduardo Kneese de Mello, Oscar Niemeyer, Helio Uchôa. Palace of Industry Ibirapuéra Park, São Paulo, 1953. Exhibition building for machinery and industrial products 800 feet in length, carried on stilts, and provided with aluminium brise-soleils.

423. Palace of Industry, Ibirapuéra Park, São Paulo, 1953. Internal access ramps to the upper display areas. The forked columns, cigar-shaped vertical members and freely curving galleries counteract the effect of a vast rectangular stretch of enclosed space.

424. Ibirapuéra Park, São Paulo, 1951–55. General layout. The flowing lines of paths and park contrast with the cubelike buildings, just as the galleries and ramps in the Palace of Industry contrast with its rectangular shape.

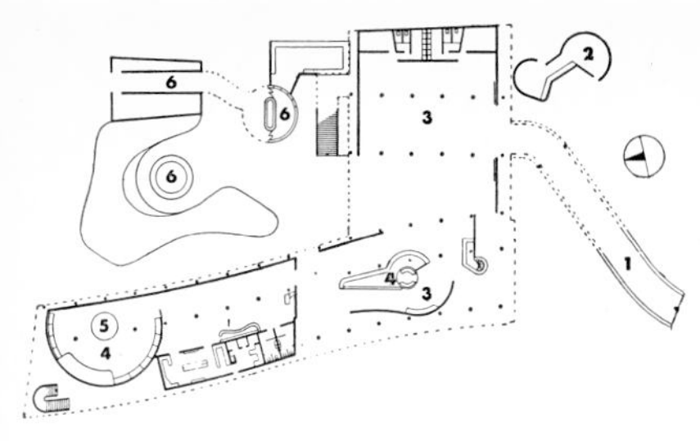

425. Lúcio Costa and Oscar Niemeyer. Brazilian Pavilion, New York World's Fair, 1939. Ground plan. 1. Access ramp. 2. Aviary. 3. Exhibition areas. 4. Restaurants. 5. Bar with dance floor. 6. Flora and fauna of Brazil.

426. Brazilian Pavilion, New York World's Fair. Access ramp to the display areas. Richly varied interpretation of space by means of the many links between interior and exterior.

modelled V-shaped stilts [433]. His free interpretation of form in details, however, is applied to buildings in their entirety. His own house, which in its singular originality explores the extreme limits of the practicable, is roofed with a curved concrete slab, supported on slender columns, and is separated from the outside world only by glass walls and opaque partitions.

Niemeyer often deliberately uses forms which strongly contrast with one another. Thus in the Palace of Industry in Ibirapuéra-Park in São Paulo (1953), in which in the middle of a long hall of simple rectangular outline he has placed a fantastic system of ramps [422, 423]. The importance of his work, of which one of the most mature examples is the interior of the Franciscan church at Pampulha (1943), lies in the way he has extended the possibilities of form recognized hitherto. Niemeyer exemplifies a complete breakaway from the exclusive use of the right angle, which had already begun to appear about 1930. His weakness as a designer lies in his delight in the unusual for its own sake and in the discrepancy in his buildings between their appearance and their structure.

In common with Niemeyer's buildings the work of a number of prominent archi-

427/428. Oscar Niemeyer. Modern Art Museum, Caracas, Venezuela. Project. 1955. Section and model. Set on a steep hillside overlooking the town, the building is in the form of an inverted pyramid, "expressing in the purity of its lines the forces of contemporary art" (Niemeyer). The ground floor contains an auditorium, the first holds offices and foyer, the second, into which a mezzanine is introduced, is top-lighted and equipped for exhibitions. Deliberate contrast between the monumental effect of unrelieved walls and the translucent roof of the upper storey.

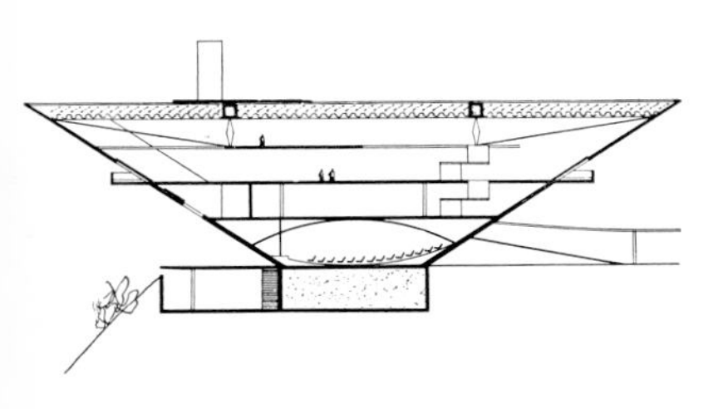

429. Osvaldo Arthur Bratke. The architect's house, São Paulo, 1953. The rectangular frame shape is enlivened by recessed walls, internal patio and lattices of reinforced concrete components.

tects bear witness to the high standing of Brazilian architecture. Lúcio Costa, associated with Niemeyer in building the Brazilian Pavilion at the New York World Exhibition in 1939 [425, 426], and also the architect of the notable flats at Eduardo-Guinle-Park in Rio de Janeiro (1948–54) [432]; Affonso E. Reidy, who designed and built the big Pedregulho housing scheme in Rio de Janeiro [81, 437, 438]; Jorge Moreira, the chief architect of the University City of Rio de Janeiro now under construction; Marcello, Milton and Maurizio Roberto, who built one of the first modern Brazilian office blocks in 1938 and from among whose later works the Santos Dumont Airport building (1944) is outstanding; and finally Rino Levi, whose principal achievement is the Central Institute for Cancer Treatment (1954) at São Paulo.

In Lúcio Costa's most important work, the flats at Eduardo-Guinle-Park, another characteristic manifestation of Brazilian art is revealed: an instinct for the lively composition of surfaces. In order to protect the flats from the glare of the sun, highly decorative ceramic grilles are inset between the externally visible frame. These give shade to the rooms behind and vivid life to the elevations [432]. In their

430. Oscar Niemeyer. Staff housing. São José dos Campos, São Paulo, 1947. Each dwelling includes a small patio placed in front of a two-storey-high living room and protected from the sun by brise-soleils of horizontal panels.

431. Staff housing, São José dos Campos, São Paulo, 1947. Plan of ground floor and upper storey. 1. Living room. 2. Kitchen. 3. Maid's room. 4. Garage. 5. Bedrooms.

432. Lúcio Costa. Flats, Eduardo-Guinle-Park, Rio de Janeiro, 1948–54. Vertical panels and close-mesh lattices screen the strong sunlight. Walls display the characteristics of textiles.

search for materials suitable for wall-cladding Brazilians have returned, like Mexicans, to early precedents and have reintroduced the "azulejo" facing of coloured tiles. Traditional elements of form, too, have been revived: the patio, sometimes covered with trellises, at others left as an open green space, plays an important part in the single-storeyed house [429–431].

Brazilian architects have freely varied those elements of modern architecture which seemed appropriate to building in Brazil, and woven them into the pattern of an older tradition. An architecture has resulted, which is remarkable for its daring experiments in form, for the great charm of its lively interpretation of open and closed surfaces and for its youthful, unaffected freshness.

433. Oscar Niemeyer. Flats, Interbau Exhibition, Berlin, 1957. Photo of model. The three-corner shape of the stilts occurs again at the back in the plan of a free-standing lift tower. The lift rises no higher than the fifth storey, which acts as a second ground floor and appears as a thick horizontal line on the front elevation. From there upwards the remaining floors are reached by stairs.

434. Paulo Antunes Ribeiro. Caramurú Building, Salvador, Bahia, 1946. Original method of sun protection. Metal grills, covered with a bronze gauze-like fabric and secured to projecting concrete brackets, are arranged in two planes in a chess board pattern.

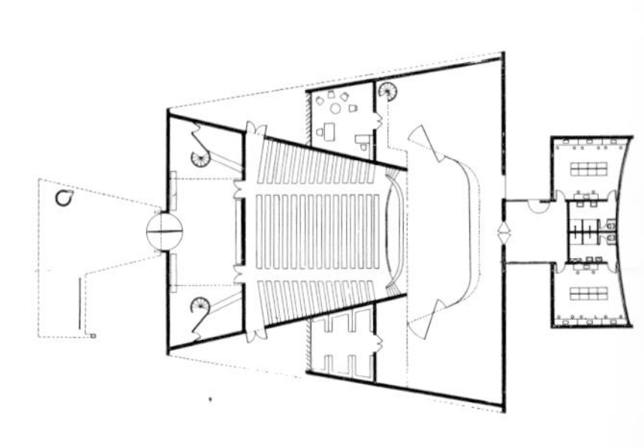

435/436. Affonso Eduardo Reidy. Community Theatre, Rio de Janeiro, 1950. Small theatre, also used for amateur performances, in an industrial suburb of Rio. Seating for 300. The angle at which the auditorium rises towards the stage corresponds to the pitch of the longer roof.

37. Affonso Eduardo Reidy. Pedregulho housing cheme, Rio de Janeiro, 1950–52. Loosely organ-:ed residential quarter, dominated on the south de by a block of flats which follows in sweeping urves the contours of the sloping site. Housing ith a social purpose; many amenities for nants; rents adjusted to incomes.

8. Pedregulho housing scheme, Rio de Jan-ro. Site plan. 1. Blocks of flats. 2. Primary chool with gymnasium and swimming pools. Recreation areas. 4. Health service clinic. Laundry. 6. Tunnel for pedestrians.

Modern architecture made an early and significant beginning in North America[72] with the buildings of the School of Chicago between 1883 and 1893 [29a–35, 439]. At first, it is true, the ideas and designs of Louis Sullivan, William Le Baron Jenney and Burnham and Root found no immediate following in their own country, but their influence on the European movement was all the stronger. In particular Sullivan's theory, the need for identity of function and form, provided an important point of departure for the new architecture in Europe. In the United States, however, increasingly powerful opposing currents made themselves felt, which turned against the functional architectural conceptions of Sullivan and led to a barren eclecticism. Only the work of the brilliant American architect Frank Lloyd Wright distinguishes the period stretching from before the turn of the century into our day [37–39, 41–52, 453, 454], and forms, in company with certain anonymous industrial architecture, a tenuous connection with the buildings of the Chicago School.

439. D. H. Burnham and John W. Root. Relianc
Building, Chicago, 1890–94.

440. George Howe and William Lescaze. Savin
Fund Society Building, Philadelphia, 193
Strongly emphasized lines. The stanchions c
the broad side of the building are revealed a
powerful vertical features, while on the narro
side the building projects beyond the axis of th
last stanchion and culminates in long ribbo
windows. The first example of a new moder
architecture which emerged in America abo
1930.

441. Reinhard & Hofmeister, Corbett, Harrison and MacMurray, Hood & Fouilhaux. Rockefeller Center. New York, 1931-40. Planned and executed as a single conception, a city group of fifteen buildings, between which wide open courts are arranged for the first time. Towering ribbons of wall, with no cornices to check their vertical thrust.

The Museum of Modern Art in New York performed a great service in reviving modern architectural thinking by acquainting the American public with developments of modern architecture in Europe by means of a series of lavish exhibitions. The first of these took place in 1932, in which a few American buildings were shown by the side of European examples. Exhibitions of the work of the Chicago School (1935), Le Corbusier (1935), Aalto and the Bauhaus (1938) followed.

Of the buildings erected in the thirties, the Rockefeller Center in New York (architects Reinhard and Hofmeister; Corbett, Harrison and MacMurray, Hood and Fouilhoux, 1931–40) offers a strong contrast to the conception of a Wall Street skyscraper, despite its overpronounced vertical articulation, even if some of its features are unconvincing [441]. The siting of the individual buildings according to an overall plan is particularly noteworthy. For the first time a large complex was so arranged that the various blocks formed a harmonious whole. The first skyscraper, in which every detail was deliberately designed to exemplify unity of form and construction, was built in 1932 by George Howe and William Lescaze: the Philadelphia Saving Fund Society Building [440].

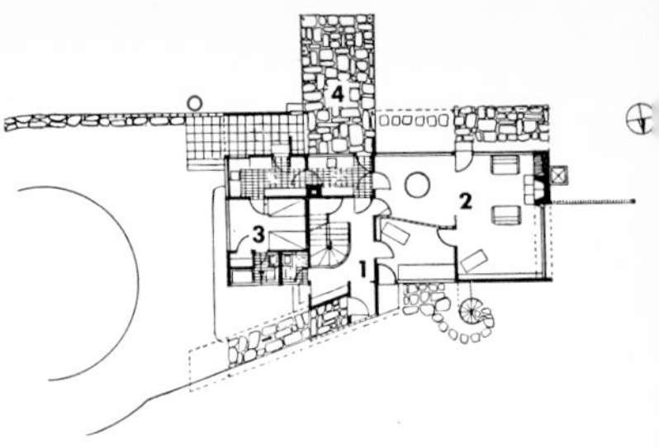

As a land of great opportunities, the United States have always attracted men of creative ability and offered them chances lacking in their homelands. Richard Neutra (born 1892) went to the U. S. A. in the twenties after working in Germany with Erich Mendelsohn. In 1927, at the time when the Weissenhof housing scheme was being carried out at Stuttgart, he built the Health House in Los Angeles, which, in the logic of its structural conception and in the planning and relationship of its living spaces, was perhaps the first domestic building in North America to translate elements of modern European architecture into a native idiom [445]. By the middle of the thirties Neutra had achieved such wide recognition that he was commissioned to build an experimental school in Los Angeles (1935) [447]. Neutra designed this school as a pure "Pavilion" building and, in so doing, started a revolution in North American school construction.
Neutra's rapidly expanding practice, which has latterly achieved particular distinction in the domestic field (House in the Desert, 1946; Warren Tremaine House, Montecito, California, 1949), illustrates the gradual change of attitude in the United States [446, 448]. Clients were more often found who sympathized

442. Walter Gropius and Marcel Breuer. Gropius' house, Lincoln, Mass., 1937. Dovetailing of internal and external space. Deep projecting roofs. Timber cladding and porch (protected from mosquitoes by wire netting) reflect local tradition.

443. Gropius's house, Lincoln, Mass. Ground floor plan. 1. Main entrance and hall. 2. Principal living-room. 3. Bedroom. 4. Porch.

444. Marcel Breuer. The architect's house, New Canaan, Conn., 1947. Projecting balcony and sun terrace suspended from cables.

445. Richard Neutra. Health House, Griffith Park, Los Angeles, 1927. Neutra's buildings spread modern architectural ideas in North America. The under part of the house is of reinforced concrete, with a steel skeleton above. The steeply sloping site was used for swimming pools and other forms of recreation.

46. Richard Neutra. Warren Tremaine House Montecito, California, 1949. Interior and exterior re linked by the uniform level of floor and site nd by projecting roof slabs. Vegetation and eological formation share in the architectural conception. The building, however, is sharply istinguished from its natural setting by the use f materials with clearly defined tectonic quali- ies.

47. Richard Neutra. Corona School, Bell, Los ngeles, 1935. A block of five classrooms (at- ached to an older building) with lighting from wo sides, which can be extended into the open. he building and its flexible plan illustrate an ducational principle in which the teacher hares in the activities of a group.

48. Warren Tremaine House. Windmill-sail plan. Main entrance. 2. Guest rooms. 3. Living-din- g area and Library. 4. Kitchen and utility rooms. Bedrooms. 6. Terrace on West side. 7. Swim- ing bath.

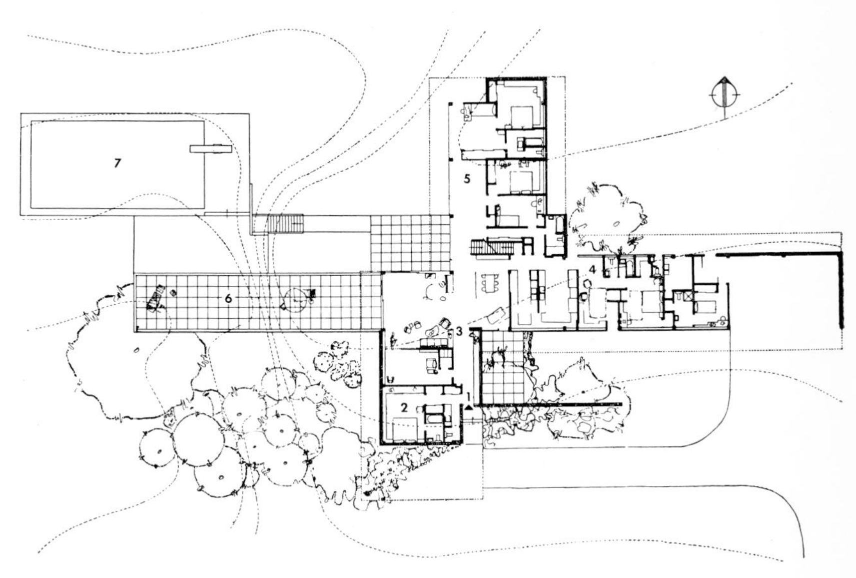

449. Charles Eames. Case Study House, Santa Monica, California, 1949. Prefabricated skeleton frame into which are fitted plaster panels, and transparent and translucent glass.

450. Case Study House, Santa Monica, California, 1949. The bedrooms are placed at an intermediate level and open on to the living room which is the full height of the house. The subtle interplay of surfaces recalls Japanese buildings.

451. Philip C. Johnson. The architect's house, New Canaan, Connecticut, 1949. Enormous glass panes set in a steel frame and mounted on a brick foundation. House open on all sides, only the service core being walled in. Spacious site conditions are the essence of a solution of this kind. Johnson is a pupil and collaborator of Mies van der Rohe.

with modern architectural ideas. The appointment of Gropius and Mies van der Rohe to American architectural schools is a measure of this swing of opinion. At Harvard Gropius at last found the climate which he needed to develop his teaching principles [124] unhampered by the difficulties that had beset his work at the Bauhaus. In 1938, only a year later, Mies van der Rohe was called to the Illinois Institute of Technology in Chicago [137, 138, 142a, 142b, 236]. Both have left an enduring influence. That of Mies, which is more apparent in his designs and buildings than in his work as an architectural teacher, can be seen in Eero Saarinen, Gordon Bunshaft and Philip Johnson [463–465, 229, 459, 451]; Gropius and his former student and subsequent collaborator, Marcel Breuer, have provided a particular stimulus to Paul Rudolph, Hugh Stubbins and his pupil, Pei [452, 461, 462], whilst Bruce Goff's work has been inspired by Wright. America gave European architects the chance to put their ideas to work in big schemes. The different relationship between architect and client, the attitude of mutual confidence, and the possibilities offered by a country of highly developed industry decisively altered their attitude of mind.

52. Hugh A. Stubbins, with Werner Düttmann nd Franz Mocken. Conference Hall, Berlin, 1957. merican contribution to Interbau Exhibition. hanging roof, largely supported by two oblique-ngled reinforced concrete arches, spans the uditorium, exhibition areas, studio stage and onference hall. Modelled on the arena at Ra-eigh [258], the majestic sculptural effect of the oof construction is enhanced by the rectangular ubstructure containing the foyer and adjoining ooms. Stubbins is a pupil of Gropius.

453. Frank Lloyd Wright. Price Tower, Bartlesville, Oklahoma, 1955. From his earliest days Wright has made a deep study of the problem of the skyscraper. The tower is erected on an approximately square plan which is divided into quadrants. Three of the four resulting prisms contain offices and are featured on the outside by horizontal panels; the fourth comprises two-storey flats and is marked by vertical fins. Four reinforced concrete slabs carry the tower and project with the top of the service core above the highest storey. Vivid interplay of light and shade, brilliant colour effects of decorative copper stripes.

454. Frank Lloyd Wright. Guggenheim Museum of abstract art, New York. Project 1946. Now under construction. Section through model. Spiral ramps, supported by the outside walls, act as continuously rising display areas. Lighting through narrow external ribbon windows and a glazed internal dome. An "introverted" building.

455. Skidmore, Owings and Merrill; design by Gordon Bunshaft. Manufacturers' Trust Company, New York, 1954. Instead of the traditional conception of a bank as a rather forbidding fortress, the building is wide open; even the strong-room is visible from the street. Cantilevered floor slabs, carried on only eight internal columns, make possible the curtain walls. The precision in detailing and slender, elegant, proportions convey an impression of richness.

456. Pietro Belluschi. Equitable Life Insurance building, Portland, Oregon, 1948. In contrast to Wright's Price Tower completely flush exterior, in which the reinforced concrete frame is apparent behind an aluminium skin.

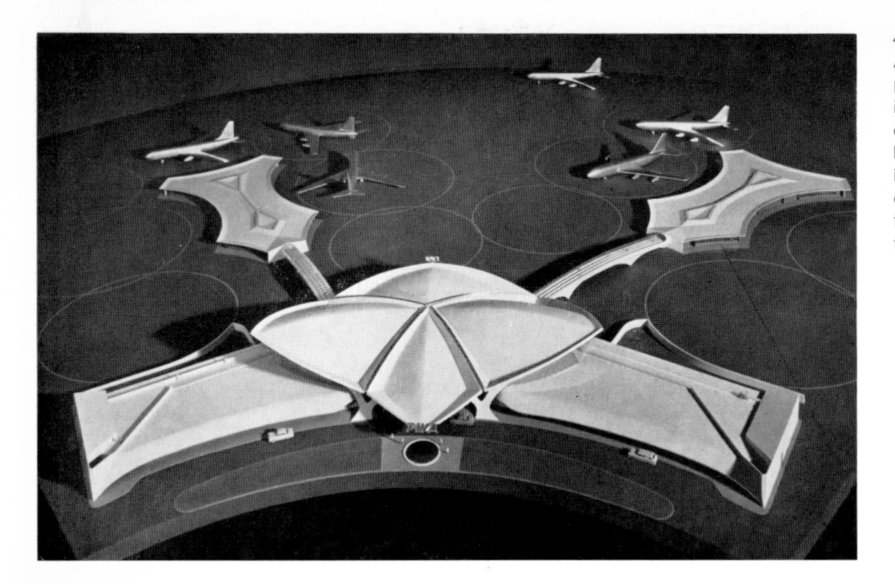

457/458. Eero Saarinen and Associates. Idlewild Airport Terminal, New York. Anticipated completion date: 1960. The passenger reception building is roofed with four shells, separated from one another by glass bands which provide top lighting. The symbolic shape of a bird in flight, in which the purposes of the building and the curve of the street are also reflected, evolved from the study of scores of models before the final form was settled.

The scope and individuality of American architecture, the full effect of which does not yet correspond, to be frank, with its practical achievements, can be appreciated in the principal work of Eero Saarinen, the General Motors Research Center at Detroit (1951–56) [463–465]. Technical perfection in details and the use of factory-produced building components are combined with a concern for human requirements. The buildings are grouped about an artificial lake. Large green spaces and a carefully chosen colour scheme ensure an open, cheerful, atmosphere. Saarinen uses prefabricated elements, and also initiates a revolution in building methods.
Factory-made components of light metal, steel and plastics gradually replace the old building materials. But this leads to the loss of individuality of form, for mass-production entails a series of identical parts. The need becomes all the greater therefore to design components which offer a wide variety of possible combinations. It is our task to master these elements and put them to the service of purposes worthy of mankind.

459. Skidmore, Owings and Merrill. Design by Gordon Bunshaft. Lever House, New York, 1952. Lever House led the way to a new era in tall building technique with its logical interpretation of the massive glass wall [229] and exquisite town manners.

460. Skidmore, Owings and Merrill. Chase Manhattan Bank, New York. Photo of model. Under construction. 60-storey office block. The stanchions of the load-bearing frame are placed both in front of the external walls and inside the central service core.

461. Ioh Ming Pei. Mile High Center, Denver, Colorado, 1956. In variety of proportion, in wall treatment, in the colour and nature of materials, widely differing interpretations of form are now possible in multi-storey office buildings of similar type. The stanchions of Lever House are behind the external wall face, in the Chase Manhattan Bank they are in front, and in the Mile High Center they are set in the actual plane of the wall itself.

462. Ioh Ming Pei. Mile High Center, Denver, Colorado, 1956. Interesting elevational treatment by means of two complementary systems: stanchions and beams with dark cast aluminium cladding and light enamelled bands, which conceal the air-conditioning ducts. The building does not occupy the entire plot, but allows space for a large court.

463. Eero Saarinen. Technical Centre for General Motors, Detroit, 1951–56. Research Administration Building. Carefully planned layout for twenty-five buildings. Meticulous detailing, superb massing, light and graceful architectural composition.

464. Technical Centre for General Motors, Detroit. Staircase. White terrazzo slabs held on steel rods.

→

465. Technical Centre for General Motors, Detroit. Steel Water Tower. The group of buildingn is arranged in a park with wide stretches of laws and water. The age-old division of commercia- and industrial quarters on the one hand, and rel creation areas on the other, gives place to a landscape for work, in which technology and nature have equal status.

Notes

The form of these notes differs slightly from those in the German original. No fresh references have of course been included, but in some cases additional bibliographical information has been supplied. It is hoped, therefore, that they will serve, not only as a record of the author's sources, but as a basic bibliography for the reader. In a very small number of instances, where the relevance of the German disappears in translation, the wording has been changed.

Some standard works on the history of modern architecture:

S. Giedion. Space, Time and Architecture. Cambridge, Mass: Harvard University Press, 1941. 3rd edition, London: Oxford University Press, 1954.
N. Pevsner. Pioneers of Modern Design from William Morris to Walter Gropius. London, 1936. 2nd edition, New York: Museum of Modern Art, 1949.
G. A. Platz. Die Baukunst der neuesten Zeit. Berlin, 1927. 2nd edition, 1930.
J. M. Richards. An Introduction to Modern Architecture. London, Baltimore and Melbourne: Penguin Books, 1940. 3rd (revised) edition, 1956.
B. Taut. Die neue Baukunst in Europa und Amerika. Stuttgart: Hoffmann, 1929.
A. Whittick. European Architecture in the Twentieth Century. Volume 1 (up to 1924); Volume 2 (1924–1933). London: Crosby Lockwood, 1950 and 1953.
B. Zevi. Storia dell'architettura moderna. Turin: Einaudi, 1950. 3rd (revised) edition, 1955. Contains comprehensive bibliography.

Books of special value for their illustrations:

S. Giedion. A Decade of Contemporary (New) Architecture. Zürich: Girsberger, 1951. Record of buildings erected between 1937 and 1947. 2nd edition, 1954.
A. Roth. The New Architecture. Zürich: Verlag für Architektur, 1948. Twenty important buildings of the thirties.
A. Sartoris. Gli elementi dell'architettura funzionale. Milan: Hoepli, 2nd edition, 1935. Arranged according to countries.

[1] The term used here in the original German is "Eisenbeton" (or "iron concrete") as opposed to "Stahlbeton" (or "steel concrete") which is the term normally employed to-day in German-speaking countries for reinforced concrete. Nowadays of course steel is the accepted agent of reinforcement.

[2] Extract from La Presse, 1850.

[3] O. Johannsen. Geschichte des Eisens. Düsseldorf, 1953. Comprehensive account from the early beginnings of iron production in Egypt and Mesopotamia to our day.
An iron blade was found in the pyramid of Cheops, which was built about 2600 B. C., and a dagger discovered in Ur dates from the period 3100 years before Christ.

[4] F. Gresbeck. Bahnbrecher der Eisenhütte. Düsseldorf, 1954. "... as early as 1315 ... the Dauphin's officers were protesting against the stripping of the forests of Burgundy, for which they held the iron works of that province responsible ... Even in 1792 the timber needs of the French iron industry were given as six million cords, which was twice as high as firewood requirements" (Gresbeck, p. 6).

[5] J. Gloag and D. Bridgwater. A History of Cast Iron in Architecture. London: G. Allen & Unwin, 1948.
G. C. Mehrtens. Eisenbrückenbau. Volume 1, Leipzig, 1908.
A. G. Meyer. Eisenbauten, ihre Geschichte und Ästhetik. Eßlingen, 1907.

[6] Henri Labrouste in a letter to his brother Théodore, November 1830. Quoted in S. Giedion. Space, Time and Architecture.

[7] H. Straub. Geschichte der Bauingenieurkunst. Basel: Birkhäuser, 1949. English translation: A History of Civil Engineering. Leonard Hill, 1952.

[8] Forerunners of the Machinery Hall are to be found in the train sheds of St. Pancras Station, London (1868), designed by Sir G. G. Scott, and the main station at Frankfurt am Main (1888), built by J. W. Schwedler.

[9] The Tall Office Building artistically considered. First published March 1896, and reprinted in Louis H. Sullivan, Kindergarten Chats and other Writings. New York: Wittenborn, Schultz, 1947. This is also the source of the subsequent quotations.
John Szarkowski. The Idea of Louis Sullivan. University of Minneapolis Press, 1956.

[10] F. Kimball. Alte und neue Baukunst in Amerika, der Sieg des jungen Klassizismus über den Funktionalismus der neunziger Jahre. Wasmuths Monatshefte, 1925, p. 225.

[11] H.-R. Hitchcock. In the Nature of Materials. The Buildings of Frank Lloyd Wright, 1887–1941. New York: Duell, Sloane and Pearce, 1942. Good summary of Wright's work. Reprint: London: Paul Elek, 1958.
E. Kaufmann. An American Architecture. Frank Lloyd Wright. New York: Horizon Press, 1955. London: Architectural Press, 1957.
G. C. Manson. Frank Lloyd Wright to 1910. The First Golden Age. New York: Reinhold, 1958.
W. M. Moser. Sechzig Jahre lebendige Architektur. Frank Lloyd Wright. Winterthur: Winterthur AG, 1952.

[12] See: "F. L. Wright zur Frage, warum die Fachleute das Wesen seiner Architektur so schwer begreifen." W. M. Moser. Sechzig Jahre lebendige Architektur, p. 76.

[13] From: Die neue Baukunst in Europa und Amerika, p. 37.

[14] From an address by Frank Lloyd Wright to business men in 1892. Reproduced in: W. M. Moser. Sechzig Jahre lebendige Architektur, p. 5.

[15] S. Giedion. Space, Time and Architecture, p. 420.

[16] S. T. Madsen. Sources of Art Nouveau. Oslo: Aschehoug, 1956. Comprehensive account of the movement. Excellent bibliography.
N. Pevsner. Pioneers of Modern Design from William Morris to Walter Gropius.
F. Ahlers-Hestermann. Stilwende, Aufbruch der Jugend um 1900. Berlin: Gebr. Mann, 1941. New edition, 1956. Outstanding appraisal of the German contribution.

[17] Otto Wagner. Moderne Architektur. Vienna, 1896. 1898–1902. Vols 2 and 3.
Quoted by: G. A. Platz. Die Baukunst der neuesten Zeit, p. 15.

[18] Henry van de Velde, quoted by F. Schumacher. Strömungen in Deutscher Baukunst seit 1800. Cologne: Seemann, 1955, p. 110. (Reprint of earlier edition).
H. Curjel. Henry van de Velde, zum neuen Stil. Munich: Piper, 1955. Selection of van de Velde's writings.

[19] Year books of the German Werkbund, Jena, 1912–17.
Die Form, magazine for design, Berlin.
These publications offer views of the work of the Werkbund.

[20] A. Loos. Ins Leere gesprochen. Articles in Viennese newspapers and magazines between 1897 and 1900. Paris, Zurich, 1921; Berlin, 1925.
A. Loos. Gesammelte Aufsätze. Innsbruck, 1931.

[21] H. P. Berlage. Quoted by: G. A. Platz. Die Baukunst der neuesten Zeit, p. 16.

[22] Quoted by: F. Ahlers-Hestermann. Stilwende, p. 86.

[23] Quoted by: F. Ahlers-Hestermann. Stilwende, p. 93.

[24] From a lecture given in April 1930. Recorded in: Th. Heuss. Hans Poelzig, das Lebensbild eines deutschen Baumeisters. Tübingen: Wasmuth, 1939. New edition, 1948.

[25] Antonio Gaudí. Quoted in: J. L. Sert. Gaudí visionnaire et précurseur. L'Oeil, No. 2, 15th February 1955, p. 33.
J. F. Ráfols. Gaudí 1852–1926. Barcelona: Canova, 1929. New edition, 1952.
J. L. Sert. Introduzione a Gaudí. Casabella, No. 202, August-September 1954, p. 48 et seq.

[26] Publication celebrating fiftieth anniversary of firm of Wayss and Freytag AG, 1875–1925. Stuttgart, 1925. Chronological record of Monier patents and more important developments in reinforced concrete.

[27] Les bétons agglomérés appliqués á l'art de construire. Paris, 1861. In this work Coignet – long before Monier – describes the application of reinforced concrete to the production of various building components.

[28] The American Thomas Hyatt published his basic discoveries in London in 1877. Although they reveal that he understood many of the principles of reinforced concrete construction, he attracted little attention. Neither Monier nor Coignet seems to have been acquainted with his work.

T. Hyatt. Account of experiments with Portland cement-concrete . . . Privately printed in London, 1877.

[29] Whilst Hennebique was above all responsible for structural innovations, the theoretical bases of reinforced concrete were worked out in Germany. In 1886 the firms of G. A. Wayss and Freytag and of Heidschuch initiated a series of experiments in Berlin, the results of which were coordinated by M. Koenen into a first theory and formula for reinforced concrete building. Koenen's work was carried further by Emil Mörsch and elaborated into a comprehensive theory of reinforced concrete construction.
E. Mörsch. Der Eisenbetonbau, seine Theorie und Berechnung. Stuttgart: Wittwer, 1902. English translation: Concrete-steel construction (revised and enlarged from 3rd German edition by E. P. Goodrich). New York, 1909.

[30] In: Industriebau, Entwicklung und Gestalt. Published by the Kulturkreis im Bundesverband der deutschen Industrie, Wiesbaden, 1953, p. 12.

[31] S. Giedion. Walter Gropius. Stuttgart: Hatje, 1954. London: Architectural Press, 1954.

[32] See structural calculations for the building, which are still in the hands of the Fagus Works.

[33] W. Gropius. Architektur, Wege zu einer optischen Kultur. Frankfurt, 1956, p. 15. Original edition, New York: Scope of total Architecture, Harper. London: Allen & Unwin, 1956.

[34] From a speech on the occasion of the seventieth birthday of Walter Gropius on the 18th May 1953. Quoted in: S. Giedion. Walter Gropius, p. 21.
The following provide information on the aims and methods of the Bauhaus:
H. Bayer, W. and I. Gropius. Bauhaus 1919–1928. 1st edition, New York: Museum of Modern Art, 1938. 2nd edition, Boston, Mass.: Branford, 1938. Reprint by Branford, 1952. London: G. Allen and Unwin, 1939. Stuttgart: Hatje, 1955.
Published in the series of Bauhaus Books, Volumes 1–14. Munich: A. Langen, 1925–30.

[35] W. Gropius. Bauhausbauten Dessau, Volume 12 of Bauhaus Books. Munich: A. Langen, 1930.

[36] Quoted in: W. Gropius. Architektur, Wege zu einer optischen Kultur, pp. 76–78.

[37] Philip C. Johnson. Mies van der Rohe. 1st edition, New York: Museum of Modern Art: Theobald, 1947. 2nd edition, 1953. Stuttgart: Hatje, 1957.
L. Hilberseimer. Mies van der Rohe. Chicago: Theobald, 1956. Comprehensive bibliographies.

[38] Published in: Philip C. Johnson. Mies van der Rohe. New York, 1947.

[39] Mies van der Rohe, in: Technische Hochschule des Staates Illinois in Chikago. Bauen + Wohnen 1956, p. 225.

[40] Le Corbusier. Oeuvre Complète. Six volumes (to date). Zürich, 1937–57. Contains all Le Corbusier's projects and buildings, and lists of his books and writings.

[41] Vers une Architecture. Paris: Crès, 1923. German translation: Kommende Baukunst. Stuttgart, Berlin, Leipzig: Deutsche Verlagsanstalt, 1926. English: Towards a New Architecture. London: Architectural Press, 1927.

[42] Les 5 Points d'une Architecture Nouvelle. In: Le Corbusier. Oeuvre Complète, Volume 1, p. 128.

[43] Vers une Architecture. Also source of subsequent quotation. See also note 41.

[44] In the introduction to: Le Corbusier. Oeuvre Complète, Volume 3, p. 9.

[45] K. R. Lorenz, in: Querschnitt durch die internationale Architektur der Gegenwart. From publication issued on twenty-fifth anniversary of Deutsche Heraklith-AG, 1953.

[46] In: Vers une Architecture. See also English and German editions.

[47] H. L. C. Jaffé. De Stijl 1917–31. The Dutch Contribution to Modern Art. Amsterdam: Meulenhoff, 1956. Also London: Tiranti. Principal reference source for "De Stijl" movement.
Th. van Doesburg. Grundbegriffe der neuen gestaltenden Kunst. Volume 6 of the Bauhaus Books. Munich, 1925.
P. Mondrian. Neue Gestaltung. Volume 5 of the Bauhaus Books. Munich, 1925.

[48] K. Malewitsch, in: Die Gegenstandslose Welt. Volume 11 of the Bauhaus Books. Munich, 1927, p. 98.

[49] In: Die neue Architektur und ihre Folgen. Wasmuths Monatshefte, 1925, p. 503 et seq.

[50] In: Neue Schweizer Rundschau, 1929, p. 536. Quoted in: De Stijl, Katalog 81 of the Stedlijk Museum. Amsterdam, 1951.

[51] The buildings of the twenties, with their characteristic cubic, rectangular form, are comprehensively recorded in: A. Sartoris. Gli elementi dell' architettura funzionale.

[52] In: Walter Gropius. Flach-, Mittel- oder Hochbau? Paper submitted to Third International Congress (CIAM), Brussels, November 1930. Published in: Rationelle Bebauungsweisen, Ergebnisse des dritten Internationalen Kongresses für Neues Bauen, compiled by S. Giedion in collaboration with V. Bourgeois. C. van Eesteren and R. Steiger. Stuttgart, 1932, p. 26 et seq. Also source of subsequent quotations.

[53] R. Wolters. Neue deutsche Baukunst. Berlin: Volk und Reich, 1943. Also: Prague, 1943. Collection of examples of Nazi architecture.

[54] E. and C. Neuenschwander. Alvar Aalto and Finnish Architecture. London: Architectural Press. Zürich: Verlag für Architektur, 1954.
Contains a number of Aalto's buildings and projects, especially of the period 1950–51.
S. Giedion. Space, Time and Architecture, p. 565 et seq.
Special issue of Werk, 1940, No. 3–4.
Pier Carlo Santini and Göran Schildt. Alvar Aalto from Sunila to Imatra: Ideas Projects and Buildings. Zodiac. No. 3, p. 26 et seq.
No adequate monograph on Aalto has so far appeared.

[55] A. Whittick. Eric Mendelsohn. London: Leonard Hill, 1940. Second (expanded) edition, 1956. Contains the whole of Mendelsohn's work.

[56] Machine made America. Special issue of the Architectural Review, 1957, May. Genesis and aesthetic possibilities of the curtain wall.
J. Peter and P. Weidlinger. Aluminium in Modern Architecture. Two volumes. Louisville: Reynolds Metal Co., 1956.

[57] Bauersfeld gave a complete account of the first experiments in shell construction in an unpublished lecture on the 12th December 1942 in Berlin.

[58] Pier Luigi Nervi. Costruire Correttamente. Milan: Hoepli, 1955. English translation: Structures. New York: Dodge Corp., 1956.
The Works of Pier Luigi Nervi. London: Architectural Press, 1957. Stuttgart: Hatje, 1957.

[59] Felix Candela. Aujourd'hui, art et architecture, 1957, No. 13, p. 48 et seq.
Esther McCoy. Concrete Shell Forms – Felix Candela. Arts and Architecture, 1957, May, p. 16 et seq.

[60] Konrad Wachsmann. Vom Bauen in unserer Zeit. Baukunst und Werkform, 1957, No. 1, p. 26 et seq.
Hans Curjel. Ein Beispiel dreidimensionaler Struktur. Werk, 1954, No. 10, p. 377 et seq.

[61] J. M. Richards. Europe rebuilt (1946–56). Architectural Review, 1957, March, p. 158 et seq. Critical review of the standard of contemporary architecture in various European countries.

[62] J. Gloag and D. Bridgwater. A History of Cast Iron in Architecture.
N. Pevsner. Pioneers of Modern Design from William Morris to Walter Gropius.
E. D. Mills. The New Architecture in Great Britain 1946–53. London: Standard Catalogue Co., 1953. Detailed description of new English buildings; short summary of developments between 1925 and 1946.
J. M. Richards. An Introduction to Modern Architecture.
Special issue of Werk, 1947, No. 4, pp. 105 et seq. Introduction by A. Roth. Many illustrations.

[63] S. Giedion. Bauen in Frankreich: Eisen, Eisenbeton. Leipzig: Klinkhardt und Biermann, 1928. Account of developments in the nineteenth century.
Special issue of: Werk, 1947, No. 2. Contains buildings of the thirties and Perret's theory of architecture.
Special issue of: Werk, 1957, No. 5. Principally concerned with reconstruction after World War II and with new (and old) architecture in North Africa.
La Contribution française à l'évolution de l'architecture. Two special issues of: L'Architecture d'aujourd'hui, 1953, Nos. 46 and 47.

[64] J. P. Mieras and F. R. Yerbury. Dutch Architecture in the 20th Century. London: Benn, 1926. Also in German: Holländische Architektur des 20. Jahrhunderts. Berlin: Wasmuth, 1926. Picture

book giving a good idea of the Dutch position at the start of the twentieth century.
J. J. P. Oud. Holländische Architektur. Volume 10 of the Bauhaus Books. Munich, 1926.
A. Behne. Holländische Baukunst in der Gegenwart. Berlin, 1922.
H. L. C. Jaffé. De Stijl 1917–31. The Dutch Contribution to Modern Art. See also note 47.
Guido Canella. L'epopea borghese della scuola di Amsterdam. Casabella, 1957, No. 215.
J. P. Mieras. Na-oorlogse Bouwkunst in Nederland. Amsterdam and Antwerp: Kosmos, 1954.

[65] F. Schumacher. Strömungen in Deutscher Baukunst seit 1800. Leipzig: Seemann, 1935. Cologne: Seemann, 1955. Book by a co-founder of the Werkbund written partly from personal experience.
G. A. Platz. Die Baukunst der neuesten Zeit.
H. Bayer, W. and I. Gropius. Bauhaus 1919–1928. Editions in English, see note 34.
G. Hatje, H. Hoffmann and K. Kaspar. Neue Deutsche Architektur. Stuttgart: Hatje, 1956. Also in English: New German Architecture. London: Architectural Press, 1956. Records developments since World War II.

[66] M. Bill. Moderne Schweizer Architektur 1925–45. Basle: Werner, 1949. Review of buildings of the thirties.
H. Volkart. Schweizer Architektur. Ravensburg: Maier, 1951. Deals particularly with the forties.
G. E. Kidder Smith. Switzerland Builds. London: Architectural Press. Also New York, Stockholm: Bonnier, 1950.
A. Roth. Zeitgemässe Architekturbetrachtungen. Werk, 1951, No. 3, p. 65 et seq. Critical appraisal of contemporary Swiss architecture.
M. Bill. Robert Maillart. Zürich: Girsberger, 1949. 2nd edition, 1955. Comprehensive monograph.

[67] S. E. Rasmussen. Nordische Baukunst. Berlin: Wasmuth, 1940. Critical comparison of Swedish and Danish architecture, including the late neoclassical phase.
Nordisk Arkitektur 1946–49. Stockholm: Byggmästaren, 1950. Published on the occasion of the Fifth Nordic Building Conference in Stockholm, 1950. Series of illustrations of Finnish, Danish, Swedish, Norwegian and Icelandic architecture.
Nordisk Arkitektur 1950–54. Published on the occasion of the Sixth Nordic Building Conference in Helsinki, 1955.
Pays Nordiques. Special issue of: L'Architecture d'aujourd'hui, 1954, No. 54.
G. E. Kidder Smith. Sweden Builds. London: Architectural Press. New York and Stockholm: Bonnier, 1950.
G. Holmdahl, S. I. Lind, K. Ödeen. Gunnar Asplund, Architect, 1885–1940. Stockholm: Byggmästaren, 1950. With an essay by H. Ahlberg.
Special issue of: Werk, 1949, No. 9.

[68] See note 67.
K. Millech in collaboration with K. Fisker. Danske Arkitekturstromninger 1850–1950. Copenhagen: Østifternes Kreditforening, 1951. Standard work on Danish architecture of the period.
Special issue of: Werk, 1948, No. 9. With detailed article on the regional factors in Danish architecture by C. D. Furrer and a contribution by K. Fisker on "Die Moral des Funktionalismus".
J. Pedersen. Arkitekten Arne Jacobsen. Copenhagen: Arkitektens Forlag, 1954, 2nd edition, 1957.

[69] See note 67.
E. and C. Neuenschwander. Finnische Bauten – Atelier Alvar Aalto. For English edition, see note 54.
Pier Carlo Santini and Göran Schildt. Alvar Aalto from Sunila to Imatra: Ideas Projects and Buildings. Zodiac, No. 3, p. 26 et seq.
Wiederaufbauarbeit in Finnland. Werk, 1946, p. 104 et seq.
Special issue of: Casabella, No. 211. Complete summary of present-day Finnish architecture. Appreciation of the work of Eliel Saarinen.
Special issue of: Baukunst und Werkform, 1956, No 6. Review of buildings by young Finnish architects. Extracts from a lecture by Aalto: "Between Humanism and Materialism", given before the Zentralvereinigung of Viennese architects.

[70] P. Nestler. Neues Bauen in Italien. Munich: Callwey, 1954.
C. Pagani. Architettura Italiana Oggi. Milan: Hoepli, 1955. Special issue of: L'Architecture d'aujourd'hui, 1953, No. 48.
B. Zevi. Storia dell'architettura moderna. Turin: Einaudi, 1955, p. 209 et seq. Contains an account of Italian architecture and its links with the modern European movement.
G. E. Kidder Smith, Italy Builds. London: Architectural Press, 1955. New York: Reinhold. Milan: Edizione di Comunità.

[71] P. L. Goodwin. Brazil Builds: architecture old and new, 1652–1942. New York: Museum of Modern Art, 1943. Standard work on Brazilian architecture.
H.-R. Hitchcock. Latin American Architecture since 1945. New York: Simon & Schuster, 1955.
H. E. Mindlin. Modern Architecture in Brazil. London: Architectural Press, 1956. Also editions in French and German. Comprehensive pictorial record.
S. Papadaki: The Work of Oscar Niemeyer. New York: Reinhold, 1950. Also: London: Chapman & Hall.
S. Papadaki. Oscar Niemeyer. Works in Progress. New York: Reinhold, 1956. Contains Niemeyer's work since 1950.

[72] Frederick Gutheim. 1857–1957. One hundred years of architecture in America. New York: Reinhold, 1957. Also: London: Chapman & Hall.
L. Mumford. Roots of contemporary American Architecture. New York: Reinhold 1956. Contains essays on modern – especially American – architecture by leading architects and architectural writers.
E. Mock. Built in USA., 1932–1944. New York, 1944.
H.-R. Hitchcock and A. Drexler. Built in USA: post-war architecture. New York: Simon & Schuster, 1952. Good survey of recent American architecture, but excluding the new conceptions in commercial buildings and large halls.
Special issues of: L'Architecture d'aujourd'hui, 1953, Nos. 50/51.
G. C. Argan. Marcel Breuer. Milan: Görlich, 1957.
W. Boesiger. Richard Neutra – Buildings and Projects. Zürich: Girsberger, 1951. 4th edition, 1955.
R. Neutra. Mensch und Wohnen: Life and Human Habitat. Stuttgart: Koch, 1955.
R. Neutra. Survival through Design. New York, 1954. Also: London: Oxford U.P. Contains Neutra's theory of architecture.

Index

The numbers in brackets refer to illustration numbers.

Sources of Illustrations

Aero Pictorial Ltd., London 270
Aertsens, Michel 435, 437
Anderson, Yngre 369
Architects' Journal, The, London 266
Architectural Review, London:
  Dell and Wainwright 19, 263, 268, 269
  Galwey, de Burgh 274, 275, 277–280
  National Buildings Record 16, 58, 264, 267
  Tempest Ltd., H. 272
Archives Photographiques, Paris 22, 27, 241
Aromé, Messina 411
Asplund, Hans, Stockholm 360
Aviatik Beider, Basel 344
Backström, Sven, Stockholm 367
Baldessari, Luciano, Milan 402, 403
Bentham, Trustees 21
Bildarchiv der Beratungsstelle für Stahlverwendung, Düsseldorf 7a–11, 15, 20
Bildarchiv Neues Bauen an der Architekturabteilung der Technischen Hochschule, Stuttgart 1, 57, 96, 167, 169, 172, 185, 187, 216, 222, 238
Bill, Max, Zürich 352
Blaser, Werner, Basel 40
Boer, São Paulo 424
Borremans, L., Cachan/Seine 292
British Features, Bonn 281
British Railways, London 13
Burg, Garrit, Rotterdam 316
Casabella, Archivio, Milan 406
Casali, Milan 237, 407, 409
Checkman, Louis, Jersey City N.Y. 233
Chevojon, Paris 28, 82, 87, 191
Chicago Architectural Photographing Company 29b, 30–32, 439
Council of Industrial Design, The, London:
  Early, M.W. 26
Damora, Robert, New York 444
Dessecker, Studio, Stuttgart 337
Deutsche Versuchsanstalt für Luftfahrt, Berlin-Adlershof 244
Dyckerhoff & Widmann Archiv, Munich 94, 112, 238, 239, 242
Eldh, Göteborg 365
Farbwerke Hoechst AG, Werkfoto 103, 105
Fiat, Direzione Stampa e Propaganda, Turin 214, 401
Finsler, Hans, Zürich 346, 347
Flygfoto Oscar Bladh AB, Bromma 366, 368
Foto Marburg 67, 70, 106
Foucault, Marc 25
Fuller, Buckminster, Forest Hills 75, N.Y. 259
Garcia Moya, M. 243
Gautherot, Marcel 81, 155, 156, 419–421, 434
Gerlach, Vienna 73, 75
Gherardi-Fiorelli, Rome 404
Gomis Archivio, Barcelona 78, 80
Hammerschmidt, Aarhus 373–376
Havas, Helsinki 393, 395, 397
Hedrich-Blessing Studio, Chicago:
  Engdahl, Bill 34
  Hedrich, Bill 232, 252
Heidersberger, H., Brunswick 341
Held, Louis, Weimar 63
Heller, F.W., Telgte 335
Herdeg, Hugo P., Zürich 193, 194, 345
Hervé, Lucien, Paris 88, 145–153, 157, 160–163, 287, 288, 298–300
Hochschule für Gestaltung, Ulm 353
Hubmann, Franz, Vienna 158, 336
Interbau, Pressestelle Berlin:
  Diederichs, Berlin 452
  Jacobs, Berlin 125, 388
  Kessler, Berlin 334
  Wimmer, Berlin 296, 433
Järvi, Jorma, Helsinki 398
Jestein, L., Paris 23
Josuweck, Josef, Cologne 333
Korab, Baltazar, Birmingham, Mich. 457, 458
Krøll, Knud, Aarhus 377
Krupp, Friedrich, Werksarchiv 17
Kunstgewerbemuseum, Zürich 61, 66, 68, 69, 74
Lang, Erwin, Los Angeles 256
Langley, J. Alex, New York 229
Lehtikuwa, Helsinki 396
Lengauer, Munich 192
Lennart af Petersens, Stockholm 370
Levi, Florence 405
Lissitzky, El 323
Luckhaus Studio, Los Angeles 445
Ludwig-Roselius-Sammlung in der Böttcherstrasse, Bremen 107
Mango, Roberto, Naples 260
Mas, Barcelona 79
Meier-Ude, Klaus, Frankfurt/Main 327
Moosbrugger, Bernhard, Zürich 159, 343
Moser Archiv, Werner M., Zürich 37–39, 41–43, 45, 46, 48
M.R.L., Paris 284, 293, 294
Neuenschwander, Eduard, Zürich 197
Oudgaarden, L. van, Rotterdam 312
Petz, Gudula, Frankfurt/Main 340
Pfau, Arthur, Mannheim 332, 338
Photoflight Ltd., Elstree 271
Photographic, Detroit 463–465
Presseamt der Stadt Kassel 186
Rijksvoorlichtingsdienst, The Hague:
  Agtmaal, J.G. van, Hilversum 304, 313
  Cas Oorthuys, Amsterdam 315
  Doeser-Fotos, Laren 171, 174, 176, 307, 309, 310
  Gemeentelijke Woningsdienst 110, 305, 306
  KLM Aerocarto N.V., Amsterdam 175
  Persfotodienst, Amsterdam 314
  van Ojen, E.M., The Hague 76, 173, 223, 224, 303, 308
  Versnel, Jan 77
Scheidegger, Ernst, Zürich 143b, 302
Schmölz, Hugo, Cologne 225
Schwab, Gerhard, Stuttgart 217
Science Museum, The, London 14
Shulman, Julius, Los Angeles 447, 449, 450
Sianesi, Eduardo, Milan 417
Sörvik, Gothenburg 359
Spreng, Robert, Basel 226, 227, 245
Staatliche Landesbildstelle, Hamburg 109
Steiger, Siegfried, Stuttgart 378
Stoller, Ezra 132, 455, 460, 462
Strüwing, Copenhagen 379, 382–385
Sundahl AB, Nacka (C.G. Rosenberg) 361–363
Suomen Rakennustaiteen Museo, Helsinki 188, 195, 196, 199, 203, 204, 206, 207, 387, 389, 391, 394,
Terragni-Fonds 215, 400
Thomas Airviews, New York 441
Troberg, Efro, Helsinki 392
Troeger, Eberhard, Hamburg 342
Underhill Studio, New York 36
USIS Photo Unit, Bad Godesberg 33, 35, 44, 47, 49–52, 124, 126, 140, 164, 230, 231, 258, 446, 453, 459
Valastro, S.C., Westminster, Col. 461
Vasari, Rome 412
Viollet, Paris 5, 24, 89, 282, 283
Vrijhof, J.A., Amsterdam 311, 317–319
Waldvogel, Fredi, Zürich 356
Welt der Arbeit, Landesredaktion Hessen, Frankfurt/Main 211
Wiking, Hälsingborg 364
Wolgensinger, Michael, Zürich 349–351
Zanella & Moscardi, São Paulo 423
Zumstein, Bern 354

Photos not enumerated above are from the publishers' own collection. The original sources were in most cases the following publications:

  The Works of Pier Luigi Nervi
  New German Architecture
  Sigfried Giedion: Walter Gropius
  Philip C. Johnson: Mies van der Rohe
  American Architecture Since 1947

The publishers would like to record their appreciation of the generous help given by many institutions and individuals in preparing the illustrations, and by the following in particular:

Acropole, São Paulo
AEG, Technisch-literarische Abteilung, Berlin
Architectural Review, London
Bauen und Wohnen, Zürich
Beratungsstelle für Stahlverwendung, Düsseldorf
Max Braun, Frankfurt
Julien Cain, Bibliothèque Nationale, Paris
The Council of Industrial Design, London
Casabella, Milan
Dyckerhoff & Widmann, Munich
Editorial Gustavo Gili, Barcelona
Professor Evers, Technische Hochschule Darmstadt
Farbwerke Hoechst AG, Frankfurt
Reinhard Gieselmann, Karlsruhe
Hugo Häring, Biberach an der Riss
Interbau Pressestelle, Berlin
Kompass-Verlag, Zürich
Friedrich Krupp, Werksarchiv, Essen
Kunstgewerbemuseum Zürich
Professor Eduard Levsen, Kiel
Ludwig-Roselius-Sammlung in der Böttcherstrasse, Bremen
Sir Leslie Martin, London
Meulenhoff & Co NV, Amsterdam
Frau Léna Meyer-Bergner, Basel
Werner M. Moser, Zürich
  for material from Moser, Frank Lloyd Wright, 60 Jahre lebendige Architektur, Winterthur 1952
Eduard Neuenschwander, Zürich,
  for material from Neuenschwander, Alvar Aalto and Finnish Architecture, 1950–51, Zürich 1954
Ing. C. Olivetti & C., S.p.A., Direzione Stampa e Edizioni, Ivrea
Presseamt der Stadt Kassel
Reinhold Publishing Corporation, New York
Rijksvoorlichtingsdienst, The Hague
A. Salto, Libreria artistica industriale, Milan
W. Sandberg, Stedelijk Museum, Amsterdam
Senat der Freien und Hansestadt Hamburg, Staatliche Pressestelle
Suomen Rakennustaiteen Museo, Helsinki
U.S. Information Service, American Embassy
Verlag Gebr. Mann, Berlin
Verlag D.W. Callwey, Munich
  for material from Nestler, Neues Bauen in Italien, Munich 1954
Verlag Girsberger, Zürich
  for material from Boesiger, Le Corbusier, Oeuvre complète, six volumes so far, Zürich 1937–57
  and Boesiger, Richard Neutra, Zürich 1951
Welt der Arbeit, Frankfurt

Cover design: Hans Haderek
Composition and printing: Ensslin-Druck, Reutlingen (Württemberg)
Blocks: Felix Köhring, Flensburg; JUP Industrie- und Presseklischee, Renner & Kähne, Berlin-Tempelhof; Scham & Storsberg, Ulm/Donau
Paper: Papierfabrik Scheufelen, Oberlenningen (Württemberg)